Born Ag̲̲a̲ W9-BCN-449

FIGURE 1. Surrendering to Jesus.

Born Again in Brazil

THE PENTECOSTAL BOOM AND THE PATHOGENS OF POVERTY

R. ANDREW CHESNUT

Rutgers University Press

New Brunswick, New Jersey, and London

Library of Congress cataloging-in-Publication Data

Chesnut, R. Andrew.
    Born again in Brazil : the Pentecostal boom and the pathogens of
poverty / R. Andrew Chesnut.
       p.   cm.
    Includes bibliographical references and index.
    ISBN 0-8135-2405-9 (cloth : alk. paper). — ISBN 0-8135-2406-7
(pbl. : alk. paper)
    1. Pentecostal churchs—Brazil—History—20th century.
2. Spiritual healing—Brazil—History—20th century. 3. Brazil—
Church history—20th century. 4. Poor—Brazil—Religious life.
I. Title.
BX8762.A45B625   1997
289.9′4′098109049—dc21   97-9191
                                                    CIP

British Cataloging-in-Publication information available

Composition by Colophon Typesetting

Manufactured in the United States of America

To Viviana, a gringa mexicana, *and the believers of Belém*

CONTENTS

ACKNOWLEDGMENTS

I am deeply indebted to a number of individuals and institutions whose intellectual, moral, and financial support enabled me to conduct research in Brazil and write this book. First and foremost, I owe my most profound gratitude to my Pentecostal informants in Belém who not only shared their faith and life stories with me but also welcomed me into their homes. Between steaming glasses of *cafezinho*, they revealed the most intimate details of their personal histories to a perfect stranger and foreigner. Also among Belenense Pentecostals, I am especially grateful to Paulo Machado, pastor-president of the Assembly of God, Dr. Jader Gomes, Eliel Negreiros and Pastor Antonio Amolina. To protect the identities of these four individuals, as well as those of my ninety informants, I have used pseudonyms in lieu of their real names.

Pastor Paulo granted me practically unlimited access to individual members, historical records and worship services. Eliel served as my primary contact in the Assembly of God, taking me to worship services in the *baixadas* at least once a week and providing key information on Assembly history and politics. Both Pastor Antonio and Dr. Gomes helped me locate ecclesiastical documents at the seminary.

At the Federal University of Pará, Anaiza Vergolino, chair of the anthropology department, went beyond the normal call of duty in facilitating my affiliation with the university as a research associate and, most significantly, offering her house as collateral so that my wife and I could rent an apartment in Belém. Moreover, she generously shared her expertise on Umbanda with me and took me to two *terreiros*.

In Rio de Janeiro both academicians and Pentecostals supplemented my research in Belém. The majority of scholars with whom I met were in some way connected with the Instituto Superior da Religião (ISER), Brazil's premier research institute on religion. The staff there, particularly Xica and Laize, went out of their way to retrieve bibliographic information for me. Cecilia Mariz, professor of sociology at Rio de Janeiro State University and fellow scholar of Pentecostalism, heads a long list of academicians who shared the findings of their research with me. Cecilia opened her home to me and my wife in both Rio and Recife and invited me to present my work at UERJ. Among the other researchers in Rio who assisted me are Maria Campos Machado (Dodora), Rubem Cesar Fernandes, Waldo Cesar, Franciso Rolim, and Jorge Luiz Domingues.

Staff at the Fulbright office in Copacabana were extremely helpful in negotiating the country's byzantine bureaucracy. Marcia, the secretary, took me to my first Pentecostal worship service in Brazil: at her church, Nova Vida.

Cyro Satiro and Geremias do Couto at the Assembly of God publishing house (CPAD) graciously allowed me to examine six decades' worth of the *Mensageiro da Paz*, the church's national journal. Cyro even furnished office space and fresh *cafezinho* to facilitate my research.

As in Rio, scholars and church leaders in São Paulo also contributed to my understanding of the Pentecostal boom. Ricardo Mariano and Flavio Pierucci at the University of São Paulo versed me in Pentecostal politics, while Paul Freston of the State University at Campinas gave me an insider's view of Protestantism in Brazil. The consummate insider, José Wellington, president of the General Convention of the Assemblies of God in Brazil, provided me with contacts at CPAD and with his business card, which opened countless temple doors throughout Brazil.

In the United States, the support of several individuals and institutions made my research possible. Grants from the IIE Fulbright and from the Latin American Center and International Studies and Overseas Programs at UCLA generously funded my field work in Brazil. My former dissertation advisor at UCLA, the late E. Bradford Burns, encouraged me to pursue my interest in Latin American popular religion. Virginia Garrard-Burnett and several anonymous readers provided useful comment on the manuscript.

Four people merit special mention for their unconditional support. My wife, Viviana, accompanied me to the Brazilian Amazon. Her rapport with Pentecostal women in Belém gave me entree into a realm of the faith that might have eluded me had the "gringa mexicana" not been there. For these and countless other reasons, I dedicate the book to her. My parents also made significant contributions to bringing the project to fruition. My father, who wrote his dissertation on a similar topic twenty-five years ago, served as an ex officio advisor in reading the manuscript and instructing me in the finer points of Protestant theologies. A librarian, my mother instilled in me her passion for research and an appreciation of the religions of the spirit(s). Finally, my manuscript benefited greatly from the editorial expertise of my friend and former colleague at UCLA, writer Randal Malat.

PART I

The Spirit of Brazil

Introduction

❧

$\mathcal{A}$ spiritual revolution is transforming the socioreligious landscape of Latin America. From the *ciudades perdidas* (shantytowns) of Tijuana to the *favelas* (slums) of Rio de Janeiro, evangelical Protestantism, particularly Pentecostalism, has replaced Catholicism as the leading form of popular religion in thousands of *bairros* on the urban periphery.[1] In some countries, such as Brazil, estimates suggest that on an average Sunday Protestant churchgoers outnumber their Catholic compatriots. But in few Latin American nations have Protestants multiplied as rapidly as in Brazil. Home to three-fifths of Ibero-America's Protestants, Brazil has seen its Protestant population almost quadruple from 1960 to 1985 (Stoll 1990: 337). As of 1990, one of every six Brazilians claimed affiliation with a Protestant denomination (Stoll 1990: 8). In Brazil's second largest city, Rio de Janeiro, *crentes*, the great majority of whom (91 percent) are Pentecostal, have founded an average of one church per workday since the beginning of the decade (Fernandes 1992: 19).[2]

Such is the ascendancy of this charismatic branch of Protestantism that other Christian churches have had to "Pentecostalize" to survive the fierce competition of the new religious marketplace in Brazil. Many members of the mainline Protestant churches, such as the Presbyterian, have seceded from their parent denominations to establish "reformed" (*renovada*) or Pentecostal congregations. These churches preserve much of their denominational heritage while integrating the Pentecostal gifts of the Spirit. Similarly, the most dynamic movement in the Brazilian Catholic Church is no longer the anemic CEBs (Christian Base Communities) but the charismatic movement, which also adopts Pentecostal practice. Only the African-Brazilian religion of Umbanda has held its ground in the battle for Brazil's souls.

Like Umbanda, its principal religious rival, Brazilian Pentecostalism is a faith of the poor and disenfranchised. Several of the larger denominations, after decades of ceaseless proselytization, have won a considerable number of middle-class converts, but the bulk of believers reside on the margins of society. Researchers at ISER (Instituto Superior de Estudos da Religião) in Rio de Janeiro discovered in 1988 that the proportion of evangelicals living on the impoverished west side of the city is three times greater than on the affluent south side, famous for its chic districts of Leblon, Ipanema, and Copacabana. Copacabana, in fact, has one of the lowest ratios of crente temples in the greater metropolitan area, with only 1.3 per 10,000 inhabitants (Fernandes 1992: 10 and 12). Why Pentecostalism has had such overwhelming success in appealing to the poor of Brazil and much of Latin America constitutes one of the principal questions of this work.

Competing Paradigms of Pentecostal Growth

Since Christian Lalive D'Epinay and Emilio Willems's pioneering research in the 1960s on the growth of Protestantism in Chile and Brazil, a new generation of scholars has formulated novel hypotheses in response to variations on the same fundamental question posited above. The concept of anomie, which sociologists of religion Rodney Stark and William Bainbridge have defined as "the state of being without effective rules for living," was key to the analyses of the first generation of scholars (217).[3] Most contemporary observers have rejected the anomie theory as crucial to understanding the Pentecostal boom, yet no single theoretical paradigm predominates.

Two of the most incisive works are comparative studies of Brazil's three major popular religions: Pentecostalism, popular Catholicism, and Umbanda and its African-Brazilian variants. Based on research conducted primarily in Recife, sociologist Cecilia Mariz (1994b) asserts that the vertiginous growth of both Pentecostalism and CEBs (Christian Base Communities) is best explained not by anomie but by how the two religions motivate Brazilians to cope with poverty. Anthropologist John Burdick (1993) presents a similar theory, but where Mariz speaks specifically of poverty, Burdick characterizes both Pentecostalism and Umbanda more generally as "cults of affliction."

Two other notable studies of Pentecostalism in Latin America seek not to compare charismatic Protestantism with its competitors in the religious marketplace but to explain its broad appeal through research in several countries of the region. Concentrating on Protestantism in Central America, especially Guatemala, anthropologist David Stoll (1990) points to political oppression as the primary impetus propelling meteoric evangelical growth. Politics also enter into British sociologist David Martin's equation for evangelical growth in Latin America but take a back seat to sociological factors. Although he avoids the term "anomie," Martin (1990) echos Lalive D'Epinay and Willems's theory that Pentecostalism empowers and offers security to the victims of modernization. In the political realm, Martin concurs with Stoll regarding the appeal of "apolitical" Protestantism, which he ascribes to the inherent "peaceability" of this branch of Christianity.

A New Theory of Pentecostal Growth

In order to gain a fuller understanding of why Pentecostalism since the early 1960s has experienced such enormous success in attracting Latin America's popular classes, I spent a year in the Amazonian city of Belém, the cradle of Brazilian Pentecostalism, conducting ninety life history interviews with impoverished believers residing in the *baixadas* (the Amazonian term for *favela*). My Amazonian informants, members of the Assembly of God (Assembléia de Deus [AD]), the Four-Square Gospel Church (Igreja do Evangelho Quandrangular [IEQ]), and the Universal Church of the Kingdom of God (Igreja Universal do Reino de Deus [IURD]) are not escaping rampaging armies or suffering anomie. Rather, they seek immediate solutions to their health problems stemming from poverty. Illness is one of the most common and life-threatening manifestations of poverty in Latin America. In Belém, insufficient caloric intake, unsanitary living conditions, and tropical heat create a fertile breeding ground for the gastrointestinal and infectious diseases that plague the poor throughout the third world.

Unlike its major religious competitors, Pentecostalism, in all its many denominations, offers the powerful remedy of faith healing. The great majority of my informants in Belém converted to Pentecostalism during or shortly after a serious illness. In the case of female converts, as the following faith healing testimonial of Arlette Silva illustrates, it is not only their own sickness that leads them to become crentes but also the health crises of family members.

> My son was hospitalized with severe hemorrhaging, and the doctor said he had seventy-two hours to live. I took him home, and a woman asked if I wanted to take him to church, and I said I had no money, but the woman lent me money for bus fare. Upon entering church, I fainted with my son in my arms, and when I came to, he was on the table being cured. I accepted Jesus and give testimony everywhere that He has the power to do anything.   (*Estandarte* 5/86)

Thus, this study posits that the dialectic between poverty-related illness and faith healing provides the key to understanding the appeal of Pentecostalism in Brazil and much of Latin America. Although somatic maladies predominate over other forms of affliction in the life histories of my informants, I expand the concept of illness beyond its physical basis to include the most common expressions of social distress present on the urban periphery. Pentecostalism's message of healing power reverberates among the popular classes, particularly women, whose already precarious household economies are further debilitated by alcoholism, unemployment, and domestic strife.

While the dialectic between the diseases of poverty and faith healing has launched the Pentecostal take-off at the ground level of individual believers, the skilled exercise of organizational and political power has facilitated rapid expansion of the ecclesiastical institution. Specifically, I will bring to light new historical information on church-state relations in Brazil during both the twenty-one-year military dictatorship and ensuing civilian rule. Nowhere else in the country did relations between the Catholic church and the military regime become as strained as in Amazonia. By the beginning of the 1970s, the Amazonian church, particularly in the state of Pará, had developed into one of the regime's most active opponents. Though the generals' violent response to church political activity is well documented, I have discovered that the regime's campaign of violence and intimidation constituted one part of a two-pronged strategy to combat the Catholic church in the region. Having lost its historical religious client, the authoritarian state turned to the largest Protestant church in Amazonia, the Assembly of God in Belém, to replace the Catholic church as its primary sacred propagandist and apologist.

Making History

On the basis of bibliographic research, I had incorrectly hypothesized before arriving in Brazil that the relation between poverty and millenarianism was crucial to understanding the rise of Pentecostalism in Latin America's largest nation. Given Brazil's rich history of millenarian and messianic movements, it seemed that charismatic Protestantism captured the same kind of apocalyptic hopes for a new order that had inspired the faithful at Canudos and Contestado. However, through my work in Belém, I began to realize that (1) millenarianism plays only a minor role in the Pentecostal boom, and that (2) material deprivation per se, while generally a necessary condition for conversion to Pentecostalism, is not a sufficient one. If poverty were the sole prerequisite for affiliation with a Pentecostal church, up to 60 percent of all Brazilians (the approximate percentage of the population living in poverty) would be crentes.

Clearly, other factors figured into the equation of accelerated Pentecostal growth. And more than any other research tool, ethnography allowed me to identify illness as the main missing variable. While I had discovered valuable historical documents in the Central Temple of the AD in Belém, they alone would not tell the entire story of Pentecostal conversion. Oral history would fill the informational lacunae left by church records.

To this end, I formulated an interview schedule that I hoped would illuminate the mechanics of conversion to Pentecostalism. Combining openended and closed questions, I sought to discover what factors in ordinary believers' lives had brought them to the doors of a crente temple. I reasoned that through approximately one hundred oral histories I would be able to detect definite patterns of conversion to Pentecostalism.

Although I had learned from experience that research in Latin America required flexibility on the part of the scholar, I aimed to select a survey population that would reflect both Pentecostal demographics and historical knowledge. This implied a concentration of both women, who comprise about two thirds of the Pentecostal population in Brazil, and older believers, those with at least twenty years of church affiliation. In accord with the AD's status as Latin America's largest Protestant denomination, the majority of my informants would be Assembleianos, followed by members of two of the largest and most dynamic churches, the IURD and IEQ.

Cognizant of the potential barriers I could face as a non-Pentecostal North American researcher, I had wisely begun to establish contact with Brazilian Pentecostals in Los Angeles. In an ironic reversal of roles, both the IURD and Brazilian AD have planted churches in the United States. Los Angeles, with its large Brazilian and Latin American immigrant communities, has become a center of AD and IURD mission work. One of the pastors whom I met at a Brazilian Assembly of God in suburban Alhambra turned out to be the son of José Wellington, the president of the AD in Brazil. After I had explained the purpose of my research, the young pastor handed me both his father's and his own business cards and promised to arrange an interview with the chief Assembleiano at his headquarters in São Paulo.

My contact in Los Angeles proved to be invaluable. I spent my first two weeks in the country in Rio de Janeiro meeting with scholars at ISER and visiting the national headquarters and publishing house of the AD. I then proceeded to São Paulo, South America's megalopolis, where I was warmly received by Pastor José Wellington, whose son in California had lived up to his word. The president of the General Convention of the Assemblies of God in Brazil seemed pleased by my desire to research the history of Pentecostalism in his country but wanted to know about my religious affiliation. I explained to him, as I would to countless others, that although not a Pentecostal, I had been raised as an *evangélico* by my father, a Presbyterian minister. Satisfied with my response, he did not ask if I still practiced the faith; I in fact do not, but did not volunteer this information. On other occasions, when my *filho de pastor* (pastor's son) explanation failed to satisfy the curiosity of my interviewees, I revealed that while I sympathized with the Presbyterian faith, I did not actively practice it. A few of my informants seized the opportunity to proselytize me but usually desisted when I further explained the aim of my research.

In Belém, the *pastor-presidente* (pastor-president) of the AD, Paulo Machado, seemed genuinely impressed that I had met with his superior José Wellington in São Paulo and had his business card as proof. With little inquiry as to the nature of my research, Pastor Paulo granted me access to church historical records and interviews with members. Salient among the historical documents were the Administrative Acts (Atas do culto administrativo da AD em Belém), which contained the minutes of weekly organizational assemblies from 1930 to 1993. The Acts allowed me to trace the general course of church history over a period of six decades. In particular, the administrative notes yielded unparalleled information on church political activity between 1962 and 1993.

The official voice of the AD in Belém, the monthly journal *O Estandarte Evangélico* (The Evangelical Standard), also proved to be a key source of institutional, political, and social information during the last three decades. Founded as a newspaper for Assembly youth, the journal rapidly evolved into the mouthpiece for the *ministerio*, the governing body of the church. Of particular interest to me were thirty years of uninterrupted conversion testimonials. Though the journal ranged in size from eight to twelve pages through the years, it never lacked a page filled with *testemunhos*. Poring over some four thousand individual testimonials through the span of three decades, I was able to corroborate the patterns of conversion to Pentecostalism emerging in my ethnographic interviews. Approximately 80 percent of the testimonials published in the *Estandarte* relate to illness and faith healing.

The AD's own institutional histories, both national and regional, proved to be reliable sources of dates, places, and names, but the heroic and supernatural accounts of the founding and development of Pentecostalism in Brazil exclude the role of common members. Nevertheless, the posthumously published diary of one of the two Swedish founders of the AD, Daniel Berg, revealed that the link between illness and conversion had existed from the very beginning. Some of the first converts to the church were Belenenses stricken with tropical diseases. The two brief histories of the AD in Belém, written by appointed committees, are basically encomiums to past and present pastor-presidents but also provide useful information on church organization and historical milestones.

Statistical data on church growth and membership came from two primary sources. Membership files dating from 1930 painted a biographical portrait of the thousands of Belenense men and women who had adhered to the faith. Without access to these files, I would not have been able to determine the occupational status of common crentes and the gender ratios of church membership. Containing quantitative data on membership and the construction of new temples, the annual reports (*Relatórios Anuais*) allowed me to chart church growth from 1968 to 1993. I delighted in the discovery that from their inception in the late 1960s, the reports had registered the incidence of *cura divina* or faith healing in all the houses of worship scattered throughout the city and in the Templo Central.

An articulate young Assembleiano from the baixada bairro of Guamá, Eliel Negreiros, whom I had met at the Central Temple, offered to assist me in any way he could. Aware that worship services would provide the greatest opportunity to meet prospective informants and observe/participate in Pentecostal congregations, I asked Eliel to take me to *cultos* (worship services) at temples in the shantytowns. During the better part of a year, Eliel, who seemed to be somewhat of a celebrity in the baixada churches, and my wife and I trudged through the labyrinthine and often flooded mud paths of the slums on our way to Sunday night services that were considered short if they ended in two hours.

I quickly realized that detached observation is next to impossible among Brazilian Pentecostals, particularly at the small houses of worship where I was often the first foreigner to visit. Foreign visitors, I learned, rarely venture out of the comfortable confines of the mother church. *Dirigentes* (pastors of local congregations) so routinely called "the young couple from America" (that my Mexican wife and I were of different nationalities confused many crentes) to the pulpit "to give a word" that on the rare occasions when we were not invited forward, I wondered if something was wrong. From the pulpit I would attempt to explain the nature of my research and would inform the congregation that at the end of the service, I would approach a few worshipers to schedule interviews. My wife would then refuse persistent requests to sing an evangelical hymn in English or Spanish. Considering her background as a nominal Catholic, this would have been a difficult feat. Despite my good command of Portuguese and reasonably clear explanation of my research, ordinary believers usually mistook us for young American missionaries.

My concern about not being able to gain access to closed Pentecostal communities was rapidly allayed when worshipers lined up at the end of services to request an interview. Not even in the best-case scenario had I imagined that hundreds more people would volunteer than I could ever possibly hope to interview. With an eye out for older and female members, I would schedule a week's worth of interviews every Sunday night. Since these impoverished crentes do not live in a world of datebooks and calendars, I reasoned that it would be safer to schedule interviews at informants' homes. Hence, even if they were to forget our appointment, I stood a chance of finding them at their residences. Furthermore, by interviewing them at home, I would get a better sense of the believers' socioeconomic status. For the few women who seemed uncomfortable with the idea of a foreign man visiting them at home, I arranged alternative sites, usually their local church.

Though the interviews generally lasted between ninety minutes and two hours, I would customarily spend the entire morning or afternoon socializing with believers and their families, often accepting their invitation to stay for lunch. During these informal *bate-papos* (chats), I often learned as much, if not more, about my informants and their faith than during the recorded interviews. This was also the time for me to reciprocate, fielding questions ranging from my view of the Holy Spirit to my estimation of Team USA's chances in the World Cup of soccer. Would they win any games?[4]

In designing the interview, I had attempted to strike a balance between open ended and closed questions. The latter would form part of a survey of Pentecostal norms and attitudes, while the former would hopefully shed light on the conversion process and allow the individuality of my informants to surface. After the first few interviews, I soon realized that I would have to struggle to fit many of the closed questions into the schedule. As people denied a voice outside the impoverished baixadas, the vast majority of my informants, particularly the women, regarded our interview as their first and perhaps only opportunity to tell their life story, albeit in an extremely abbreviated form. For many, the narration of their own history had a definite cathartic effect, not unlike their ecstatic worship in church. Childhood memories of scarcity and hardship brought many to tears, which then quickly gave way to intoxicating effervescence when they recalled their conversion and baptism in the Holy Spirit. Some of my interviewees even broke into glossolalia at this point.

Even though I commenced every interview prepared to engage in dialogue, most believers became so immersed in the pathos of their own narrative that I often felt like an extension of the tape recorder in my hand, registering my informant's every word but pronouncing precious few of my own. Given that many of the ninety crentes would have recounted their life histories ad infinitum, I gradually learned to interject at strategic moments with key questions. Had I not begun to take a more active role in the interviews, many important questions would have remained unanswered.

Belém: Bethlehem of Brazilian Pentecostalism

Due to the city's historical significance in the Pentecostal movement, Belém, the capital of the Amazonian state of Pará, seemed to be the ideal research site. The largest Pentecostal denomination in the Western Hemisphere, the Brazilian Assembly of God, was founded in 1911 by Swedish immigrants in the steamy former rubber capital. Two additional factors brought me to Belém. First, through preliminary research, I determined that within Brazil, the state of Pará had experienced some of the nation's highest Protestant growth rates. Moreover, because the evangelical presence in the state was negligible at the time of the Swedish missionaries' arrival, Pará had one of the highest ratios of Pentecostals to mainline Protestants. Given that Pentecostals, and not their historical brethren, have sparked the religious revolution in Latin America, I preferred to carry out my field research in a region where Assembleianos and Quandrangulares (members of the IEQ) predominated.

Another reason for choosing Belém relates to prior research on the growth of Protestantism in Brazil. The vast majority of scholars conducted their studies of evangelical communities in Rio de Janeiro and Recife. As both the nation's second city and cultural capital, as well as home to ISER, Rio de Janeiro is a natural laboratory for the study of religion. Wanting to navigate uncharted waters, I looked to the flooded lowlands of the Amazon basin, where no social scientist had yet examined the crente boom. My plan to study Pentecostalism in an urban environment narrowed the choice to the two metropolises of the Brazilian North, Belém and Manaus. With its superior academic infrastructure and unique Pentecostal history, the Paraense capital was the obvious choice. Finally, my research, which called for extensive ethnographic interviews with ordinary members, required spending considerable time in Brazilian shantytowns. The baixadas of Belém and Manaus seemed much less formidable than the favelas of Rio de Janeiro or São Paulo, the former of which, by the time of my arrival in August of 1993, had become a war zone in the battle between drug gangs and the police.

The Secular City

Distorted economic development in Belém, in its modern phase, can be traced back to the rubber era. The rubber boom and bust thrust Belém and much of Amazonia into the volatile marketplace of international capitalism during the last quarter of the nineteenth century and first decade of the twentieth. Charles Goodyear's invention of vulcanization spurred the world's insatiable appetite for *Hevea brasiliensis*. Refugees from the drought-stricken Northeast poured into Amazonia to work as *seringueiros* (rubber gatherers), gathering and processing the white resin from the trees into large black balls of rubber. Exploiting the labor of the seringueiros, who worked as virtual indentured servants, the *seringalistas* (rubber plantation owners) amassed spectacular fortunes. The opulent opera house in Manaus and Teatro da Paz in Belém stand as testament to the boom that enriched a handful of rubber barons. As rapidly as technological innovation beyond Brazil's borders ignited the rubber boom, ecological imperialism contributed to the bust. Englishman Henry Alexander Wickham smuggled rubber tree seeds out of Brazil and took them to Ceylon, where efficient plantation production was able to undersell Amazonian rubber by the first decade of the twentieth century (Burns 291). Except for the brief resurgence in demand during World War II, Belém returned to the economic and geographic isolation of "ante hevean" Amazonia.

Belém's isolation ended in 1960 with the inauguration of the Belém-Brasilia highway. The economic integration of Amazonia through colonization and industry formed an integral part of President Juscelino Kubitscheck's grandiose "fifty years in five" plan for economic development. Government planners sought to earn precious foreign exchange by exploiting the region's vast natural resources. The Transamazonian Highway would also bring in hundreds of thousands of impoverished northeasterners to colonize the "last frontier." Colonization served the dual purpose of diminishing the mounting pressure for agrarian reform and populating the sparsely inhabited region. In accord with Brasilia's geopolitical interests, a more densely populated Amazonia would deter foreign intrusion.

Amazonia, as it had during the rubber era, watched from the sidelines as decisions regarding its own economic development were made exogenously. Responding to fiscal incentives from the federal government, such as the PIN (National Integration Program) and PoloAmazonia (Agricultural and Agromineral Poles of Amazonia), multinational and national capital descended on the territorial giants of Pará and Amazonas. Corporate capital reinserted the region into the global economy, and through extractive industry brought it into the financial orbit of the industrial behemoth São Paulo. Mining, exemplified by Carajas, the immense iron-ore and hydroelectric complex in southern Pará, and the extraction of nonrenewable natural resources such as timber, expanded the frontiers of capitalism.

For those living on the Amazonian frontier, the expansion of extractive industry meant the attenuation of preexisting economic structures. Subsistence farmers and agricultural workers were driven off the land by corporate capital and cattle ranchers in alliance with the state. Victims of an authoritarian model of development, thousands of rural families fled to Belém, where they settled in the baixadas of the city's periphery. The great influx of migrants from the interior of the state swelled the existing slums and pushed the limits of the urban frontier.

Unprepared for the massive migration, state and municipal government was notable for its absence in the baixadas. While the bulk of the city planning budget was spent on middle- and upper-class neighborhoods, slum dwellers built their own *barracas* (wooden shacks with thatched palm roofs that replicate the simple dwellings nestled on the banks of the *igarapés* [streams] and rivers that snake through the Amazon) and pirated electricity. Despite the lack of basic services and the squalid living conditions, Paraenses from the interior continued to settle in the baixadas throughout the 1970s and 1980s. Belém's total population doubled between 1960 and 1980, while the bairros of the shantytowns increased between four- and eightfold. Terra Firme, where many of my Pentecostal informants lived, went from 4,201 inhabitants to 28,281 (IBGE 1980b). Only 8.6 percent of Belenenses were migrants in 1970, but by 1980 the number had leapt to 31.9 percent (IBGE 1980a: 149). In his study of Belém's baixadas in 1985, Thomas Mistchein discovered that 60.5 percent of residents were migrants from the interior of the state, 64.2 percent of whom came from rural areas (62–64). Interviewees in the study explained their migration to Belém in terms of agro-extractive hardship and the lack of basic services in the interior, primarily health and education (118).

The service sector has traditionally driven Belém's economy. In 1990, 42.6 percent of the work force in the Amazonian capital labored in services, while only 14 percent held manufacturing jobs and 17.2 percent earned their wages in commerce (Mitschein 62). Food processing, lumber, and textiles make up Belém's fragile industrial base. The city also functions as the principal commercial entrepôt of the region, receiving agricultural and extractivist products from its hinterland. Black pepper, cacao, dende oil, and heart of palm are shipped abroad from the city's fluvial port.

The predominance of the service sector in the local economy results in wages insufficient for purchasing the basket of basic goods necessary for survival. Of those working in services, 75 percent earned less than twice the minimum wage. Galloping inflation during the 1980s reversed any gains in income made in the 1970s. Purchasing power in 1989 was 79 percent less than in 1980 (Souza 78). The city's fragile production base also consigns most residents of the baixadas to the informal economy, where wages are depressed and labor rights are not respected. Between 60 and 65 percent of the economically active population of the city's slums earn their living in the informal economy.[5]

Poverty in Brazil

While several Pentecostal denominations in Brazil have attracted growing numbers of those employed in the formal economy, Pentecostalism in general remains a religion of the informal periphery. The complex relationship between this religion of the Spirit and poverty holds one of the keys to understanding its unbridled growth during the past four decades. More generally, the rise and fall of almost all forms of religion in Brazil and the rest of Latin America can be explained on the basis of their relationship to poverty-related illness. In-depth analysis of Pentecostalism's main religious rivals in Brazil falls beyond the scope of this study, but I will demonstrate how Pentecostalism's response to the afflictions of material deprivation has determined its success in recruiting Brazil's poor.

Distorted development, since the colonization of Brazil by Portugal down to the present day, has favored an elite few while pushing the majority to the economic margins, where they engage in a determined struggle for survival. Dominion over the nation's vast natural resources and dynamic industry affords members of the elite a lifestyle on a par with the wealthy of the countries of the OECD while half the population suffers the consequences of low wages, underemployment and unemployment, malnourishment, and disease. Economic inequality, measured as national income distribution, plagues most countries of the third world (and increasingly certain developed nations). Brazil, however, has been one of the world leaders in socioeconomic inequity. From a Gini coefficient of 0.5 in 1960, the South American colossus declined to .652 in 1989. Only Honduras and Sierra Leone had higher coefficients (Souza 55).[6] The richest 1 percent of the population in 1993 captured the same share of national income as the poorest 50 percent.

Poverty in Brazil and throughout Latin America is a multifaceted problem that cannot be measured by a single social or economic gauge. Rather, a set of macrosocial indicators provides a more integral portrait of what it means to be poor in Brazil. Illness, one of the most common manifestations of poverty, will be discussed at length in part 2. Above all, poverty is the inability to meet the basic human needs of shelter, food, health, and education. The fact that basic human needs are, in part, determined by culture does not invalidate the above definition. Despite the polemic on definitions of poverty that fills volumes of social science literature, researchers have been able to quantitatively measure poverty by such yardsticks as daily caloric intake and annual income.

Born into the lower echelons of a highly stratified society in which interclass mobility is the exception to the rule, disprivileged Brazilians are forced to sell their labor at depressed wages. The huge labor surplus, even in the context of economic growth, ensures that salaries will not rise significantly. In fact, with consistently high inflation since the 1970s, workers have watched their purchasing power plummet. In 1988 the minimum wage had fallen 21 percent from 1980 (Souza 68). Despite some divergence, considerable consensus exists on the definition of poverty in Brazil on the basis of income. A per capita income of one-half the minimum wage will be the standard employed in this study. According to the FAO (Food and Agriculture Organization of the United Nations), 50 percent of all Brazilians were poor in 1990 (Souza 56). Approximately a quarter of the population lived in extreme poverty, with a per capita income of less than one fourth the minimum wage.[7]

Poverty in Brazil also depends on gender and geography. The global trend toward the feminization of poverty is especially acute in Brazil. In the 1970s the percentage of poor households in urban areas headed by women rose from 19.6 percent to 29.8 percent (Pastore 44). Institutionalized gender discrimination relegated women to the low-paying tertiary sector of the economy at twice the rate of men. In 1970 more than two-thirds of economically active women were employed in the service sector, compared to less than one-third of working men (Barroso 18). More Brazilian women work as domestic servants than in any other occupation. Besides notoriously low remuneration, domestics are often subjected to long hours and sexual harassment.

As deplorable as material conditions are on the urban periphery, poverty in Brazil and much of Latin America is inordinately concentrated in the rural areas. Sociologist José Pastore, delimiting poverty at the level of one quarter of the minimum wage, found that 10 percent of all urban households were impoverished in 1980, while 36 percent of rural families could not afford to purchase the basket of goods required to meet their basic needs (86). The great majority of my Pentecostal informants in Belém, despite occasional nostalgia for the rustic way of life in the Amazonian interior, stated that their standard of living had improved in the baixadas. Poverty in Brazil also correlates with geographic region. Inhabitants of the less industrialized Northeast and North are more likely to be poor than their compatriots of the South and Southeast. The North in 1980 claimed 4.4 percent of all Brazilian families but 5 percent of the nation's poor families (Pastore 83). Though they do not suffer material poverty to the same degree as their rural counterparts, impoverished city dwellers are confronted with the familiar but more potent demons of jealousy, marital infidelity, and domestic conflict, among others (Burdick 1990: 156). These demons, of course, existed in the countryside but did not torment people with the same intensity as in the cities. Urbanization concentrated people in high-density spaces that sharpened both domestic and extradomestic conflict, particularly in the favelas and baixadas. Whereas the Amazonian *lavrador* (agricultural worker) might have to row an hour upstream to drink a few rounds of cachaça (sugar-cane rum) with his friends at a general store, the day laborer in Belém's baixadas need only walk to the corner bar, where intoxicating spirits flow seven days a week. Moreover, urban spouses have a much greater pool of potential paramours for extramarital affairs. Many Pentecostal women, in fact, enter the church seeking a solution to their husbands' philandering. Social indicators fail to capture these less tangible dimensions of urban poverty, but they are as significant as more measurable phenomena, such as unemployment and illness, in the conversion testimonials of Brazilian Pentecostals.

The Believers of Belém

Pentecostals seek spiritual power that will free them from material deprivation. Like half of their compatriots, the great majority of crentes struggle to meet their basic needs. Their evangelical faith affects the way in which they subjectively experience poverty, but the objective conditions are the same for believers and nonbelievers. Research on Latin American Pentecostals uniformly identifies the great majority of crentes as members of the lower classes. However, their exact socioeconomic position among the lower classes has been the subject of intense debate. In Brazil, scholars have generally characterized Pentecostals as the "poorest of the poor," those who suffer absolute poverty (Mariz 1994b and Cesar). Mariz, in her comparative study of Umbanda, Catholic Base Christian Communities (CEBs), and Pentecostalism, located crentes at the bottom rung of the lower class and members of the CEBs at the top.

Outside of Brazil, researchers have not in general classified Pentecostals as the most destitute of the poor or differentiated them economically from their nonreligious peers who occupy the middle rungs of the lower class (Aguilar et al. and Galliano). Analyzing the socioeconomic status of Salvadoran Protestants, Edwin Aguilar and his colleagues found them to be indistinct from their nonreligious peers. Yet others have portrayed Latin American Pentecostals as social climbers within the confines of their own class (Stoll 1994 and Mariz 1992). Mariz posits that Pentecostals' ascetic behavior allows them to reduce consumption of nonessentials, such as alcohol, which can consume up to 30 percent of the household budget of the Latin American poor.

Socioeconomic data collected on Pentecostals in Belém demonstrate the need to distinguish between preaffiliation and postaffiliation economic indicators. Moreover, there are interdenominational differences in terms of the class composition of church members. In Belém and throughout Ibero-America, Pentecostal churches tend to recruit members from the lower to middle ranks of the poor. Unlike the CEBs, which attract affiliates from older more established bairros, Pentecostal churches flourish in the baixadas and invasion sites that have mushroomed since the 1950s.[8]

Data on median family income in Belém and the location of the AD's 165 temples reveal a direct correlation between the geography of income and temple distribution. In other words, an inverse relationship between the number of temples in a given bairro and household income means that the poorer an area is, the more churches it will have and vice versa. Batista Campos, the upper-middle-class neighborhood where I resided during my research, had a median household income of 15.8 minimum wages and a total population/AD temple ratio of 19,566/1. In contrast, one of the poorest bairros of the baixadas, Sacramenta, with a median household income of 3.8 minimum wages, had a population to temple ratio of 2,227/1, the highest in the city. As of 1991, no AD houses of worship were to be found in several historic middle-class districts, such as Reduto and Cidade Velha. The landmark 1992 census of Protestantism in Rio de Janeiro conducted by ISER confirms

FIGURE 2. Assembleiana children lunching in the bairro of Sacramenta, Belém.

the correlation between the geography of Pentecostal temple distribution and household income.

Pentecostals in Belém experience intraclass and occasionally interclass mobility. By eliminating expenditures associated with the male prestige complex, Assembleianos were able to climb from the lower and middle ranks of poverty to the upper echelons, and some Quandrangulares migrated from poverty, defined as per capita income of one-half the minimum wage or less, to the lower rungs of the middle class.[9] Median per capita income was .6 minimum wage for the Pentecostal population surveyed. Analysis by church affiliation shows household income varying significantly along denominational lines. Members of the IEQ earned almost twice what their Assembleiano brethren did. While crentes of the AD occupied the upper ranks of poverty, with a per capita household income of .5 minimum wage, Quadrangulares, averaging a household income of .9 minimum wage, reached into the lower ranks of the middle class. Paul Freston, one of the few scholars to discuss interdenominational variations in the socioeconomic status of Latin American Pentecostals, has ranked Brazilian Protestant churches according to the class composition of their members. Of course, mainline Protestant churches, such as the Methodist and Presbyterian, rank highest. Socioeconomically, the Pentecostal denominations rank as follows, in descending order: IEQ, IURD, AD, CC (Christian Congregation), BPC (Brazil for Christ), DEA (God Is Love) (Freston 113).

Oral histories of Belenense Pentecostals verify the centrality of poverty in believers' lives. Queried about their greatest existential problem, interviewees mentioned financial hardship more often than any other difficulty. Ovidio Pinheiro, for example, a seventy-seven-year-old retired night watchman and member of the AD, said, "Money is my greatest problem, because there isn't enough money to buy food every day. And that becomes a problem, wondering how to get food. The Lord knows that those who don't have a good salary don't always have good days. Their spiritual life is fine, but the family finances are bad." Reflecting their higher household incomes, Quadrangulares cited family conflict slightly more often than financial difficulty in their responses.

Like their non-Pentecostal neighbors in the baixadas, crentes' meager income derives from their concentration in the informal and service sectors of the local economy. Most men had worked in agriculture and/or fishing in the interior. As lavradores, they cultivated manioc and beans and gathered Amazonian fruits for domestic consumption. In Belém, these rural migrants, with minimal formal education, found employment that allowed them to raise their standard of living modestly but still did not provide enough to meet basic needs. Most Pentecostal men, like their non-Pentecostal contemporaries, followed a pattern of employment that involved working in both the formal and informal sectors of the economy but more frequently in the latter.

The bulk of Pentecostal men, according to data from AD membership records in Belém and interviews with individual members, labor in the low-paying service sector. The most common jobs are security guard, carpenter, shop clerk, janitor, house painter, bus and truck driver, and day laborer. More crente men worked as security guards than in any other occupation. In Brazil guards of public and private property risk life and limb (drivers of armored vehicles went on strike in 1994 because so many of their colleagues were dying in armed assaults). After security guard, joblessness ranked as the second most common occupational status. José Castro, the leader of a small AD congregation in the baixada of Sacramenta who had been working since the age of nine, had lost his job as an armed guard at a bank four months before our interview. He described how he survived without steady employment. "When I get a job I work only about two to three days, and then I wait for another, always praying that the Lord will let me be self-employed [*conta propria*]. I take any kind of job that is offered to me. I work in carpentry, painting, construction; I do everything." In summary, 61.5 percent of Pentecostal men interviewed worked in the informal sector at the time of their interview, and 65.2 percent were employed in services.

The service sector claimed an even greater proportion of Pentecostal women. Of economically active crente women, 77.4 percent were employed as domestic servants, nannies, laundresses, and seamstresses, working long hours and receiving much less than the minimum wage. More than a third (38.7 percent) of Pentecostal women had at some time worked as *domesticas*. Some even worked for middle-class Pentecostal families, where their compensation was often no better than in non-Pentecostal homes. Claudia Gomes, a single twenty-one-year-old member of the AD, labored sixty hours a week for one-third the minimum wage, approximately US$22 a month. Next to domestic service, Pentecostal women were most frequently employed as door-to-door salespersons, selling clothes and cosmetics. As independent agents of U.S. multinational corporations, principally AMWAY and Avon, the women determined their own work schedules.[10] Flexible work hours allowed women to augment the household income substantially without abandoning their role as homemaker and caregiver.

Even the sizeable minority of women (40.3 percent) who did not work outside the home usually supplemented their household income by making and selling snacks and sweets, such as popsicles, cakes, and *salgadinhos* (fried croquettes filled with cheese or meat). Pentecostal men enthusiastically embraced this type of microenterprise, because it augmented family earnings without drawing their spouses or common-law wives (*amigas*) out of the home and into the *rua*, the street, where the evil world offers temptation at every corner. Of the 60 percent of the women who worked outside the home, only 16.1 percent held jobs in the formal sector of the economy. These women tended to have more schooling than their sisters in faith.

Research on Pentecostals in Belém corroborates sociological studies on evangelical Protestantism and Pentecostalism in Latin America that discovered Pentecostal workers to be concentrated in the service sector (Rolim 1985, Guimaraes, and Page). Rolim argues that crentes, in comparison to their non-Pentecostal peers, are disproportionately represented in services. Data from Belém, however, show no significant sectoral difference between Pentecostals and their impoverished contemporaries. Bryan Roberts, one of the first scholars to perceive the proliferation of evangelical Protestantism in Latin America, found Guatemalan Protestant men more likely to be self-employed than nonevangelicals (757). Though my own research in Belém does not confirm Roberts's findings, many believers of both sexes aspired to become microentrepreneurs. Unsurprisingly, members of the IURD and IEQ, where prosperity theology achieves its maximum expression, were particularly enthralled by the idea of running their own businesses. On Mondays at the IURD temples in Belém, telegenic evangelists bedecked in high-powered business suits led those who "desired to be self-employed, and prosper in work" in the Prosperity Campaign (Corrente da Prosperidade). José Cardoso, a twenty-seven-year-old furniture maker and AD member who lived in the invasion site of Pantanal, explained two advantages of self-employment. "I always used to ask the Lord to help me be self-employed. It's not good to have a boss. Besides, it gives you more time for evangelizing."

Another salient characteristic of the Pentecostal population in Belém is their status as migrants. An overwhelming majority (75.1 percent) of informants were not born in Belém.[11] Of my interviewees, 60.2 percent had migrated to Belém from the interior of the state, while 15.9 percent came to the city from neighboring states, primarily Maranhão. Those born in Belém, less than one-fourth of the total, tended to be younger than the others, the majority under thirty. When queried as to their reasons for migrating to Belém, almost half (49 percent) cited the lack of employment opportunities in their place of origin. Another significant portion, 18.4 percent, mentioned the underdeveloped educational system of the rural areas as a reason for abandoning the interior. Illness also sent inhabitants of the riverine communities of the interior to the state capital in search of medical treatment. One of nineteen siblings, Felipe Fernandes, a thirty-three-year-old baker and AD member, vividly described the hardships of life in the Amazonian province of Igarapé-Mirim.

> Well, our situation was somewhat precarious, since we didn't have good conditions for survival. I remember Dad rowing from Vila de Mamangau Grande to Vila de Maiouata to buy a little can of farina milk, and when he returned home we were all waiting with little cups.

It was hard back then. I also remember Dad would say, "Look, I bought a little piece of jerky for each of you. First eat the açai. When you are down to the last spoonful of the delicious açai, then you can eat the jerky." He couldn't bear that situation anymore, the lack of food and money, so we left for Belém.

In contrast to much of the literature on Pentecostalism in Latin America, research in Belém does not point to rural-to-urban migration as an impetus to evangelical affiliation. Physical migration can serve as a springboard for social, cultural, and religious change, but the fact that a large proportion of informants had already become Pentecostals before arriving in Belém exposes fissures in the anomic-migrant theory. Brazilian Pentecostalism does claim a greater proportion of urban practitioners than rural ones, but to characterize it as an "urban phenomenon," as some have, is to exaggerate.[12] The omnipresence of the AD in the Brazilian *campo*, coupled with the concentration of mainline Protestantism in the cities, puts the claim to urbanism in doubt. Moreover, those migrants who did join Pentecostal churches in Belém typically did so only after five to ten years of living in the baixadas. Latin American Pentecostalism is indeed a religion of the poor but is only slightly more urban than rural.

In addition to their status as service workers and migrants, Pentecostals in Belém and across Latin America are predominantly female. The ramifications of this gender imbalance will be explored in depth in part 2, but here it suffices to say that the corps of dedicated ushers, Sunday school teachers, choir directors, and visitors (*visitadoras*) are the lifeblood of the Pentecostal movement. With the great exception of the IEQ, men compose the hierarchy of Pentecostal churches. However, female members largely run the daily affairs of the churches. At several services I attended, women and girls filled the left side of the sanctuary while only a scattering of men and boys worshiped on the right.

Crente females in Belém and most of Latin America outnumber males by a ratio of two to one. Many of my interviewees explained the gender disequilibrium in terms of a widely held belief that there are ten females in Belém for every male. Census figures for 1990 reveal the actual ratio to be approximately fifty-one to forty-nine. Urban lore aside, Pentecostalism in Latin America is largely a religion of and for women. It must be noted, however, that this gender gap is not peculiar to Pentecostalism. Catholicism and African-Latin American religion are also sustained by female believers.

With the exception of public *festas* and ceremonies related to the

Catholic saints, nonindigenous Latin American men have traditionally regarded religion as pertaining to the private female sphere of home and family. So prevalent is this belief that devout Catholic and Umbandista men, particularly those aspiring to the priesthood, are often suspected of being homosexuals. While Pentecostal men are exempt from such suspicions, they too are often mocked by their coworkers and former drinking partners for abandoning the comportment that has traditionally formed an integral part of Latin American conceptions of masculinity. Abstinence from alcohol, tobacco, prostitution, and gambling can call into question the believer's manliness. Given Pentecostalism's repudiation of the male prestige complex, it falls to subsequent chapters to explain its success in attracting poor Brazilian men.

The Pentecostal Boom in Three Dimensions

This book is organized into three parts. Part I traces the historical development of Pentecostalism in Brazil, with particular emphasis on the social and economic context in which it has flourished. Chapter 1 commences with the birth of Pentecostalism in Los Angeles and follows its implantation and three stages of growth in Belém and the rest of Brazil. Drawing heavily on oral history, part II demonstrates that the dialectic between faith healing and illness in the conversion process is key to understanding Pentecostalism's remarkable success among the poor in Brazil and much of Ibero-America. In accord with the manner in which my informants constructed their own narratives, this section is divided into the three stages of the conversion process: preconversion, conversion, and postconversion. Wherever possible, the voices of my crente informants resonate through the text, articulating their faith in their own words.[13]

In chapter 2 I show how the preconversion world of illness and affliction prepares impoverished Belenenses to accept the Pentecostal message of divine healing. For analytical purposes, I classify illness into three categories: physical, social, and supernatural. Poverty, in varying degrees, underlies all three types of disease. The core of the argument, chapter 3 analyzes the three main steps in the conversion process: a sudden health crisis, faith healing, and affiliation with the Pentecostal community. Exploring the mechanics of the conversion process, such as the contractual agreement that the petitioner enters into with Jesus or the Holy Spirit, I posit that to convert to Pentecostalism is to heal the maladies of poverty.

Chapters 4 and 5 focus on health maintenance, or how converts are able to preserve their physical, psychological, and spiritual well-being in the midst of ubiquitous illness. In the fourth chapter, I advance the thesis that spiritual ecstasy, manifested in both the gifts of the Spirit and baptism in the Holy Spirit, and mutual aid networks fill impoverished Pentecostals with an overwhelming sense of divine power. But ecstatic worship and congregational support are not the only ways in which crentes tap into the healing force of the Holy Spirit. Chapter 5 considers the ideological dualism and moral asceticism of Latin American Pentecostalism, which require adherents to renounce the earthly vices that frequently culminate in illness. Pentecostal Manichaeism demonizes the street, where many *favelados* (shantytown residents), particularly men, face the temptations of liquor and prostitution, among others.

Power also emerges as a central theme in part III. However, here the analysis shifts from the microlevel of the individual believer to the macrolevel of the church as a religious institution. In chapter 6, which explores the internal organizational structure of Pentecostal churches, I employ the AD in Belém as a case study to explain how such an ostensibly authoritarian and centralized organization can allow such a high degree of member participation. This section starts at the apex of the ecclesiastical pyramid and descends through the institutional ranks, examining the major church offices and groups.

Whereas the subject of chapter 6 is the internal organization of ecclesiastical power, relations with the external world are the primary concern of chapter 7. Specifically, I trace the political history of the AD in Belém, averring that the region's largest Protestant church replaced the Catholic church as the military regime's primary religious client in Amazonia during the twenty-one-year dictatorship. Finally, in the conclusion I attempt to synthesize the principal arguments set forth in the book.

CHAPTER 1

A Prophetic History

❧

The Birth of Pentecostalism in Los Angeles

The perennial hopes and popular religiosity of disenfranchised African Americans gave birth to Pentecostalism. William Joseph Seymour, an African-American itinerant preacher from Louisiana, arrived in Los Angeles in early 1906 at the invitation of an Angelino church worker, Neely Terry, whom he had met at a Holiness mission in Houston, Texas (Anderson 60). Engulfed in the Holiness revival sweeping through the independent missions and churches of working-class Los Angeles, Seymour used the pulpit at Terry's storefront church, the Santa Fe Holiness Mission, to preach the doctrine of baptism in the Holy Spirit.[1] Seymour's novel message that glossolalia was the "seal" or external manifestation of baptism in the Spirit found little receptivity among the humble congregation. Such was Seymour's rejection that the mission padlocked the doors to prevent his return (Cox 54).

Undaunted by the hostile reception, Seymour sought out home prayer meetings where he could continue to preach the gifts of the Holy Spirit and the imminence of the apocalypse. The African-American laundresses and domestic servants who gathered to worship in the modest homes of a rundown section of the city responded enthusiastically to the one-eyed evangelist's message of Pentecostal salvation. The news that Seymour himself and one of his followers had spoken in tongues spread quickly through the Holiness community, attracting greater numbers of spiritual seekers to the home worship services on Bonnie Brae Street. Growing crowds and heightened fervor led Seymour to rent a vacant stable on Azusa Street, where he preached to the faithful and the curious from a makeshift pulpit of packing boxes.[2] Although attendance rose steadily during the spring of 1906, it took a natural disaster to spark the Azusa Street revival of Pentecostal lore. The San Francisco earthquake of April 18 shook the religious soul of the nation. Seymour's millenarian teachings gained newfound relevance amid the apocalyptic fears provoked by the temblor (Anderson 65–67). Hundreds of nervous Angelinos flocked to Seymour's charismatic mission, where they ignited the Pentecostal conflagration that rages across the globe almost a century later.

The Pará Prophecy

Within five years of the Azusa Street revival, the religion that had captured the spiritual and existential aspirations of African-American wash-women in Los Angeles arrived in Brazil via third-class steamer. Two Swedish Baptist immigrants, Gunnar Vingren and Daniel Berg, who had met and been baptized in the Holy Spirit in Chicago, were to be the agents of Pentecostalism's expansion to Brazil. Like their coreligionists in Los Angeles, both Berg and Vingren were of proletarian origin. Berg labored as a foundryman, and Vingren pastored a small Baptist church in South Bend, Indiana. Eager to win converts to the Pentecostal movement, the two Swedes received a prophecy instructing them to conduct mission work in a place neither had ever heard of: Pará. Emilio Conde, writing the first history of the Assembly of God in Brazil, mystified the event that brought the Swedish evangelists to the Amazon.

> Sometime later, Daniel Berg went to visit Pastor Gunnar Vingren in the city of South Bend. On that occasion in a prayer meeting, God spoke through a prophetic message to the hearts of Daniel Berg and Gunnar Vingren that they should depart to preach the Gospel and the blessings of the Pentecostal awakening. The place mentioned in the prophecy was Pará. No one present had heard of such a place. After the prayer meeting, the two young men went to a library to consult a map that would show them the location of Pará. Thus, they discovered that it was a state in the North of Brazil.   (Conde 14)[3]

Berg and Vingren, determined to fulfill the prophecy, scraped together enough cash for third-class fare on a steamer sailing from New York to Belém. Arrayed in wool suits, the Swedish Pentecostals arrived in the torrid climate of Belém on November 19, 1910. The North American pastor of the city's Methodist church directed them to the local Baptist temple, where the minister, who spoke English, agreed to shelter them in the church basement for approximately two dollars a night. The two missionaries spent the ensuing months participating in worship services and prayer meetings at the Baptist church and at Belém's three other Protestant houses of worship. Portuguese lessons also consumed much of their time, as neither had arrived in Brazil with any notion of the language (Vingren 1991: 31–32).

Although Berg and Vingren had affiliated with the Baptist church of Belém, their Pentecostal message of baptism in the Holy Spirit contradicted Baptist doctrine, which held that the outpouring of the Holy Spirit described in Acts was an historical event not to be repeated in modern times. For a number of months the Swedish Pentecostals held small prayer meetings with groups of ten to fifteen members of the Baptist church. The Baptist pastor tolerated the unsanctioned prayer circles until one of the faithful, Celina Albuquerque, was baptized in the Spirit and spoke in tongues in May of 1911. An act of faith healing started the chain of events that culminated in a church schism and the birth of the Western Hemisphere's largest Pentecostal denomination. Gunnar Vingren recorded the historical occasion in his diary.

> During that week we had prayer meetings every night in a sister's home who had an incurable illness on her lips. We felt sad. We were saddened because she could not attend services at church. The first thing I did was to ask her if she believed that Jesus could cure her. She said yes. So we told her to get rid of all the medicine she was taking. We prayed for her, and the Lord Jesus healed her completely. At the ensuing prayer meetings she began to pray for baptism in the Holy Spirit. On Thursday, after the service, she continued praying at home. Her name was Celina Albuquerque. She continued praying at home with another sister. And at one o'clock in the morning, sister Celina began to speak in new tongues and spoke for two hours.
>
> (Vingren 1991: 36)

Threatened by the new doctrine and its charismatic disciples, the Baptist pastor convened a special assembly on June 13 and excommunicated Berg and Vingren and their eighteen followers (Vingren 1991: 37). The two Pentecostal missionaries, unfazed by their expulsion, organized the small band of believers into the Apostolic Faith Mission and in 1918 registered the church in Belém under the name of "Assembléia de Deus" (Vingren 1991: 97).

Despite its North American origins and Swedish cultural imprint, the AD quickly won many converts through its emphasis on faith healing. Early twentieth-century Belém was an incubator of disease. Equatorial heat and one of the globe's highest precipitation rates made Belém an efficient breeding ground for malaria, yellow fever, cholera, tuberculosis, meningitis, and even leprosy. Shortly before Berg and Vingren's arrival, lepers throughout Amazonia had flocked to the Amazonian rubber capital upon news of a miraculous medicinal root that could purportedly cure the disfiguring disease (Conde 17). Many of those suffering from Hansen's disease turned to

Pentecostalism after discovering that the root was less than miraculous. In his memoirs, Berg described the heavy toll that the lethal convergence of an insalubrious climate and poverty exacted on the city's inhabitants.

> It was common at the time for lepers to walk the city streets with great risk of infecting other people. We saw sick people without hands or feet or with ears and noses destroyed by the illness. The number of sick people in the streets was a depressing sight. In addition there was yellow fever. An epidemic came from the interior; it started with a few cases but a short while later spread through the whole city.
>
> The lines of sick people at the hospitals grew longer with each passing day, and the funeral processions to the cemeteries grew at short intervals. It was wrenching to see the poor classes, treated so harshly in life, laden with the added burden of sickness. Some who had lost family members to illness came to visit us in our small room, seeking comfort in the word of God.   (Berg 43)

To win converts to their Pentecostal faith, Berg and Vingren spent much of their time making house calls on the sick.[4] Berg reports receiving calls at their basement room after midnight from distraught relatives of the infirm. Even if the afflicted eventually succumbed to malaria, yellow fever, or another tropical malady, the therapeutic value of prayer, anointment with oil, and laying on of hands proved real. With little access to the city's precarious health care facilities and neglected by the Catholic church, many ill Belenenses and their families came to the Assembly of God as a last resort.

Despite frequent and often violent persecution by sectors of the Catholic church, Berg and Vingren's indefatigable proselytizing in Belém and the surrounding area won hundreds of new converts to the fledgling church. To avoid the sticks and stones and epithets hurled by hostile crowds, the first baptisms were performed clandestinely around eleven o'clock at night in the turbid waters of the rivers and igarapés that cut through the region (Vingren 1991: 38). Vingren recorded only 13 baptisms in 1911, the founding year of the church. By 1914, the number of Belenenses who had affiliated with the Pentecostal church through the nocturnal baptisms had jumped to 190 (Vingren 1991: 65).

The approximately two hundred Pentecostals were so economically disprivileged that they could not afford to rent a space for worship. Berg, who had been supporting both Vingren and the mission work by selling Bibles door to door and working part-time as a smelter at the Port Company of Pará, drew on his own funds to rent a building in 1914 (Vingren 1987: 19–20).[5] A limited cash flow, however, did not impede steady expansion in the early years. By the mid-1920s the congregation had grown such that the first temple, with space for twelve hundred worshipers, was constructed and inaugurated in 1926. By 1930, after two decades of ceaseless evangelization in Belém, the new denomination boasted three temples and a thousand worshipers. Radiating from the capital along the Belém-Bragança railroad, lay evangelists had founded fifty churches in Belém's hinterland, in towns such as Capanema, Quatipuru, and Bragança (Vingren 1991: 42, 50).

But the sparsely populated backlands of the state of Pará were not the primary concern of the Swedish missionaries. Since the 1920s, Berg and Vingren had been making increasingly frequent trips to the burgeoning metropolises of the Southeast, Rio de Janeiro and São Paulo. Although the church in Belém continued to serve as the base of operations from which missionary efforts were launched throughout Amazonia and the Northeast, the transfer of AD headquarters in 1930 to Rio de Janeiro relegated the Belém church to a more regional role.

The Second Front: The Christian Congregation in São Paulo

In the Southeast the AD did not play the pioneering role that it had in the North and Northeast. While the Swedish evangelists preached salvation and healing to impoverished Amazonian *caboclos* (miscegenated backlanders), an Italian immigrant delivered the Pentecostal message to his transplanted compatriots in São Paulo. Luis Francescon, like his Scandinavian coreligionists, had converted to Pentecostalism in Chicago. Francescon, who had received his own prophecy, headed south to Argentina and Brazil, where recently arrived Italian immigrants swelled the ranks of the working-class districts of São Paulo and Buenos Aires. An artisan, Francescon spoke the colorful language of his proletarian brethren.

Francescon's new religious idiom had the same effect on Paulista Presbyterians that Berg and Vingren's doctrine of Spirit baptism had among Baptists. In June of 1910, a year before the founding of the AD, Francescon accepted an invitation to preach at the Presbyterian Church of Brás, São Paulo's largest Italian bairro. His sermon, delivered in Italian, exhorted Presbyterians to seek baptism by the Holy Spirit. Francescon's homily provoked his expulsion from the church and a full-blown schism. Within months, the Italian-American preacher and twenty adherents had founded the Christian Congregation (Congregação Cristã), the first Pentecostal church in Brazil. The church took root in the bairro of São Brás and followed the migratory routes of Italian immigrants through the interior of the state of São Paulo. As the immigrants acculturated to Brazilian life, the CC adopted Portuguese in its worship services and began to attract native Brazilians (Read 23–26).

Severing the Ties of Dependency

The end of the first period of classic Brazilian Pentecostalism coincides with major transformations in the national economy and body politic. The global financial crisis of 1929 sent coffee prices plummeting and made imports prohibitively expensive. The coup d'état which brought Getulio Vargas to power in 1930 marked the shift from an economy dominated by agro-export interests to one led by industrialists. Capitalizing on the high cost of imports, Brazilian industrialists, backed by the state, launched the initial phase of import-substitution industrialization, in which goods that were previously imported would be manufactured domestically. The crash of international capital markets forced Brazil to look inward, and beyond coffee, in its quest for economic development.

While Vargas dismantled the coffee monoculture that had retarded the nation's economic and political development, the Assembly of God brought the first era of Pentecostal history to a close by severing the ties of dependency on foreign missions. Because they took decades to nationalize, the historic Protestant churches and faith missions that had been proselytizing in Brazil before the arrival of the CC and AD were unable to attract the masses. North American and European missionaries did not believe that their Brazilian brothers were prepared to govern their own churches. Having perhaps learned from the errors of their Protestant brethren, the Swedish leaders of the AD, meeting in Natal at the first General Convention in 1930, decided to nationalize their church. Brazilian pastors were to head the central churches of each district. Ecclesiastical leaders at Natal also decided to transfer national headquarters from Belém to Rio de Janeiro (AD em Belém 1986: 25).

During the second period of the classic era of Pentecostal history, from 1930 to 1952, the AD and CC continued to be the only major denominations in the country. Without significant competition from other Pentecostal churches or the ineffectual historical churches and faith missions, the AD and CC began to harvest a bounty of nominal and disaffected Catholics. Membership rolls show accelerated growth starting in the early 1930s. The CC, due to its inception in densely populated São Paulo, expanded at a quicker pace than the AD until the Second World War. William Read, one of the first scholars to examine the proliferation of Pentecostalism in Latin America, charted the remarkable development of both the CC and AD. The CC had 36,644 Brazilian members, the majority Paulistas, in 1936, the first year in which statistics were available. Only fourteen years later, in 1950, church membership had mushroomed to 132,297, an increase of 261 percent (Read 29). After two decades of proselytizing, the AD had a modest membership of 14,000 in 1930. Almost twenty years later, in 1949, this figure had increased over eightfold, to 120,000 (Read 120). Total Pentecostal growth from 1932 to 1955 gives an even clearer picture of the accelerated rate of expansion. Twenty-nine times more believers claimed Pentecostal affiliation in the mid-1950s than in 1932 (Endruveit 45). Despite the CC's faster growth in the early years, church expansion was highly regionalized; that is, it was concentrated in the states of São Paulo and Paraná. In contrast, the AD by 1940 had already established temples in all states and federal territories (Landim 51).

Rubber Bust and Pentecostal Boom in Belém

In Belém the construction of the Central Temple in 1926 symbolized the consolidation and permanence of the Pentecostal movement. The attendance of Governor Dionisio Bentes de Carvalho at the cornerstone-laying ceremony lent legitimacy to the Pentecostal movement and presaged the political linkages with the state which would become of crucial importance in the 1960s. Although the General Convention at Natal had mandated that Brazilian ministers serve as the head pastors of the central temples, the AD in Belém decided to retain their senior pastor, missionary Nels Nelson, thus continuing the legacy of Swedish leadership. By 1930, the church had developed to the point where Nelson found it necessary to institute a weekly administrative assembly. A secretary kept detailed minutes of the meetings.[6] The popularity of the Pentecostal message among the city's lepers led the church in 1932 to establish a sanitary commission charged with the task of restricting their access to the temples (Acts 1932). Hansen's disease provoked such fear that even a church which won converts on the basis of faith healing was willing to forgo the conversion of these social pariahs.

If the Pentecostal message found a receptive audience during the euphoric climate of the rubber boom years, "post-*Hevean*" Belém, reeling from the rubber bust, embraced the gospel according to the AD even more ardently. The collapse of the rubber industry in 1912 not only threw the Paraense capital into an economic tailspin but also sent thousands of northeastern seringueiros back to their home states of Ceará and Maranhão. Many of the seringueiros, returning to their native lands in the impoverished Northeast, planted the hearty seeds of Pentecostalism in one of Brazilian Catholicism's most fertile soils.

Despite a net population loss in Belém, the AD grew rapidly from the 1920s through the 1940s. Decades of meteoric population growth, spurred by the rubber economy, came to an abrupt halt in the early 1920s. Belém's 236,400 inhabitants recorded in the 1920 census dwindled to 208,706 in 1940 (Penteado 205). Yet membership data show impressive net gains for the AD during the same period. According to Gunnar Vingren, AD membership in Belém leapt from seventy in 1916 to the one thousand who in 1930 worshiped in the city's three Pentecostal temples (Vingren 1991: 65). As wartime demand for rubber began to resuscitate the region's depressed economy, the Administrative Acts of 1942 reported seventeen hundred baptized faithful on the membership rolls. Implementing a strategy of evangelization that continues today, church workers and laity recruited the great majority of converts from the peripheral zones of the city.

The AD, as a church of the poor that expanded among those who had been pushed to the margins of economic, social, political, and religious life, erected well defined boundaries that served to separate itself from the world.[7] A rigid code of conduct kept the evil world at bay while creating a sense of group solidarity and distinctiveness. During the 1930s and 1940s, the first two decades in which records were kept, frequent disciplinary action, including reprimands and expulsions, filled the pages of the Administrative Acts. From the beginning, Pentecostal women outnumbered men by a ratio of about two to one, but women were singled out disproportionately for discipline. Almost 90 percent of all disciplinary action during the 1930s and 1940s was directed at female members of the AD. By far the most common reason for censure involved alteration of the woman's "veil." Literal interpretation of 1 Corinthians 11:15 proscribed any cutting or trimming of women's hair.[8] Waist-length hair and ascetic apparel differentiated Assembleiana women and girls from their less conservatively dressed neighbors. The strict dress code also applied to men, but the few males who were disciplined had usually been caught engaging in male prestige activities such as drinking and gambling.

In a free religious market, invective against potential or actual competitors often forms an integral part of boundary maintenance. Spiritual leaders denounce the rival sect or church as heretical and admonish members to avoid contamination by the diabolical doctrine. Since the AD exercised such complete hegemony in Belém's alternative religious arena, it is not until the late 1940s that a religious rival is mentioned. In 1947 Pastor-President Nels Nelson warned his flock of the "pernicious sabbath doctrine" preached by Seventh-Day Adventists (Acts).

Persecution by the Catholic Church

Inchoate Protestant sects, however, were not the Assembly's primary concern. Since Vargas's ascent to power in 1930, the Brazilian Catholic church, under the dynamic leadership of Dom Sebastião Leme, had reasserted its position in society. After decades of waning influence, the church sought to establish a conservative presence in the upper echelons of society and government. The new model of church, known as neo-Christendom, successfully forged an alliance with the state founded on the pillars of education, morality, anticommunism, and anti-Protestantism (Mainwaring 27).

The rapid expansion of Pentecostalism and, to a lesser extent, Spiritism transformed the Catholic church's attitude of benign neglect into a policy of persecution. With the Estado Novo's elimination of any communist threat, real or imagined, Pentecostalism by the late 1930s had become one of the Catholic church's principal enemies. Brazilian bishops meeting at the Brazilian Plenary Council in 1939 developed a vehicle for launching a frontal offensive against the dynamic crentes. The bishops charged the newly created ecclesiastical department, the Defense of the Faith (Defesa da Fé), with the task of compiling demographic data on Protestant churches, particularly Pentecostals. Given the unreliability of national census figures on the Protestant population, the Defense of the Faith sought more accurate information on the size of its rivals.

Of greater concern to the AD and CC was the second prong of the Catholic offensive. The church directed violent attacks on Pentecostal temples and believers. Some of my older informants, at the behest of their local priest, admitted to stoning Protestant houses of worship in their youth. Local government often colluded with the church in persecuting Pentecostals (Rolim 1987: 65). Violence, however, was extremely localized, and few *crentes* lost their lives.

Anti-Protestant crusades in Belém and the state of Pará were probably not as virulent as in other regions, due to the beneficence of the state governor. Commenting on the governor's good will in his memoirs, Nels Nelson wrote: "After the revolution of October 1930, we have had a good governor. He is Catholic but a great friend of the evangelical church. . . . His name is

Major Joaquim Magalhaes Cardoso Barata. He has helped all crentes in the best possible way. There was never so much liberty to preach the gospel as during his rule. Thanks be to God" (Vingren 1987: 47). Catholic repression, paradoxically, added fuel to the engine of Pentecostal growth. A seemingly omnipotent enemy provided a rallying point around which Pentecostals converged in solidarity (Rolim 1985: 68).

Church Growth in the 1940s

The revitalization of the local economy sparked by wartime demand for rubber failed to deliver tangible benefits to those whose labor made the boom possible. Precarious living conditions combined with neglect by the Catholic church made the Pentecostal message of immediate healing and salvation increasingly popular on Belém's urban periphery. In just five years, AD membership more than doubled, from 1,700 in 1942 to 3,529 in 1947 (Acts). According to the demographic census, which undoubtedly underestimated the nation's vibrant Protestant community, the number of faithful who identified themselves as Protestants in the state of Pará almost doubled during the 1940s. The 1.2 percent of all Paraenses who claimed evangelical affiliation in 1940 jumped to 2.2 percent in 1950 (IBGE 1992: 27). AD growth at the national level mirrored northern patterns. Membership rose twofold, from 60,000 in 1943 to 120,000 in 1949 (Read 120). The CC, despite its proscription of the use of mass media for proselytization purposes, followed suit, doubling its membership rolls during the same period from 50,223 to 105,838 (Read 29). But rejection of mass media, particularly radio, curtailed CC expansion in the next chapter of Pentecostal history, which commenced in the early 1950s.

The Modern Era

The emergence of the International Church of the Four-Square Gospel (Igreja do Evangelho Quadrangular) meant the end of four decades of hegemony of the classic type of Pentecostalism represented by the AD and CC and marked the beginning of modern Pentecostalism.[9] Until the National Evangelization Crusade in 1953, which led to the founding of the IEQ two years later, Pentecostal churches recruited new members almost exclusively through preexisting family and neighborhood networks. The AD had begun to take its message to the airwaves, but neither it nor the CC had ever attempted to win thousands of converts at once by staging massive public crusades. The IEQ, in contrast to its more conservative Brazilian rivals, had mastered modern techniques of mass communication in its North American crusades.

Founded in Los Angeles by Canadian evangelist Aimee Semple McPherson in 1922, the IEQ integrated Hollywood showmanship into its evangelistic campaigns. A pioneer in the use of radio, Aimee secured her own station in 1924 (Freston 83). The enigmatic and flamboyant McPherson crisscrossed the country filling tents and auditoriums with the faithful and the curious (Cox 123–128). Deemphasizing the ascetic codes of conduct of classic Pentecostalism, McPherson offered the promise of healing for the physically ill and those afflicted by the economic demons of the Great Depression. Her rousing services were essentially sessions of collective faith healing.

Harold Williams, an actor (in Hollywood Westerns) turned missionary, brought the Four-Square Gospel to Brazil in 1953 via the National Evangelization Crusade. Drawing on his proselytization skills honed under the tutelage of Aimee, Williams launched the nondenominational crusade in São Paulo with friend Raymond Boatright, another actor-cum-preacher. The crusade introduced a quintessentially North American method of evangelism, the tent revival, to the Brazilian evangelical camp. The novelty of the revivals, which featured Boatright on the electric guitar belting out gospel hymns to the infectious rhythm of "rockabilly," drew wide press coverage, large crowds, and the initial support of many Pentecostal leaders (Freston 82 83). The collective healing sessions that had formed the core of Aimee McPherson's ministry in the United States became the cornerstone of the crusade.

The demand for healing, particularly in urban Brazil, surged partly in response to the stress of rapid social change. Brazil in the early 1950s was suffering the process of modernization. State-directed industrialization and vertiginous urbanization characterized the transformation of the economy and society. Industrial output rose by 140 percent during the decade (Frase 475). Economic policy favoring industrialization led to divestment in the agricultural sector, which sent waves of economic refugees to the cities. Accelerated urbanization had already begun in the 1930s, but by the 1950s significant numbers had migrated to the metropolises of Rio de Janeiro, São Paulo, Belo Horizonte, and other regional centers. Capital-intensive industrialization failed to employ the majority of these unskilled rural migrants.

Bypassed by the modernization project, these new urban residents erected wooden and cardboard shacks in the favelas and baixadas of metropolitan Brazil and sold their undervalued labor on the informal market. The squalor of the slums bred the familiar diseases of rural poverty. Urban poverty exacerbated the pressures on the household unit. Prostitution, alcohol, and

FIGURE 3.   A typical *barraca*, or shack, in the baixada of Guamá, Belém.

gambling existed in rural areas but multiplied on the urban margins. These favelados, excluded from the modernization process, responded enthusiastically to modern Pentecostalism's timeless message of healing.

Opposition on the part of envious Pentecostal leaders ended the crusade. Williams then founded the Crusade Church (Igreja da Cruzada) in 1954, which was reorganized the following year as the IEQ (Freston 83). Despite its dramatic beginning, the IEQ experienced slow growth until the 1970s. The IEQ had demonstrated extraordinary evangelistic acumen by giving a modern sheen to the Pentecostal message. However, Brazilian soil had become less receptive to religious organizations with foreign roots.

The drive toward modernization in Latin America has invariably been linked to populist nationalism. Populist-nationalist leaders, such as Vargas, Lazaro Cardenas in Mexico and Juan Peron in Argentina, sought to develop their countries by diminishing ties to the global market and turning inward. Import-substitution industrialization and the expropriation of foreign petroleum and mining interests were key ingredients in the nationalist recipe for modernization. Reflecting the dialectical relationship between society and religion, the nationalist zeitgeist favored the development of a totally Brazilian church.

Manoel de Mello, a magnetic northeasterner from the state of Pernambuco, emerged as the first Brazilian founder of a major Pentecostal church. Mello, a lay preacher, left the AD and joined the National Evangelization Crusade, in which he quickly rose to national prominence. Crowds numbering close to one hundred thousand pressed into tent meetings in São Paulo to hear the gospel and experience the miraculous healings performed by the spirited evangelist. Mello's enormous popularity transcended the amorphous crusade and led him to found his own church in 1955 (Read 144–145).

Brazil for Christ (Brasil para Cristo [BPC]) perfected the strategies of mass evangelism introduced by the crusade. Whereas the crusade had brought healing campaigns out of the churches and into the public arena, BPC took the message from tents to rented stadiums, theaters, auditoriums, and gymnasiums (Freston 87). The BPC's extensive use of radio complemented and reinforced its evangelistic mission. Mello's rustic demeanor and gospel hymns set to *sertanejo* rhythms (country music from the Northeast) made his morning radio program tremendously successful with transplanted northeasterners living in São Paulo, the industrial center of the nation (Read 147). Unlike the North American founder of the IEQ, Mello spoke the salty language of the Brazilian *povo* (folk).

Consonant with the spirit of the times, Mello became the Pentecostal populist par excellence. His great influence over hundreds of thousands of believers attracted the attention of politicians, who viewed him as a potential political broker and his legions of followers as prospective electorate. The sertanejo preacher's quest to build a monumental temple in São Paulo led Pentecostalism into the Brazilian political arena for the first time. Cognizant of Mello's desire to construct the temple, a shrine to religious populism, Deputy Ademar de Barros approached him with an enticing deal. Mello, in exchange for a generous piece of city property, mobilized BPC in support of Barros's candidacy for president. BPC airwaves broadcast news of Barros's "gift" to the church's estimated five million listeners. In all-night prayer vigils, worshipers implored the Holy Spirit to aid in Barros's election.

The prayers for Barros's campaign went unanswered, and intense pressure from the Catholic church led the shrewd politician to betray the BPC. A demolition crew, sent without previous warning, unleashed its wrecking ball on the newly constructed temple, razing it in a few hours (Read 151). What appeared to be a devastating setback, however, was but a minor obstacle in Mello's political ascent. At the height of his influence in 1962, Mello was able to marshal his flock to elect his assistant, Levy Tavares, federal deputy. Another BPC pastor was elected state deputy in 1966. Echoing the populist sentiment of the time, Mello justified his political activity in terms of global struggle. "While we convert a million, the devil de-converts ten millions (sic) through hunger, misery, militarism, dictatorship" (Hollenweger 104). As the military dictatorship became entrenched in power in the mid-1960s, Pentecostal involvement in national politics became less conspicuous.

The third major church spawned during the era of modern Pentecostalism synthesized elements of classic and modern Pentecostalism while presaging the development of postmodern Pentecostalism in the late 1970s. In the classic pattern of schismatic Pentecostal growth, pastor David Miranda exited BPC to start his own church in São Paulo in 1962. The God Is Love Pentecostal Church (Igreja Pentecostal Deus É Amor [DEA]), unlike its modern counterparts, adopted the ascetic ethos of the AD and CC. The DEA Regulation Handbook for Members is a compendium of draconian ecclesiastical laws dictating personal conduct, dress, and relations between the sexes. For example, Item U6 regulates feminine footwear. "Concerning sisters wearing high heels, worldly shoes, or boots that reach the knee, with the exception of work boots: The Ministry does not agree, based on Isaiah 3:16, Ecclesiastes 6:11, and Jude 12. Whoever does not obey will be expelled from communion until she complies." An addendum in 1987 further stipulated that heels shall not exceed four centimeters in height. Regulations on footwear and eyeglasses, however, coexisted with modern evangelization methods. Miranda elevated faith healing to the point where some researchers have classified God Is Love as an "agency of divine healing" rather than a church (Mendonca and Velasques).

Miranda, shunning television, which he believed pernicious, took to the airwaves of radio to a degree no other Pentecostal evangelist ever had. In 1986 Miranda occupied half of all programming on Radio Tupi in São Paulo. At the end of the 1980s his daily program, *Voz da Libertação* (Voice of Liberation), was broadcast on more than five hundred stations, including at least five of his own (Landim 62).

Within the temple walls, liturgical innovations paved the way for the postmodern Pentecostalism that would emerge a decade and a half later. Although classic Brazilian Pentecostalism exhibited certain syncretic beliefs and practices, DEA raised syncretism to new heights. Borrowing from Roman Catholicism and the African-Brazilian religions of Candomblé and Umbanda, God Is Love recovered the thaumaturgy eliminated centuries ago by the Protestant reformers. Exorcism became a main attraction at DEA services. Not only did pastors expel demons from their human hosts but also invoked the "evil spirits" of Umbanda such as Tranca Rua to be then collectively exorcised by the frenzied congregation.[10] Visual imagery in the temple also broke with the extreme austerity of classic Pentecostal houses of worship.

The regional concentration of modern Pentecostalism in the Southeast, particularly the burgeoning metropolis of São Paulo, meant the continuing dominance of the AD in Belém and in most other areas of the republic. In Belém, Francisco Pereira do Nascimento ended the era of Swedish leadership in 1950 by becoming the first Brazilian to occupy the position of pastor-president. During his ten-year tenure, the church expanded its physical presence in the bairros of the baixadas such as Condor, Arsenal, Matinha, and Jurunas. The church construction boom of the 1940s accelerated in the 1950s, when Assembleianos erected six temples, an 87 percent increase over the previous decade. On the other hand, membership growth for the first and only time in the history of the AD in Belém lagged behind total population growth.

In the 1950s Belém experienced its greatest growth since the crash of the rubber market. From 1949 to 1962 the city's population grew 60 percent, while the church's increased by only 27 percent. Half a century after its founding, the AD boasted 4,023 members (*Estandarte* 10–11/64). The diminished growth rate during the 1950s stemmed, in part, from the neglect of proselytization in favor of the construction of temples. No structural changes occurred in Belenense society, economy, or religion that would have reduced the flow of converts to the AD.

Following the example of his Four-Square compatriot in São Paulo, U.S. missionary Carlos Hultgren brought the AD in Belém into the modern age with radio. Hultgren donated audio equipment to the church, and in late 1955 Radio Marajoara broadcast the first installment of *The Voice of the Gospel*. One of the first set of broadcasts to air attempted to convert listeners through healing. The program, "A Word to the Sick," exhorted the infirm to surrender to the restorative power of the holy microwaves. "If you are sick, put your hand on the radio and pray with true faith, by which you will be radically healed" (*Estandarte* 1/81). Radio evangelization helped to launch the membership boom of the 1960s that continues unabated in the mid-1990s.

The Upsurge of Church Growth in the 1950s

The acceleration of the modernization process in the 1950s corresponded with the take-off of Pentecostal growth in the first years of the decade. While all denominations shared in the growth, the AD was the primary beneficiary. From 1949 to 1962, AD membership increased by a factor of five, reaching 702,750 (Read 119–120). Astronomic growth rates continued in the 1960s. Brazilian Pentecostals multiplied by a factor of thirty-three from 1955 to 1970 (Endruveit 45).

Though the mushrooming favelas of the urban periphery continued to serve as the main suppliers of Pentecostal converts, church growth was not limited to the urban margins. Some of the fastest growth has occurred in the areas of agricultural colonization, particularly in the Center-West. To stave off pressure for agrarian reform and secure its tenuous grip on the sparsely populated region, the military regime provided fiscal incentives for impoverished agricultural workers, especially northeasterners, to colonize the Center-West and parts of the Amazon. Territorial migration from the heavily Catholic Northeast to a region where the church had no established presence facilitated religious migration. Unlike the omnipresent Jesus and Holy Spirit of Pentecostal churches, the saints of popular Catholicism tend to be fixed to particular locales and do not travel easily.

The portable divinity of Pentecostalism thrived on the fluid frontier of capitalist expansion. The Pentecostal churches of the states and territories of the agricultural North (Amazonia) and Center-West experienced record growth in the 1960s. While crentes doubled their ranks nationally between 1960 and 1970, they increased by 291 percent in the Center-West. Pentecostal affiliation grew over 400 percent in the Federal District and Acre. Matto Grosso led the country with the unprecedented expansion rate of 605 percent. In contrast, the northeastern state of Ceará whence many *colonos* hailed, exhibited one of the lowest growth rates, 33 percent (Rolim 1985: 110).

In addition to the wrenching modernization process, a favorable political climate created by the military regime and its clash with the Catholic church fortified Pentecostalism. Both Pentecostal churches and Brazilian Catholicism welcomed the military takeover in 1964, which abruptly ended almost twenty years of formal democracy.[11] By 1968, the Catholic church's attempt to stanch the flow of converts to the AD, BPC, IEQ, and DEA brought it into direct conflict with the generals. Led by Dom Helder Camara, the CNBB (National Council of Brazilian Bishops, the highest authority of the church in Brazil) embarked on a strategy to incorporate the disenfranchised and nominally Catholic masses into the church. In the spirit of the landmark reforms of the Second Vatican Council (1962–1965), the CNBB adopted a "preferential option" for the poor: the disprivileged povo replaced the elite as the object of church evangelization efforts.

Common enemies brought the military regime and Pentecostal

churches together in a tacit alliance. Decades of persecution, coupled with boundary maintenance, had given rise to fervent anti-Catholicism in Pentecostal quarters. Catholicism, Pentecostals argued, was the source of Brazil's underdevelopment. Next to the Catholic church stood communism as the great red devil. Ten years before the onset of the Cold War, the AD denounced the persecution of Christians in the USSR. In the article "Bolsheviks Battle against Christianity," the AD mouthpiece *O Mensageiro da Paz* alluded to the Red Army as "the army of the Antichrist" (2/35). With the backdrop of the Cuban revolution and guerrilla insurgency in Brazil, the red menace of the 1930s seemed much more ominous in the late 1960s and early 1970s. In exchange for resources from the state, AD pastors in Amazonia delivered votes and religious legitimacy to the authoritarian project.

The Boom in Belém

The proliferation of the city's slums, beginning in the early 1960s, corresponds with the take-off of Pentecostal growth in Belém. Recovering from the sluggish growth of the 1950s, AD church membership raced ahead of population growth during the 1960s. Expanding its membership roll by 178 percent, the AD grew three times faster than the city. Statistics for the past three decades (1962–1990) demonstrate nothing less than an explosion in church affiliation. While the population of the former rubber capital increased by a striking 212 percent, the Assembly augmented its membership 934 percent, to 41,589 faithful. Adding the congregants who participate in church life but have not been baptized by immersion, the AD community in Belém approached 70,000, more than 5 percent of the metropolitan population.

The shifting of church resources into proselytization in the 1960s halted the flurry of temple building of the preceding decade. Only four temples were inaugurated in the 1960s. The diminished pace of construction then accelerated dramatically with the ascent of Paulo Machado to the presidency of the AD in Belém in late 1968. From the church's founding in 1911 to 1970, Assembleianos raised seventeen temples. In contrast, 101 churches, an average of 5 per year, were built from 1970 to 1990.

The expanded use of mass media as a method of evangelization accompanied the boom of the early 1960s. Since 1930, when the *Boa Semente*, the AD's monthly journal, was transferred to Rio de Janeiro and renamed *O Mensageiro da Paz*, the church in Belém had no official organ of news and propaganda. Pastor-President Alcebiades Pereira Vasconcelos (1961–1968),

FIGURE 4. An Assembly of God temple in the bairro of Guamá.

a journalist by trade, founded *O Estandarte Evangélico* (The Evangelical
Standard) in June 1962. Created as a vehicle for winning adolescent converts,
the paper detailed church activities, explained Pentecostal doctrine, and,
above all, recorded testimonies of faith healing. The strategy of proselytizing the afflicted is revealed in the poem that opened the first issue.

> In pain and suffering you sustain me, Lord,
> Because you always protect me,
> You please my soul and you never dishearten,
> You never forsake mortals,
> Human beings (who trust in God), lift your voices to the
>   heavens,
> When in desperation,
> And He will never abandon you. (*Estandarte* 6/62)[12]

The ascent of Paulo Machado to the presidency of the AD in Belém in
December of 1968 marks the beginning of a new phase in Belenense Pentecostal history. Still without serious evangelical competition and over eight
thousand members strong, the AD, led by Machado, commenced a period of
profound institutionalization.[13] At the base, the small congregations in the
baixadas continued to operate as sects, drawing a radical distinction be-

tween church and world. In the larger churches, particularly the Central Temple, the middle-class need for social legitimation led the church to form political alliances and bureaucratize its administrative apparatus. Pastor Paulo, contradicting traditional Pentecostal belief in the imminence of the parousia, had adopted a long-term institutionalist perspective on evangelization. In a weekly administrative assembly, the senior pastor estimated that it would take fifty years to evangelize Belém (Acts 1970).

Institutionalization also affected charisma. Acting as a priest rather than a prophet, Pastor Paulo admonished his flock to exercise extreme caution with the spiritual gifts of prophecy and vision (Acts 1973).[14] Prophecy and vision provoke such fear in powerful Pentecostal pastors because the recipient of these divine gifts, almost always female, can challenge the authority of the priests. Bishop Macedo of the IURD refers to prophecy as "the main door through which demons enter Pentecostal churches" (Macedo 1993: 11).

The inauguration of the Amazonian Seminary of the Assembly of God in Belém, Pará in 1973 provides further evidence of institutionalization. To use Weber's distinction, seminaries produce, not prophets, but priests, skilled in biblical exegesis and elocution. The decision to organize a seminary had generated much polemic in the church in the late 1960s. Opponents argued that seminary graduates would be more cerebral and less likely to be guided by the Holy Spirit; they would resemble Presbyterian or Methodist ministers, theologically savvy but spiritually obtuse.[15] Debate on the naming of the theological institution reveals the leadership's concern with social prestige and class. In justifying the use of the word "seminary" rather than "biblical institute," the pastor-president asserted that the former would "appeal more to different social classes" (the middle classes). Moreover, the appellation "biblical institute" would, according to the head pastor, imply inferior theological training (Acts 1973). The borrowing of Catholic and mainline-Protestant terminology to confer status did not stop at the gates of the seminary. In 1988 the *Estandarte Evangélico* began to allude to the Central Temple as the "Cathedral of Faith."

The days when an uneducated *caboclo* pastor filled with the Spirit could easily rise to the top of the AD pastorate were coming to an end. Middle-class Pentecostals in the Central Temple and larger churches had little tolerance for the rustic Portuguese of unlettered preachers. By the latter part of the 1980s, church leaders themselves had become concerned about the growing gulf between clergy and laity. In a letter to the AD State Assembly of Pará, Pastor Paulo warned of the "tendency toward professionalization of the ministry" (Acts 1987). But the pastor-president's actions only reinforced the apparently irreversible trend. Just three months after the missive to the state assembly, Machado required all members of the ministry to enroll in a course on "Church Administration and Ministerial Activities" (Acts 1987).

Increasing interest in winning middle-class converts attended the process of institutionalization. Founded in 1976, ASSEHNPLELP (Association of Evangelical Businessmen and Professionals of the State of Pará) functioned as a sort of evangelical Rotary Club.[16] Protestant businessmen and professionals, the majority Pentecostal, gathered monthly to lunch at posh *churrasquerias* ("all you can eat" steak houses) and deliver five-minute conversion testimonials. Members were encouraged to invite nonevangelical men of their same class. In a highly stratified society, ASSEHNPLELP allowed members of the middle class to adhere to the faith without having to mix with the *populares* who compose the great majority of AD membership.[17]

In addition to the process of institutionalization, another key development during Pastor Paulo's tenure was the emergence of a new religious rival. Umbanda, by the early 1970s, had grown to the point where Assembly leaders identified it as the principal non-Protestant competitor. Despite radical theological and liturgical differences, Pentecostalism and Umbanda are both popular religions that place healing and spirit possession at the core of their practice. In their preconversion quest for health, many Pentecostal proselytes consult with a *mãe-de-santo* (mother of the saint) or *pai-de-santo* (father of the saint) at an Umbanda *terreiro* (center). If the Umbanda spirits fail to resolve the problem, the afflicted often seek out the Holy Spirit of Pentecostalism. Foreshadowing the holy war against African-Brazilian religion that would erupt in the 1980s, Pastor Paulo exhorted his brethren to double the number of AD congregations. "The followers of Satan are expanding" (Acts 1973). Only a few years before, North American anthropologists Seth and Ruth Leacock discovered 140 Umbanda terreiros registered in Belém (47). The AD, in comparison, had twenty-nine houses of worship in 1970 (Relatório Anual 1971).

Even more unsettling for Brazil's oldest AD was the arrival of its first significant Pentecostal competitor. Conspicuously absent from the Administrative Acts of 1973 and 1974 is mention of the inauguration in Belém in November 1973 of the International Church of the Four-Square Gospel. Paulista missionary and present head pastor Josué Bengston took to the city's airwaves to announce the campaign of miracles in which the Holy Spirit was purportedly curing thousands of Belenenses of their earthly afflictions. The IEQ evangelist drew hopeful crowds but condemnation from the AD. In a case of historical déjà vu, the same church that had been denounced as heretical by the Baptists sixty years ago accused the Pentecostal newcomer of being a "diabolical false prophet" (Bengston).

Vitriol from the AD had a negligible effect on the IEQ. Surpassing the AD's impressive growth rate, the IEQ in only twenty years has gained thirty thousand members and established over 150 houses of worship. The leadership of the AD, despite its public condemnation of the IEQ, incorporated one of its rival's most successful approaches to evangelization into its arsenal of proselytization strategies. The IEQ brought the "campaign" (*campanha*), an adaptation of the Catholic novena, to Belém.[18]

The Postmodern Era

While modern Pentecostalism was just arriving in Belém via the IEQ, Edir Macedo, a former employee at the Rio de Janeiro state lottery (LOTERJ), was ushering in the postmodern era, the latest stage in Brazilian Pentecostal history. Like millions of his coreligionists, Macedo was raised Catholic but also frequented Umbanda terreiros in his youth. He "accepted Jesus" in his adolescence at the Pentecostal church New Life (Nova Vida). Malcontent as a lottery bureaucrat, Macedo left his job in 1977 to found his own church and inaugurated in that same year the Church of Divine Grace (Igreja da Benção) in a former funeral parlor. Months later the bishop registered the church under its current name, the Universal Church of the Kingdom of God (Igreja Universal do Reino de Deus [IURD]).[19]

Classified as a Neopentecostal church by some scholars and an agency of divine healing by others, the IURD fits more appropriately under the rubric of postmodern. The hegemonic beliefs and practices of classic and modern Pentecostalism are syncretized with elements of Umbanda and reinterpreted through the lens of television culture. A loose foundation of traditional Pentecostal doctrine supports a multilevel theological and liturgical edifice that integrates discrete elements of the sacred and secular. Although divine curing forms an integral part of the IURD ministry, it is much more than an agency of divine healing in which immiserated urbanites offer their tithes in exchange for miracles. The term Neopentecostal accurately denotes a new generation of Pentecostalism but does not clearly distinguish between the churches of the modern era on the one hand, such as the BPC and IEQ, and the IURD on the other.

The practice of *libertação* (literally "liberation" but more accurately defined as exorcism) vividly illustrates the postmodern syncretism at work in the IURD. Unlike members of classic Pentecostal churches, most people who attend the IURD have had significant experience in Umbanda or one of the African-Brazilian religions. During a typical IURD service, the pastor puts a new spin on an old Catholic rite. Instead of exorcising individuals, the preacher leads the congregation through a collective exorcism, singing "It's time for the demons to leave" to the melody of the theme song of the Xuxa television show (Jardilino 29).[20] Stomping their feet and throwing their arms back over their shoulders, the frenzied congregants are not chasing away any ordinary demons. These are the *exús* of the pantheon of Umbanda spirits, such as Tranca Rua. Unfazed by the mass exorcism, several Umbanda "demons" possess four or five worshipers. In a scene recalling the movie *The Exorcist*, the possessed fall into a dissociated state of consciousness. Uniformed ushers rush to the victims and drag them by their arms or hair to the altar, where the minister performs a highly theatrical exorcism. Before liberating the individuals from their demonic invaders, the exorcist queries the demons as to their identity. Evasive at first, the demons eventually succumb to the greater power of the IURD thaumaturge and reveal themselves to be exús. The fleeing exús leave their exhausted human host in a prostrated heap. The dramatic display of spiritual power awes the congregation.

For the younger generation of urbanites without ties to the rural regions, the IURD's further relaxation of classic Pentecostalism's puritanical moral code is more in harmony with their lifestyle. Young working women, in particular, must dress fashionably to a certain degree if they are interested in keeping their jobs. The traditional denominations' proscriptions against modern coiffures, cosmetics, and dress are likely to lead working women to the IURD or similar churches, where there are no such restrictions. Criticizing what he sees as the dogmatism of many Pentecostal churches, Bishop Macedo explained his thinking on faith and customs.

> We have few relations because other Pentecostals are too fanatical, mixing faith with customs. One thing has nothing to do with the other. Traditional Pentecostals, for example, base themselves on doctrine rooted in the customs of the time of Jesus. We, on the contrary, do not prohibit anything. In the IURD it is prohibited to prohibit. People are free to do what they understand to be right. A man can have ten wives or a woman ten husbands. People are free to drink, smoke, to do what they understand to be right. Our obligation is to teach them that they, on their own accord, have to make the decision whether or not to do this or that. ("O dinheiro é um bem" 6)

The increasing immiseration of the lost decade of the 1980s provided the socioeconomic context in which the IURD became the nation's fastest-growing Pentecostal church. A debt crisis, runaway inflation, and chronic unemployment and hunger raised the misery index for the poor and for large sectors of the shrinking middle class. Between 1982 and 1987 domestic consumption declined 25 percent (Burns 476). A perennial world leader in social and economic inequality, Brazil in the 1980s watched its rich citizens slice for themselves an even larger piece of the economic pie in the 1980s, while the poor were sent away from the dining table. The percentage of national income accruing to the poorest 50 percent of the population dropped from an already paltry 17.4 percent in 1960 to an astonishing 11 percent in 1990 (Burns 471).

Impoverished and ill favelados and growing numbers of the attenuated middle class responded enthusiastically to the IURD triad of exorcism, prosperity, and healing. Imported from North American Pentecostalism, prosperity theology or the "health and wealth gospel," as it is known in the United States, claims that Christians are entitled to material as well as spiritual blessings. If Christians find themselves in a state of material deprivation, it is because of a lack of faith. Bishop Macedo even denies Jesus' humble origins. "Jesus never was poor. He [Jesus] said: 'I am the Lord of lords, the King of kings.' A king is never poor" ("O dinheiro é um bem" 6). Thus genuine faith in God will result in refrigerators, houses, jobs—whatever the believer prays for. The former lottery official intelligently perceives that in the context of diminishing purchasing power, the prospect of striking gold either through the lottery or the church holds enormous appeal.

Notwithstanding the powerful attraction of libertação and prosperity theology, it is the weekly services dedicated to faith healing that attract the largest crowds. Tuesday nights at the IURD's central temple in Belém were standing-room-only as the physically, spiritually, and emotionally afflicted fervently sought a divine remedy for their ailments. Like prosperity, the blessing of health depends on the supplicant's faith. Interviewed in 1990, the spiritual leader of the IURD explained the healing process: "Extraordinary cures are common in the IURD. People with cancer given no hope by doctors also have been cured. Of course I can't say that all the sick whom we pray for are healed. It depends on the person's faith. If a person believes, he/she is cured" ("O dinheiro é um bem" 7). By the early 1990s over a million Brazilians in approximately one thousand churches believed sufficiently to become members of the IURD (Freston 98). Reversing the traditional direction of missionary work, the IURD has established eleven temples in the

FIGURE 5. A Universal Church of the Kingdom of God temple in Belém.

United States, one of which occupies the old Million Dollar Theater in downtown Los Angeles, the birthplace of Pentecostalism.

Thus from Los Angeles to Brazil at the beginning of the twentieth century and from Brazil back to Los Angeles at its end, Pentecostalism has rapidly become the South American nation's most dynamic popular religion. Pentecostal proselytization methods and liturgy evolved through the different eras of growth, but the core of the message remained unchanged. "Accept Jesus as your savior and you will be healed." For those denied a role in the exclusive modernization process and neglected by the Catholic church, the promise of faith healing in the Pentecostal churches has appealed enormously. Moreover, the Pentecostal pastor has offered healing not only of physical ailments but also of the emotional and psychological wounds of urban poverty. If at the end of this century Pentecostalism is poised to replace Catholicism as the foremost popular religion in Brazil, it is largely due to its spiritual offensive against the pathogens of poverty.

PART II

Exorcising the Demons of Poverty

CHAPTER 2

The Preconversion World of Illness

❦

            Latin American Pentecostals construct their personal history along the axis of their religious conversion experience. Crentes divide their life history into three moments: preconversion, conversion, and postconversion. Without Jesus and the Holy Spirit, life before conversion was lived in the sinful world. Illness, in its broadest sense, was the consequence of living in the world without Jesus. Disease, domestic strife, and alcoholism plagued the quotidian lives of those who had not "accepted Jesus." Pentecostals place conversion at the center of their personal histories because church affiliation signifies the recovery of health; joining the church means renouncing the world of disease and affliction for a life of spiritual and material well-being. Postconversion life history is essentially health maintenance through active participation in church life. Following the Pentecostal model of the conversion narrative, the next four chapters will explain how believers recover their physical, spiritual, and mental health through conversion and church membership. The three temporal stages of Pentecostal life history, preconversion, conversion, and postconversion, will demonstrate how the struggle against poverty-related illness is key to understanding the extraordinary success of Pentecostalism in recruiting the poor of Latin America.

            Illness in its multiple forms is one of the most universal manifestations of poverty. From the atrophic five-year-old suffering from amoebic dysentery to the security guard who is too intoxicated to work, illness destroys millions of lives in the favelas and rural hamlets of Latin America. So elementary is the issue of health and illness that the quest for the former is essentially the struggle for life itself. The poor are infected by a pathogenic society that denies them the means to sustenance and then restricts their access to health care. Although physical infirmity is both the most common and most potent manifestation of illness, a more comprehensive definition of health will illuminate the mechanics of Pentecostal growth.

An expanded conception of health would include not only physical but also social well-being. Health comprises the right to employment, fair wages, potable water, clothing, and education. It also includes the right to a nonaggressive environment; one that permits a life of dignity and decency (Souza 126). Thus illness, or the absence of health, is also a social malady arising from poverty, the inability to meet basic human needs. In a situation where secular society provides adequate health care only for those with the means to purchase it, the economically disenfranchised frequently turn to the only available source of healing: the divine.

Emerging from my oral histories of Belenense Pentecostals is a specific set of pathogens that predisposes people to accept the Pentecostal message. Actual conversion does not occur until an illness has reached the crisis point. This chapter focuses on the preconversion maladies that lead a person to crisis. For analytical purposes, I have classified illness into three types: physical, social, and supernatural. Clearly, disease in Latin America is characterized by the intermingling of the three types, but their separation will facilitate a more rigorous analysis of preconversion life.

Physical Illness

Of the three classes of illness, physical affliction is the most potent manifestation of poverty, and the one that most often brings individuals into contact with Pentecostal churches. Physical illness plagues millions of poor Brazilians. The most frequent maladies that visit the poor result directly from hunger and unsanitary living conditions. Dehydration, malnourishment, parasites, and infectious diseases thrive in the favelas of Brazil. In the baixadas of Belém, where children play in the contaminated waters of the igarapés and creeks, the tropical climate, joining forces with hunger, facilitates the spread of tuberculosis, whooping cough, leprosy, measles, meningitis, malaria, and hepatitis (Souza 131). Testament to the toxic mingling of climate and poverty, the state of Pará leads the world in dermatological diseases. In 1994, 80 percent of all Paraenses under the age of twenty had been infected with some type of mycosis ("Pará é recordista em micoses").

Of even graver consequence is pandemic hunger. An IBGE study on Brazilian mothers and children found that in the North 42.3 percent of children under the age of five were suffering from malnutrition. In Belém an astonishing 68 percent of students in the public elementary schools arrived hungry to class ("Nortista vive a tragedia da fome"). Studies on poverty in the United States have demonstrated the devastating consequences of mal-

FIGURE 6. Houses on the banks of an igarapé in the baixada of Terra Firme.

nutrition in childhood. A deficient diet can severely retard both a child's physical and intellectual development.

Along with children, poor Brazilian women bear the brunt of physical infirmity. In fact, illness was the primary impetus impelling women to affiliate with Pentecostal churches in Belém. Of my female interviewees, 45.8 percent had come to Pentecostalism through sickness, while 25 percent of males had. In addition to the familiar diseases of poverty, women suffer the gamut of gynecological and obstetric disorders. Nizila da Silva, a sixty-five-year-old homemaker and member of the AD, described her battle with ovarian cancer.

> When I had my other son, I got very sick. I'm only here now by the grace of God and Jesus, because my son died in me in the morning. I broke out in a cold sweat. Because I had taken so much medicine for albumen, it seems like it affected the child. He was stillborn at eight months. Afterward, I was in such bad shape that I couldn't even pick up a piece of soap to wash clothes. I couldn't work. I got really sick for about a year, and then one day I started hemorrhaging. I felt really sick. I was thin and racked with pain. Then my sister-in-law said "Why don't you go to Belém for treatment, because what you have is dangerous."

As desperate as Nizila da Silva's situation was, she and Brazilian women in general must bear the additional burden of responsibility for the health of the entire family. As wives and mothers, Brazilian women assume the culturally prescribed role of caregivers and nurturers. When a child is ill, it is the mother's duty to administer a home remedy or attempt to scrape together enough cash to buy pharmaceuticals. So crucial is the role of caregiver in the family unit that a seriously ill wife or mother can mean the psychic and moral breakdown of the household. Thousands of testimonies recorded in the *Estandarte Evangélico* and the life histories of my Pentecostal informants underscore women's familial role as health care providers. Of the plurality of women who had become Pentecostals through physical illness, almost half (45.5 percent) had not converted because of their own cure but through the cure of another, usually a family member. For example, Maria Moura de Paula "accepted Jesus" in an attempt to restore her daughter's health.

> My daughter was stricken with malaria and hepatitis while pregnant. She went to the doctor, who tried everything, but it was useless. When the doctor said it was hopeless, I lost my head and went out into the street and made a vow to the Lord. At home I invited a sister [in faith] to pray, and the Lord used her as his servant and said, "If you believe me, I will cure her, and I will give life to the baby girl." We prayed all night long, and the baby was born alive. After the birth, the mother vomited a lot of bile and was cured. (*Estandarte* 10/63)

The *Estandarte Evangélico*, the monthly newspaper of the AD in Belém, documents the ubiquitousness of disease in believers' lives. The section of the paper called "Testimonials" is a litany of almost every malady known to medical science. From snake bites to ovarian cancer, crentes relate how Jesus, the Physician of Physicians, cured them of their ailments. Assembleiana Gertrudes de Palma exemplifies how the lack of resources in the material world leads many into the spiritual realm in search of succor. "My four-year-old daughter became delirious with a sudden fever. We didn't have any money; we are poor. So I invited my husband and some crentes to pray for my child. She was completely cured at the end of the prayer" (*Estandarte* 7/73).

The Health Care Crisis

The testimonial of Gertrudes de Palma exposes the second front of the offensive against the health of the poor. Having denied almost half of its population the means to satisfy its basic needs, the Brazilian state then severely restricts access to health care. The state's meager spending on health care declined precipitously during the "lost decade" of the 1980s. The 4.2 percent of Brazil's GDP invested in health in 1977 fell to 1.8 percent in 1992. According to a report on health expenditures by the Getulio Vargas Foundation, the ratio of beds in public hospitals to the general population dropped from 1.03/1000 in 1984 to .87/1000 in 1990. Even private hospitals which attend to the middle classes and the affluent watched their number of beds shrink from 3.21/1000 to 2.85/1000 during the same period ("Crise na saúde ligada à economia").[1]

As one of Brazil's poorest cities, Belém suffers an acute and ongoing health crisis. In 1980 the Commission on the Bairros of Belém estimated that 88 percent of the city's residents had no access to health care (Pace 26). During the 1980s, the state of Pará spent an average of only 5.4 percent of its total municipal expenditures on health (Souza 134). A deficit of five hundred hospital beds in Belém in 1993 meant that patients filled hospital corridors waiting for one to become available. In late 1993 the local media reported the case of an adolescent who died of stab wounds after being denied treatment at three hospitals that claimed to have no available bed.

The nationalization of health care in 1989 theoretically extended health coverage to all Brazilians through municipal *postos de saúde* (health posts) in the poor bairros. In reality, limited hours of operation and enormous lines severely restrict access to the clinics. The fortunate few who are able to obtain medical treatment are often subjected to health care of dubious quality. Many of my informants who had received medical attention through the public system had been victims of misdiagnosis and malpractice.

One of the most common terms in the lexicon of illness of Belenense Pentecostals is the verb *desenganar.* When a doctor *desengana* a patient, he has informed her that her case is hopeless or terminal. At the public health clinics and hospitals in Belém and throughout the country, many physicians pronounce a patient's illness incurable before conducting the necessary tests. The case of Nizila da Silva, the Assembleiana cited previously, demonstrates the recklessness and dehumanizing treatment to which the lower classes are frequently subjected at state health care facilities.

> At the time I was seeing Dr. Andrade there in Guajará. When I got there, he looked at me and told me to tell him about my problem. He looked at me and examined me and said, "Look, you have cancer." And getting right to the point, he said, "Look, you people always

operate this way. You come in for treatment when it's too late. If you had come at the beginning of the illness, there might have been hope, but, you know, cancer is a very sad illness." Then I told him that I have a God that can do everything. He can cure me. Then he got up and gave me a little piece of paper to have a preventive exam. So I went to have the test. When I went to the doctor the next day, I couldn't do it, because I had a lot of blood. The doctor called me and told me to wait because he had to attend other people in front of me. When he finished with them, he called me. He picked up a needle like this and said, "Look, go home, take a bath and give yourself this injection. When I get the results of your exam, come back and I will put you in the state hospital for treatment." . . . Well, when I returned for the results, the test showed I had nothing.

Informants who were treated at hospitals or clinics ran the additional risk of contracting one of the myriad diseases that infest public health facilities. On an excursion to Marajó Island, across the river from Belém, one of my informants was stung by a stingray. At the municipal health clinic in Soure, the island's largest town, she was given an analgesic with a nondisposable syringe.

The Evil Spirits of Alcoholism

Seeking to numb the pain of poverty, the economically disprivileged in Brazil and much of the world resort to psychoactive drugs. The depressant alcohol is the drug of choice in the shantytowns of Belém and most of Ibero-America. In Brazil, almost every street has its *barzinho*, or open-air bar, where residents gather to socialize over rounds of Antartica (Brazil's answer to Budweiser) and cachaça. Barzinhos do most of their business on weekend nights but usually have a few customers at any time of day. Although women also frequent corner bars, barzinho culture is decidedly male. Relaxed by the sedating effect of alcohol, boisterous groups of men exchange stories that tend to revolve around work, soccer, and sex. Conversation centering on the latter two subjects often becomes a game of one-upmanship in which each new exploit is more fantastic than the last.

But for millions of poor Brazilian men, the jocosity of barzhinho culture degenerates into the gravity of alcoholism. The physical craving for alcohol compels the addict to spend much of his money on liquor consumption. In her research on evangelicals in Colombia, Elizabeth Brusco determined that a heavy-drinking husband can spend between 20 and 40 percent of the household budget on alcohol (1993: 147). An already impoverished household can easily slide into a state of utter destitution when the principal bread-winner not only squanders precious household income on liquor but also reduces earnings by working less or not at all. Often the difference between an impoverished household and an immiserated one is the absence of a functional spouse. Households submerged in extreme poverty are characteristically headed by women or by dysfunctional (alcoholic or ill) men.

Though a powerful physical addiction, alcoholism is also one of the most virulent social diseases. Like physical illness, alcoholism does not exclusively afflict the poor. High indices of alcoholism in OECD countries, such as France, bespeak the omnipresence of the disease. Nevertheless, the correlation between poverty and alcohol abuse is manifest. Almost half of all adult Native Americans living on reservations, the poorest ethnic group in the United States, are alcoholics, compared to approximately 10 percent of the U.S. population at large.

In the context of economic, social, political, and religious emasculation, millions of poor Latin American men attempt to escape their oppressive reality through the world's most popular psychoactive drug. But the respite found in a bottle of cheap *aguardente* (literally "fire water," a generic term for high-proof brandy, rum, and cachaça) proves ephemeral, as the abuse of distilled spirits makes reality even more unbearable. The alcoholic and his family are caught in a downward spiral of disease and poverty. José Vergolino, a twenty-nine-year-old member of the IEQ and appliance repairman, described his battle with alcoholism when he was in his early twenties.

> We used to drink round after round, you know. I used to leave the bar throwing up on the street like a dirty pig. My shoes were covered with it. My mother couldn't stand it. She was sad, anxious, and she suffered a lot because of me. But I kept on drinking. I used to buy a bottle of wine at Christmas. It was a disgrace for my family. The truth is my friend helped push me into it. "Don't be sad. Let's go to the bar. That's our fun, our moment." One day I was on my sixth round of beer when that girl arrived and started talking about Jesus.

Alcoholism in Latin America is much more prevalent among males than females, in part because it figures in the male prestige complex. The men at the barzinho socializing over round after round of beer are asserting their masculinity. The open-air bar belongs to the male-dominated public sphere of the *rua*, or street. Women too are present but are not the protagonists of this form of street drama. The drinking itself often becomes a bacchanalian contest to determine who can consume the greatest quantity of liquor. The man who exhibits little tolerance for alcohol risks a questioning of his masculinity.

More than any other reason, it is the desire to be cured of alcoholism that impels Brazilian men to convert to Pentecostalism. In Belém, a plurality (40 percent) of my male informants affiliated with a Pentecostal church on account of an alcohol problem. Given the limited options of secular treatment for alcoholism and the inability of the other major religions to provide effective spiritual aid, Pentecostalism has become Brazil's principal detox center. Secular treatment for alcoholism is limited to one private organization, Alcoholics Anonymous. This hemisphere's most visible support group for alcoholics appears to have achieved a modicum of success in Brazil but has one major drawback: demand far exceeds supply. People must often wait months before being accepted into a group.

Brazilian Pentecostalism's two principal competitors, Catholicism and Umbanda, at best provide little spiritual aid for the alcoholic. Paraense anthropologist Heraldo Maues explains how the fusion of the sacred and the profane during the Catholic festa results in a carnivalesque procession. "Catholicism does not have restrictions. This permits the revelry of people who celebrate Saint Anthony, carrying their saint and drinking cachaça, yelling 'Long live the saint' while performing a type of dance that simulates sexual acts" (Maues 147).

The free-flowing distilled spirits that are an integral part of Catholic festas give license to excessive drinking. For an individual seeking to control his drinking, festas such as Saint Anthony's are perilous. Similarly, rituals at Umbanda terreiros often involve liquor consumption. The *filhos-de-santo* (affiliates of an Umbanda center) often pass around a bottle of cachaça during breaks in the rituals. Also, when believers are possessed by certain ribald spirits, such as the Cabocla Mariana, drinking and smoking become part of the performance.

Conflicting data exist on whether or not Umbanda provides spiritual aid for those with alcohol-related problems. Diana Brown, in her study of Umbanda, found that less than 1 percent of Umbandistas surveyed had come to their present center in order to overcome alcohol abuse (95). In contrast, the Leacocks, in their study of Umbanda in Belém, found excessive drinking to be one of the most common domestic problems taken to Umbandista healers (266). My own research supports Brown's findings. Only 6 percent of Pentecostal men who visited an Umbanda terreiro at least once had gone there looking for help with alcohol abuse. Even if those suffering from al-

cohol dependency do seek out Umbanda centers in significant numbers, they
are unlikely to be cured there, since African-Brazilian religion does not forbid alcohol.

Although men suffer from alcoholism at a much higher rate than
women, wives and amigas must deal with the devastating consequences of
a male alcoholic in the family. Besides the financial drain on the household
budget, women are often the victims of alcohol-related domestic violence.
A fifth of cachaça can sharpen the rage of poverty. Maria Tavares, a seventy-
two-year-old Assembleiana, related the tribulations of life with an alcoholic
husband.

> My life before accepting Jesus? Let's say that my suffering was greater
> after I got married. When I was single, I had my problems, like not
> having a mother or father. I had to work to support myself. I had to
> live in the houses of others and work. But after I got married, things
> got worse, because like I told you before, my husband had many
> vices. He liked parties a lot and especially that business of carnival.
> In fact, he organized his own carnival troupe, which made me suffer,
> because I didn't like it. I wasn't a crente, but I didn't like it. And my
> greatest suffering came later, when he started to drink. I was very wor-
> ried about his drinking and my finances for my small children. So my
> life became very difficult. I had to work a lot, because he spent all his
> time at the bars.

Social Disease: Domestic Strife

After physical illness, domestic strife most frequently leads poor Brazilians to the doors of a Pentecostal church. Nearly one-third (29.4 percent) of
my interviewees had turned to Pentecostalism because of family problems.
As is the case with somatic affliction and alcoholism, domestic strife is not
peculiar to the poor. Marital tension, spousal and child abuse and abandonment cut across class boundaries. However, the financial stress of poverty ex-
acerbates domestic conflict among the popular classes. Both Pentecostal men
and women described a preconversion feeling of uncontrollable rage—the
rage of poverty. A profound sense of powerlessness, arising from the inability to properly shelter, feed, clothe, and educate themselves and their families, results in violent emotions that are ready to explode to the surface at a
moment's notice. Cultural conditioning usually limits female violence to ver-
bal aggression while permitting males to express their rage physically.

A result of cultural imprinting, behavior associated with the male prestige complex has a more deleterious impact in the baixadas than in more economically privileged areas. For example, the middle-class Carioca (resident of Rio de Janeiro) abandoned by her husband probably has a network of fictive kin to help her bear the possible emotional and financial shock. In the baixadas, however, spousal abandonment can mean financial disaster for the wife and family. The departure of the principal breadwinner forces the woman into a perilous situation in which she must employ a number of different strategies in order to survive.

Both spousal and paternal abandonment are two of the most common and gravest manifestations of the intersection of poverty and the male prestige complex. Approximately one-third (30.7 percent) of my informants, both male and female, had been abandoned by either their husbands or their fathers. A few women had been abandoned by both father and spouse. A much smaller number had themselves walked out on their mates (4.8 percent of all women and 11.5 percent of all men). Though myriad factors can contribute to abandonment, an affair with another woman is usually the immediate cause. The male prestige complex measures manliness partly in terms of sexual conquest. The greater the number of women that a man seduces, the greater his prestige. Traditional cultural conceptions of sex roles have assigned the wife the role of homemaker, nurturer, and caregiver but not the role of primary provider of sexual gratification. Thus, many married men in the favelas and the *bairros nobres* (upper-class neighborhoods) of Brazil seek sexual satisfaction through extramarital relationships, either somewhat stable associations or temporary liaisons, often with prostitutes. An evening out at the barzinho frequently segues into a trip to the local brothel or to one of the ubiquitous sex motels.

Rapid cultural change accompanying macrosocial and macroeconomic transformation, particularly urbanization and industrialization, has granted greater sexual freedom to Brazilian women. Women also have extramarital affairs. However, cultural norms still do not condone illicit unions for women as they do for men. In fact, discovery of an extramarital liaison by a jealous husband often leads to violence. The crime pages of *O Liberal*, Belém's journal of record, were replete with stories and gruesome photographs of women who had been beaten, mutilated, and even murdered by their husbands and boyfriends for alleged infidelity.

The financial and psychological stress of poverty augments the incidence of abandonment among poor households. In tandem with the male prestige complex, financial hardship figures into the equation of spousal and paternal desertion. Impoverished men often leave their mates for younger, childless women. The new lover or spouse will not necessarily earn any more than the abandoned wife. Therefore, the decision to desert a wife and/or family is, in part, also a matter of the economics of poverty. In abandoning his family, a husband/father relieves himself of the responsibility of supporting five or six dependents.

If abandonment disrupts the lives of middle- and upper-class women and their children, it can threaten the very survival of a poor household. The introductory chapter, examining the demographics of poverty in Brazil, revealed that female-headed households constitute the most immiserated stratum of the impoverished classes. If she has children to support, the abandoned woman is forced to superexploit her own labor to keep the household intact. Sexism in the labor market forces her to work for even lower wages than her husband earned. Often the struggle to survive involves placing one or more of the children with members of the extended family, *compadres* (godparents), or friends. If her situation improves, the mother will usually reclaim her children. But if not, they will spend the remainder of their childhood with the foster family.[2] Elene Viana, a forty-eight-year-old seamstress and member of the IEQ, stated that being abandoned by her husband was the worst thing that had ever happened to her.

> The separation of my husband was the most difficult time in my life. I was younger [twenty-four years old]. I was left with four small children, including the retarded one. I had been married for nine years when he left me. It was the worst problem in my life. I looked for help but didn't find any. Thank God I had that job in the factory then. Daily purchases came with great sacrifice. I went to live with my mother and two sisters, but they were mean to me since I wasn't with my husband anymore. My mother was very demanding and would throw my things around.

Children abandoned by their father suffer the financial and psychological effects as much, if not more, than their mother. Paternal desertion can send already vulnerable children into a profound psychological crisis. Twenty-one-year-old Hezio Nazareno, a member of the IEQ in the bairro of Jurunas, dropped out of seventh grade and began associating with gang members shortly after his father left his mother for another woman. When I asked Hezio why he had abandoned his studies, he responded:

> It was when my mother started to work, you see. My father left and never came back. It was then that my mother had to work, and we

[he and his siblings] had nobody to tell us what to do. We could come and leave whenever we wanted and do whatever we felt like, because we didn't have a mother or father to take care of us. It was then that I abandoned my studies. And at seventeen I was already wanting to spend all my time in the streets, hanging out with bad company. I didn't feel like working. A while later, I started to get involved in drugs and alcohol.

Spousal and parental desertion usually is the culmination of an extra-marital affair. However, not all affairs result in abandonment. Even if the husband does not leave his wife, the discovery of an extradomestic sexual liaison causes considerable strife. Some women accept their husband's philandering as normal male behavior, but others experience a profound sense of betrayal. Those who feel betrayed are more likely to seek consolation in religion, which is often a safer strategy for dealing with adultery than direct confrontation. Arlete Costa, a forty-six-year-old homemaker and member of the IEQ, told the story of her married friend who had the courage to confront her husband and his lover at the local bar where they were drinking together. The husband did not appreciate his wife's public challenge to his authority, so he beat her right there at the bar.

From barroom brawls to massacres of street children, violence permeates the fabric of Brazilian society. Almost all of my informants had been robbed at some time, forced to hand over their pocket change to a razor-wielding adolescent. The type of brutality suffered by my interviewees is the everyday violence of the rua. According to residents of the baixadas of Belém, gangs of adolescent *pivetes*, or delinquents, that have proliferated since the "return to democracy" perpetrate most of the violence. Many Pentecostals lamented the end of military rule, claiming that street violence had soared since 1986.

But it is not typically the violence of the rua that leads people to accept the Pentecostal God. Rather, it is the violence of the street reproduced inside the walls of the house that sends shantytown dwellers, mainly women, in search of the peace of the sanctuary.[3] Rendered financially impotent by the brutality of the social relations of production and fraught with a profound sense of powerlessness, millions of impoverished men vent their anger on their wives and/or children. Men receive mixed cultural messages about domestic violence. While the male prestige complex pronounces wife battering to be the supreme act of male cowardice (a real man never strikes a woman), it also tends to legitimize violence as a way of exercising mascu-

FIGURE 7. A veteran Assembleiana and her grandchildren.

line authority. Unfortunately, the latter message rings clearer than the former in the baixadas. Twenty-eight year old Carlos Mara, raised by his widowed mother and obliged to quit school at thirteen to work to support his family, unleashed the rage of poverty on his wife. In our interview he explained why he had joined the IURD in Belém.

> I was still drinking and partying in the street. So when I would come home from good parties, all was fine. But if I had lost money, I would fight with my wife. Any little thing she would say would offend me. I came to know the church after a very ugly fight at home, you know. I had a really nasty fight with her at home when she was pregnant with my first little daughter, and I hit her in the stomach. After that, she didn't want to live with me anymore. She said she would only stay with me if I went to church. I told her I would go but with no intention of staying there long. So I did what she wanted, and I'm still in the church today.

Carlos affiliated with the fastest-growing Pentecostal church in Brazil as a penitent perpetrator of domestic violence, but the more usual scenario is for the victims, mostly women and children, to adhere to Pentecostalism as a strategy for making peace with their violent environs. In the absence of the type of shelters for battered women that exist in the United States, poor abused women have practically no institutional support beyond the extended family and network of friends. As anthropologist John Burdick explained in his comparative study of religion in Rio de Janeiro, the Brazilian Catholic church is for many not a major source of relief from suffering, because it tends to affirm, rather than reject, secular social roles. In particular, priests and lay workers who subscribe to the tenets of liberation theology are more likely to lecture a battered woman on the exploitative economic system that pushes her husband to violence than dispense a dose of sacerdotal sympathy (Burdick 1990: 255). A Pentecostal pastor or church worker, in contrast, would tend to emphasize the evil of the situation and offer the healing power of the Holy Spirit to the battered wife. Such was the affliction of an anonymous woman who wrote to the *Estandarte Evangélico* in November 1985 that she thanked Jesus for "taking her husband away."

> The tribulation at home was great. My son and husband weren't crentes. I didn't have any freedom to serve my Lord. I wasn't legally married, and my companion didn't want to get married. My suffering was great. But I knew that it was the hand of the Lord over me, due to my disobedience for having left the church for eight years. Now with a broken home and a drunken and violent husband, I wanted to go to church, but I couldn't. It was time for me to return to the feet of Christ. The sisters of the prayer circle and the visitadoras helped me with prayers and advice. I waited for the Lord, and He didn't take long to respond. My union was legalized. My husband continued his life of drunkenness and violence, and the Lord, in order to give me the freedom to serve Him, took my husband away through death. The price was high, but I know that it was the best thing for me.

Another common form of physical violence within the household is sexual abuse. Fathers figure among the main perpetrators of the sexual molestation that takes place in the home. Many of the offenders were themselves victims of sexual abuse in childhood. In addition, the fluctuating composition of the impoverished household means that male relatives and compadres can be residing in the house for long periods. When the head(s) of the household are out of the house, the man or boy has an opportunity to molest one or more of the children. Claudia Souza, a twenty-one-year-old domestic servant and member of the AD, was raped by her forty-four-year-old uncle.

My aunt had just gone out. He [her uncle] came later, when I was sleeping. I had gone to bed. I was tired. I don't know about him, because there are people who have a spirit, something to do with incantations. Anyway, I was there sleeping; I didn't see anything. I only awoke when he had finished his business. When I woke up, my panties were off; I was naked. I asked him what had happened, and he didn't say anything. Afterward, he always wanted to grab me and kiss me, always with a knife in his hand.

Battering and sexual molestation are the physical expressions of domestic strife that fill Pentecostal churches with afflicted women and, to a lesser degree, men. Of no lesser import is the psychological toll of frequent fights, generated from the rage of poverty and from conduct associated with the male prestige complex. The pain of hunger causes emotional volatility, as Nancy Scheper-Hughes (1992) demonstrates in her pioneering work on the moral economy of hunger in the Brazilian Northeast. Emotional states vacillate wildly and what seems trifling on a full stomach can take on larger-than-life dimensions for the malnourished. And beyond the network of fictive kin and friends, institutional resources for coping with domestic conflict are practically nonexistent. Silvia Santos, a thirty-seven-year-old single mother and member of the AD, never was battered by her former husband, but he expressed his opposition to her interest in the Assembly of God in no uncertain terms. When Silvia disobeyed her spouse's edict to stay away from the AD, he responded by burning her favorite Sunday blouse and Bible.

The Impotence of Poverty

Although the great majority of my informants "accepted Jesus" in a desperate quest for relief from the physical and social illnesses of poverty, a significant minority became Pentecostals as a direct result of material deprivation. In the context of declining real wages and high levels of underemployment and unemployment, the health and wealth gospel of postmodern Pentecostal churches, particularly the IURD, reverberates through the slums of Brazil. In response to my question about why Pentecostal churches are so successful among the poor of Belém, my informants cited the quest for financial and material "resources" as the primary reason. Sixty-three-year-old Carlos Garcia, a member of the AD and an attendant at a car wash, eloquently explained how financial hardship and illness bring the poor of Belém to the

Assembléia de Deus. "People with less resources always join the church looking for financial blessings and things like cures. That is why the church grows a lot. Many stay in the church, but others don't, you know. But they generally stay, because when they start to attend church, their life begins to change. It begins to improve financially, in health, family problems. Everything begins to change."

On the front wall of the sanctuary of the largest IEQ church in the bairro of Guamá hangs a big red banner that proclaims, "Jesus, in this name there is power. You will receive power in the Holy Spirit." Banners, personal testimonies, sermons, hymns, and gifts of the Spirit give testament to the centrality of power in Pentecostal discourse and praxis. As the next chapter will show, the very act that constitutes the nucleus of Pentecostal practice, baptism by the Holy Spirit, is first and foremost an experience or "dressing" of power (*revestimento de poder*). Furthermore, when asked to define Pentecostalism, crentes responded univocally that to be a Pentecostal believer is to be filled with the power of the Holy Spirit.

Pentecostalism's invitation to personally experience divine power via baptism in the Holy Spirit can only be understood in terms of the sense of profound powerlessness experienced by the disprivileged. The pathogen of poverty, be it somatic, social, or psychological, debilitates its victims, causing them to feel too weak to change their desperate situation. They are aware that in Belém and the rest of the country, money is power and that without an adequate cash flow, they are economically impotent. Talking like a *petista* (member of the leftist Workers' Party [PT]), Rosilea Garcia, a twenty-nine-year-old member of the IURD and toy store clerk, comprehended the social relations of power that emasculated her father. When I asked what had led her father to become an alcoholic, she replied:

> Sometimes it's because of financial problems, and I'm going to tell why that is. This region is a poor state. No, that's the wrong word. This is a rich state, very rich. Belém is one of the largest, richest states [*sic*] of our region, but the government doesn't know how to give any incentives. It doesn't help people find work. Are you catching what I'm saying? It's like this: this is a very rich state in minerals. There is a lot wrong in this state, like only the powerful, called the elite, own anything. That means the miserable ones become more and more miserable. And that is why there is so much family crisis. The person who wants to give his child a present at the end of the year and can-

not. That's where fights begin. The lack of money, the lack of work, it's what led my father to drink and fight so much. You understand?

Spiritual Impotence

Belenense slum dwellers also experience a sense of powerlessness in the religious realm. For many, the Catholic saints and the spirits of African-Brazilian religion do not inject them with the supernatural antibodies needed to overcome the adversity of life in the shantytown. Regardless of the degree to which they practice their faith, almost all poor Brazilians and Latin Americans believe in the divine. Beyond the walls of the academy, atheism is a foreign concept in Brazil. Declaring oneself an atheist on the urban periphery is tantamount to revealing oneself to be a Pentecostal at a café in the Latin Quarter of Paris. From the caboclo who believes in the enchanted kingdom at the bottom of Amazonian rivers and igarapés to the Pentecostal who believes in the Holy Spirit, all poor Brazilians cleave to the idea of a divine order.

Along with Pentecostalism, popular Catholicism and African-Brazilian religion, represented by its most popular branch, Umbanda, are united by a subtext of popular religiosity that, though expressed differently in each religion, gives rise to a common weltanschauung. Above all, popular religiosity is utilitarian. Concerned with matters of daily survival, the poor seek to manipulate the supernatural, not primarily for rewards in the afterlife, but for divine aid in the here and now. In her study of Umbanda, Diana Brown discovered that the primary reason for joining an Umbanda center was the quest for health (94). Whether in Pentecostalism, Umbanda, or popular Catholicism, believers have found the contractual agreement to be the most efficacious manner of soliciting supernatural succor. Mimicking the secular patron-client relationships, poor clients attach themselves to a divine *patrão* who provides protection and occasional miracles in exchange for ritual acts of sacrifice. The supernatural patron assumes different identities in the three religions, but the relationship of exchange entered into with the Holy Spirit, the saints, or the spirits of Umbanda is similar. The granting of a petition, such as the cure of a sick daughter, requires the supplicant to express his/her gratitude in a ritual act of sacrifice. Failure on the part of the divine patron to grant the request frees the client from any obligation "to pay." The *promessa*, or vow, of popular Catholicism clearly illustrates the mechanics of the relationship of exchange. Far from the mediative power of the priest, the economically disinherited practice a form of Catholicism that revolves around worship of the saints. From the intimacy of their niche in the believer's home to their public display in processions, the saints rule the world of popular Catholicism. The saints and their devotees are bound by a contractual agreement called the *promessa*. In exchange for divine intervention, or a miracle, supplicants promise to "pay" for the aid by performing a ritual act of sacrifice, normally a procession or pilgrimage (Burdick 1990: 169, n. 11).

The massive display of religious devotion and profane festa that takes place every October in Belém's Cirio de Nazaré, Brazil's largest Catholic procession, captures the dynamics of the promessa.[4] In return for a blessing granted by the Virgin, Our Lady of Nazaré (Nossa Senhora de Nazaré), patron saint of the state of Pará and much of Amazonia, pilgrims parade behind her image through the main thoroughfares of Belém in blazing equatorial sun or driving rain. Faithful from Belém and the riverine communities of Amazonia amble behind the Virgin carrying wooden models of the houses and boats that she helped them buy. Wax replicas of feet, hands, hearts, and other body parts symbolize the healing power of the Amazonian saint.[5]

Prior to affiliating with a Pentecostal church, the majority (54.2 percent) of my interviewees identified themselves as cultural Catholics (*Católicos por nome*). As children they might have undergone the Catholic rites of passage, such as baptism and first communion, and even sporadically attended mass, but their contact with the institutional church was minimal. Their practice of popular Catholicism was limited to occasional propitiation of the saints in periods of crisis and revelry in the profane festivities that accompany religious processions. A shortage of priests, coupled with official neglect of the lower classes until the 1960s, meant that the Catholicism practiced by the Brazilian poor diverged greatly from the Romanized version practiced in the sanctuary of the cathedral.

After the cultural Catholics, the next largest group of informants (slightly more than a quarter: 27.8 percent) had been active practitioners of popular Catholicism. They had attended mass on a fairly regular basis, in addition to participating in the rituals of folk Catholicism. In accord with the gender gap in Latin American religion, almost three times as many women as men had been active Catholics (34 percent of women and 13.6 percent of men). Although Christian Base Communities had been formed in the baixadas in the 1970s and 1980s, none of the Belenense Pentecostals interviewed had belonged to one. Moreover, only a few had even heard of the CEBs. Many more were acquainted with, but had not participated in, the Catholic charismatic movement, one of the church's responses to the threat of Pentecostalism.

Owing to the legacy of persecution and discrimination, my informants in Belém, especially the women, were less candid about their past participation in Umbanda. While only 6.9 percent described themselves as former Umbandistas, 62.5 percent admitted having visited a terreiro at least once. Involvement in Umbanda varied greatly along gender and denominational lines. There was no appreciable gender difference in the small group that identified themselves as former Umbandistas (9.1 percent of all men and 6 percent of women), but members of the IEQ and IURD had three times more ex-Umbandistas among their ranks than did the Assembleianos (13 percent versus 4.3 percent). The proportion of Umbandistas differed even more between the women of the AD on the one hand and the IURD and IEQ on the other. Less than 1 percent of Assembly women claimed past affiliation with Umbanda, compared to 17.6 percent of female believers of the IURD and IEQ.

Differences among those who had frequented an Umbanda terreiro on at least one occasion were even more striking. While half of all Assembleianos had gone, 91.3 percent of Quandrangulares and "Cristãos" (Christians, i.e., members of the IURD) had visited an Umbanda center.[6] Surprisingly, a greater percentage of men than women in all three denominations had witnessed the ritual of spirit possession at a terreiro. The more aggressive prosecution of the holy war waged by modern and postmodern Pentecostal churches, particularly the IURD, against African-Brazilian religion accounts for the higher proportion of former Umbandistas in the IEQ and the IURD. Pastors of these churches have ascribed the quotidian evil that afflicts the pobres of Brazil to the "demons" of Umbanda. In Belém, for example, pastors tell worshipers that the popular, hard-drinking Umbanda spirit, the Cabocla Mariana, is the fiend destroying their lives through cachaça and prostitution.

Unlike the denominational difference in past Umbanda affiliation, the unexpected gender gap defies easy explanation. In their study of Batuque (Umbanda) in Belém in the early 1960s, the Leacocks found that active female participants outnumbered males by a ratio of three to one (103). Other research on Umbanda confirms the Leacocks' findings in Belém. The most likely explanation is that female informants tended to downplay the extent of their past involvement in Umbanda. It remains an open question as to why women would underestimate their involvement when, considering the popular association between Umbanda and homosexuality, men have a greater incentive to conceal their participation.

The reasons cited for frequenting a terreiro, in accord with the research of Diana Brown, dramatically illustrate how all popular religion in Brazil serves as an alternative source of health. Of the majority of my Pentecostal informants who admitted visiting an Umbanda center, a striking 55 percent went seeking a cure for physical illness. Employment and family-related problems also impelled people to consult the spirits, but much less frequently than sickness. Responsible for the collective health of the family and the individual welfare of each member, women sought healing at Umbanda centers at a much greater rate than men (63 percent to 38.5 percent). Men, more concerned with their role as breadwinners, implored the spirits for help in finding a job or earning a better wage as often as they asked to be cured of physical affliction. José Nilo, a twenty-nine-year-old self-employed appliance repairman and member of the IEQ, explained how he obtained a job as a janitor through "Macumba."[7]

> I went to that place and the Umbandista arrived and said, "Look, if you want to get that job, you're going to have to buy four lemons, a bit of *arruda* [rue, a medicinal plant], and a small bag of garlic. You're going to have to bring four bottles of cachaça and a bit of gunpowder. Go get everything tomorrow and then bring it here."
>
> I remember that I had an eighteen-karat gold chain that I bought on credit. I hadn't even finished making payments, and I grabbed the chain and sold it to buy those things. He told me to bring my work card, and I did. I returned to that place, and he prepared a bath and told me to get in a tub that was falling to pieces. "Listen, go that way, take your bath and throw the water out over there." I said, "Ok, I will." I wanted that job bad.
>
> Then he said, "Come back later, and don't dry yourself off." Next, he spread a whole bunch of gunpowder around me like this and took a match to it and "pow," there was a tremendous flash, and that man with a pitchfork in his hand started to shake right next to me, and I said to myself, "This stuff isn't going to work." I got up and said, "Did I get it?" And he said, "Now you can go to that place and you will get it." And I went to that place, and I got the job. The only thing is that I didn't last very long there, only around three months.

In part, it is Catholicism's and Umbanda's inability to heal the wounds of poverty that contributes to the decision to affiliate with a Pentecostal church. As a civil religion, Brazilian Catholicism is so enmeshed with national culture and society that the borders separating the sacred from the profane dissolve, as was illustrated in the aforementioned religious festa in which revelers celebrated the saint's day with cane liquor and erotic dancing. If an alcoholic is not actually encouraged to imbibe distilled spirits at such festas, he is certainly not going to find the spiritual strength to overcome his addiction in a church that does not forbid drinking. Neuza Sá, a sixty-two-year-old widow from the AD in Terra Firme, explained why she thought Catholic priests cannot be good counselors. "Doesn't the padre read the book of Deuteronomy? Because that book shows the sin of the padre: drinking and smoking. The priest smokes and drinks. He can't be a counselor."

Neither Brazilian Catholicism nor Umbanda offers the spiritual power of Pentecostalism to overcome addiction and heal the maladies of poverty. Although Umbanda speaks the language of affliction, it does not require, anymore than Catholicism does, a rupture with secular society. Because of its holistic ethos that allows for the practice of both good and evil, initiates do not have to renounce their life in the world. A man, for example, can continue to drink heavily and face no sanctions at his Umbanda center. Umbanda provides no definite moral code by which followers should live. Similarly, the Catholic church, as a civil religion, fails to create a world apart, where believers can stand in opposition to a pathogenic society that robs them of their human potential and dignity. Under the influence of liberation theology, Catholic CEBs offered a radical critique of the social, economic, and political status quo but failed to address the afflictions of poverty at their most individual and personal level.

More importantly, Catholicism, as practiced in Brazil and throughout Latin America, does not demand personal conversion or transformation as a prerequisite for affiliation. The evangelical language of conversion, which speaks of "being born again" or "accepting Jesus as personal savior," is alien to both Brazilian Catholicism and Umbanda. Brazilian sociologist of religion, Rubem Alves, in accord with Weberian theory, has persuasively argued that salvationist religion only makes sense as a response to a "sinister reality" (1979: 72). The absence of salvationist and conversionist discourse at the level of the individual means that "sinister reality" is not banished from the doors of the Catholic church. More specifically, the absence of the experience of personal conversion in both Catholicism and Umbanda translates into a lack of transformative spiritual power. How can the diseases of poverty be healed by religious agents who fail to create a new salutary world apart from the current sick one?

The necessity of creating a world apart has become evident through the examination of the preconversion world of poverty-induced illness. A pathogenic society that denies millions of its members the opportunity to meet basic human needs, particularly adequate caloric intake, infects its hosts with a multiplicity of ailments. Most salient and virulent among these is physical illness. A deficient diet weakens the organism, rendering it much more susceptible to disease. But the assault on the health of the poor is not limited to the somatic. The contagion of society also contaminates the social, psychological, and religious being. Alcoholism, domestic strife, and, to a lesser extent, religion that does not call for conversion augment the profound sense of powerlessness brought on by physical affliction. With limited access to the dehumanizing assembly-line medical "care" of the health posts, Pentecostal faith healing becomes a highly attractive alternative source of health.

CHAPTER 3

Conversion: Crisis, Cure, and Affiliation

❦

In the same way the Lord Jesus said to Satan, we too must say to illness, cancer, paralysis, or any other sickness: it is written, according to the path of my Lord Jesus, I have been healed. Thus, get out and never come back! Believe in this, and, depending on your faith, . . . from that exact moment the root of your infirmity or illness will wither, and your symptoms will start to vanish, sometimes gradually, other times instantly, depending on the size of your faith.
—Macedo, *O Espírito Santo*

*A*s crentes, poor Brazilians are able to recover their health because Pentecostalism, unlike its major religious rivals, conceptualizes religious affiliation as conversion. Religious affiliation conceived as a "positive transformation of the nature and value of a person" makes sense to individuals and groups who have been negatively evaluated by society (Stark and Bainbridge 197). Affiliation is rarely conceived of as conversion among those occupying the apex of the social pyramid because such people already enjoy a positive social evaluation. A Paulista industrialist, for instance, seeks religious continuity with his secular status. He asks God to affirm his earthly status, not to transform it. In contrast, the poor individual seeks to turn away (*convertere*) from the contagions of the diseased social body. In turning away from alcoholism, domestic strife, and deficient medical "care," the convert begins to recover her health, to restore her social, physical, and spiritual integrity.

The disease of poverty in its multifarious forms predisposes the dispossessed of Brazil and Latin America to accept the Pentecostal practice of faith healing. Nevertheless, illness itself is only a necessary, not a sufficient, condition for conversion to Pentecostalism. Before an individual accepts the preacher's *chamada*, or call, to conversion and walks to the front of the church to publicly "accept Jesus," a series of interrelated events has taken place that has brought the person to the spartan Pentecostal house of worship. No two persons follow the exact same path to the doors of a Pentecostal temple, but the life histories of my informants evidence a common road traveled by the great majority who have adhered to the faith. A closer inspection of this path and its milestones will shed new light on the dynamics of meteoric Pentecostal growth in Brazil and throughout Ibero-America.

Crisis

Illness, like hunger, is a permanent fixture of the urban periphery and rural areas, and its mere presence does not alarm people. When, however, a lingering but apparently benign condition worsens, or a sudden and virulent pathogen attacks, crisis compels the afflicted and/or his family to action. Regardless of the nature of the illness, people first tend to seek to defuse the crisis through secular channels. The gods are only implored after a cheaper or easier way of remedying the situation has come to naught (Stark and Bainbridge 85).

In the case of physical illness, Belenenses, like most Amazonians and especially the economically disprivileged, will normally draw on their vast pharmacopeia of medicinal plants, herbs, and roots before visiting a health post or attempting to scrape together enough cash to purchase pharmaceuticals. The colorful Ver-O-Peso market spilling beyond Belém's historic riverfront is a premodern pharmacy al fresco, stocking everything from basil (not for pesto but medicinal baths) to cinchona bark from which quinine is extracted. Affordable prices make these natural drugs the remedy of choice in the baixadas and even in many middle-class homes. When, over forty years ago, terminally ill Fidelis Coelho decided he would not leave his then pregnant young wife, Lucia (now a seventy-two-year-old member of the IEQ) with another mouth to feed, he concocted a three-liter batch of abortifacient. Although she had six children already, Lucia refused her dying husband's home "remedy."

The failure of a *remédio caseiro* (home remedy) to cure an illness sends the afflicted or her kin out of the casa and into the rua in search of succor. In the case of physical infirmity, the quest for medical aid usually begins at either the municipal miniclinic or the local pharmacy. Likewise, many alcoholics and alcohol abusers seeking treatment first go to AA. Sufferers of domestic strife, unable to resolve conflict on their own, typically do not knock on institutional doors in search of relief but seek solace from an empathetic family member, neighbor, or friend. At this intermediary stage of the quest for health, those able to remedy their situation through secular intervention give thanks and continue the daily struggle to survive, not knowing when the next health crisis will erupt.

For the others, the desenganados, battered wives, and alcoholics, the failure of secular or "worldly" solutions leaves the supernatural as the only remaining source of health. Only a miracle performed by the gods can save the afflicted at this point. The fulfillment of a promessa by the Virgin of Nazaré or a miraculous cure performed by the queen of Belenense Umbanda healers, the Cabocla Mariana, renews supplicants' faith in the restorative powers of their familiar deities and ends the arduous path to recovery (Leacock and Leacock 134).[1] However, the Catholic saints and the spirits of Umbanda, because they are not agents of conversion, do not possess the healing power of the Pentecostal Jesus and Holy Spirit. Rosilea Garcia, who clearly understood the social and economic etiology of her father's alcoholism, found the Catholic saints unable to grant her the transformative power she needed to resolve her own drinking problem. "Yeah, I used to go to the Catholic church but only out of tradition. I would sit and kneel like everybody else. I used to go to the Church of Nazaré. I would remain there kneeling and looking at those images [saints]. I would talk to them about what I was feeling, and nothing would happen. I would leave feeling the same as I had when I came, you understand?"

Many sufferers of the afflictions of poverty never even have the opportunity to beseech their traditional deities for aid; in their moment of crisis, a Pentecostal evangelist, visitadora, or lay missionary arrives at their home or hospital bed, bringing the message of divine healing for the corpus and animus and salvation from the sinful (i.e., sick) world. Unlike Umbanda and Catholicism, which customarily require supplicants to come to the sanctuary or terreiro to access the means of religious production, Pentecostalism, via its zealous evangelists, brings the means and goods of religious production out of the temple and into the public and private realms of street, home, and hospital. For example, José Vergolino was trying to drown his problems in drink when a young missionary from the IEQ, a friend of his sister, surprised him on his sixth round of beer.

> When she would come visit me, I would say, "I don't want to have anything to do with that church stuff. You're just talking bull. What you're saying has nothing to do with me." She would say, "OK, no problem," and leave. But she came back to my house every week, asking how I was. She was worried about me. I would say, "Look, I'm not interested in that church stuff. I have a good time going to parties and fooling around." She would say, "Oh, José, you don't have any peace in your life. You're not happy. You know only hardship. It

breaks your mother and father's heart." And I would say, "Odete, get out of here. I'm not interested in that. I want to enjoy my life." But she wouldn't give up. She kept on talking and talking to me about Jesus. And the day arrived when I really had to accept. I said, "Fine, I'll go to your church."

Thus, it is the coalescence, in a moment of crisis, of the patient, the spiritual medic, and her medicine that sets the stage for adherence to Pentecostalism. Each act in the unfolding drama of spiritual transformation brings the protagonist closer to the climax of conversion.

Contact

The afflicted, having reached the point of despair at the "closed doors" (*portas fechadas*) of secular and possibly sacred institutions, listen intently to Pentecostal proselytizers who offer an immediate and comprehensive solution to the sufferers' illnesses. The agent bearing the Pentecostal message of healing most often is a relative, friend, or neighbor (someone such as Odete, who proselytized José Vergolino), a part of the afflicted's preexisting network of kin, work, and neighborhood relationships.

Pentecostalism in Latin America recruits primarily along family lines. A plurality (43.3 percent) of my informants made their initial contact with the Pentecostal faith through a crente family member. A family member who has undergone a positive transformation in the AD or IEQ, among other denominations, is living testament to the healing powers of his charismatic religion. At the very least, the individual in crisis is more likely to accept prayers or an invitation to worship at a new church from a spouse or sibling than from a stranger.

Church recruitment in Belém does not occur principally along spousal lines, but crente women had much greater success than men in drafting their spouses into the Pentecostal fold. While only 4.3 percent of married and *amigada* (consensual union) women had been introduced to a Pentecostal church by their husbands, 25 percent of my male informants had been led to *crença* (Pentecostalism) by their wives. The gender gap—women outnumber men by a two to one ratio—partly accounts for the striking difference. Put simply, wives are statistically more likely to be believers in the first place than their husbands.

But the gender gap does not explain all. Even more crucial are the dichotomous social realms in which the two sexes operate. Men work, play, and die in the rua. Many are more attuned to the scene outside their front door than to the one inside it.[2] Hence, friends and colleagues, companions of the street, more than wives or family members, are the primary recruiters of men into Pentecostalism. Nearly one third (30 percent) of my male interviewees had been evangelized by friends or coworkers. Women, in contrast, were proselytized in the culturally constructed female domain of the household. Whereas crente kin ranked below friends and wives in recruiting men to the faith, relatives were the principal disseminators of the gospel of health among women. A slight majority (53.2 percent) of crente sisters cited a family member (excluding husbands) as the person responsible for first introducing them to charismatic Protestantism.

Some Pentecostal women in the baixada bairros of Guamá, Terra Firme, Sacramenta, Jurunas, and Condor also "accepted Jesus" through the influence of friends or neighbors but many more through kin relationships. Twenty-eight-year-old Quandrangular and homemaker Teresina Lima typifies the female pattern of conversion. Teresina's older brother and parents became converts after her younger brother's miraculous cure. Doctors at the military hospital in Rio de Janeiro told Teresina and her family that only a kidney transplant would save the life of her younger brother. Fearing for his life, Teresina decided to donate one of her kidneys to her critically ill brother. Her older brother, in an attempt to enlist divine aid, vowed to "accept Jesus" if the complicated surgery were successful. The older brother fulfilled his vow, watching his younger sibling make a full recovery. Certain that Jesus had guided the surgeons' hands in transplanting her vital organ, Teresina, her younger brother, and her parents followed her elder brother into the IEQ.

The success of low intensity proselytization among preexisting social networks does not preclude the churches from organizing the faithful into mission brigades that, depending on the groups and the occasion, evangelize both in public plazas and door to door. Visitadoras are by far the largest and most dynamic missionary brigade. In pairs, they trudge through the fetid mud paths of the inundated shantytowns to bring the good news of health and salvation to those stricken by the diseases of deprivation. Once, when I was in the middle of an interview with a wizened, tubercular informant, I had the opportunity to witness a pair of visitadoras in action. Perhaps forewarned by my interviewee or his family, the Assembleiana duo had come to proselytize me. Noticing my persistent cough, they inquired as to the state of my health. I explained that my cough was nothing more than a grippe that a little rest would cure. Not satisfied with my answer, the two *servas de Deus* (servants of God) shot up from their makeshift seats and launched into a rousing hymn

FIGURE 8. An Assembleiana preparing lunch.

that recalled the healing powers of Jesus, the *médico dos médicos*. In case that was not enough to exorcise my cold, the hymn segued into a powerful prayer for my health that joined everyone in the house in a circle of interlocking hands. Though not a believer, I perceived the therapeutic benefits of a roomful of people focusing their spiritual energy on me.

Beyond the intimacy of a small prayer circle in a believer's home, Pentecostal pastors recruit collectively during the *culto*, or worship service. At the smaller houses of worship in the baixadas, the preacher asks all visitors to stand while the entire congregation welcomes them with a melodic hymn. The pastor then mentions the presence of any distinguished visitors, such as an evangelist from the Central Temple or a North American researcher. Thus, within the first fifteen minutes of the service the visitor has lost his anonymity. For the researcher who finds himself often participating more than observing, the loss of anonymity can be a source of frustration. However, recognition is received gratefully by the visitor who has led an anonymous and often invisible life as one of the millions of João or Maria da Silvas.[3]

The message delivered to visitors in diverse liturgical forms presumes affliction. Evangelistic flyers handed out at the IURD in Belém ask in boldface, "What is your problem? Vices, finances, unemployment, illness, nervousness, depression, or family fights?" Crente pastors, often favelados themselves, know the misery of the shantytowns and assume that the visitor has entered the temple seeking relief. Also cognizant of the visitor's attempts to remedy her situation through secular and possibly sacred channels, the preacher underscores the futility of seeking a solution that does not involve Jesus and the Holy Spirit. "You who were given no hope by doctors, you who received a false cure from the demons of Macumba, there is a solution," proclaimed a preacher at the IEQ in the bairro of Guamá.

One of the most effective evangelistic techniques is the conversion testimonial. The following anonymous letter published in the *Estandarte Evangélico* for February 1990 contains the key elements that constitute a Pentecostal testimonial.

> When doctors here on earth tell us that the illness a person is feeling has no cure, that the only thing left to do is to die, I want to say that there is a greater doctor than earthly doctors, who does not take away hope and who is ready to offer healing, salvation, liberty, new life, and all that we need. Just accept Him as savior, doctor, teacher, advocate, and master of your life.
>
> I was dying of uterine cancer. I spent ten years suffering when I wasn't a crente. But I knew someone in the prayer circles was interceding for cancer patients. I then vowed to serve Jesus for the rest of my life if He cured me. He healed me immediately without needing an operation.

The individual's preconversion life was full of pain and affliction, in this case "ten years of suffering." The attempt to relieve the pain through institutional health care fails miserably. The physician's prognosis is grim; "the only thing left to do is to die." Desperate, due to the exhaustion of secular resources, the woman turns to the supernatural, gratefully accepting the prayers offered in the *círculo de oração* (prayer circle) for cancer patients. To invoke the healing powers of Jesus, the woman, drawing on her past relationships with the Catholic saints, enters into a contractual agreement, a kind of promessa, with the Doctor of Doctors.

As part of the worship service, conversion testimonial is followed by spirited hymn singing and fervent praying. The preacher then invariably leads the service to a climax with the *chamada*, or call. Non-Pentecostal visitors, *desviados* (apostates), and believers feeling "weak in the faith" are invited to come to the front of the church. Overcome by their own emotions, many sob plaintively as the pastor lays his hands on their heads and asks them if they are ready to accept Jesus as their Lord and savior.

The Cure

The patient and the healing agent (two of the three main factors in the equation of Pentecostal conversion) have brought the ailing visitor to the altar, where she has decided to "accept Jesus" and become a member of (for example) the AD. But before she commits to follow Jesus before the pastor and congregation, the third integer of the conversion equation, the cure, must be factored in. Until a cure, a miracle demonstrating God's omnipotence, takes place, the equation remains incomplete. An examination of faith healing, the powerful motor driving Pentecostal growth in Brazil and much of Latin America, will aid in solving the conversion equation.

Faith healing, even more than glossolalia, is the most universal and potent gift of the Spirit in Latin American Pentecostalism. While less than half (46.8 percent) of all Pentecostal informants in Belém regularly spoke in tongues, the great majority (86.4 percent) claimed that Jesus or the Holy Spirit had cured them of some type of ailment. From 1970, the year the AD in Belém began to register the incidence of *cura divina* in its annual reports, to 1990, the number of recorded cases of faith healing skyrocketed 3,733 percent. Demand for healing surged particularly during the "lost decade" of the 1980s, when financial shocks to impoverished households were severest (*Relatórios Anuais* 1970–1991).

On the other side of the continent, sociologists Christian Lalive D'Epinay and Hans Tennekes, in separate studies of Pentecostals in Chile, highlight the universality of divine healing. D'Epinay discovered that 98 percent of Chilean pastors surveyed had been used by the Holy Spirit to heal a believer, but only 57 percent had ever spoken in the "tongue of angels" (Wagner 122). Similarly, 56 percent of Tennekes's Chilean *crente* informants alluded to a divine cure in their conversion stories (Tennekes 34). Toba Indians of the northern Argentine Chaco also came to Pentecostalism through illness (Wilson 123). Moreover, Africans typically visit a church for the first time seeking relief from an illness that has proved resistant to folk and/or modern medicine (Cox 247).

Cura divina in its most elementary and commonest form is the curing of a physical malady through direct or indirect intervention of one of the three persons of the Trinity. Jesus, owing to his evangelical role as a curer, and the Holy Spirit, charged with miraculous power, are the principal healers in Pentecostalism. God the Father is a powerful but less tangible figure. As the biblical Jesus bestowed the gift of healing on his disciples, who cured the sick in his name, Jesus and the Holy Spirit, operating in Pentecostal churches, typically use believers, both clergy and laity, as human conductors to restore the health of the infirm.

At some point during nearly every Pentecostal church service I attended in Belém, Rio de Janeiro, and São Paulo, the preacher called the afflicted forward to be divinely cured. The pastor and his assistant(s) would lay their hands on, or cup them around, the patient's head while leading the congregation in impassioned prayer for the Holy Spirit, to flood (*derramar*) the house of prayer with a current of healing power. If the sickly petitioners were too numerous and the pastor was unable to lay his hands on each person, he then would extend his arms toward the group, functioning as a conduit for the supernatural serum unleashed by the Holy Spirit. Supplicants can also direct the divine healing power beyond the walls of the temple to afflicted family members and friends not present at the service. In continuity with Catholic tradition and Umbanda practice, the faithful at *cultos de cura divina* place photographs of the ill, bottles of water, and cooking oil, work cards, farina, and salt at the altar to be blessed. Charged with prayer, these objects function as spiritual conductors, facilitating healing in absentia.[4]

In some churches faith healing so dominates the liturgy that the sanctuary resembles a hospital. The stern *obreiras* (ushers) who patrol the pews of the IURD, IEQ, and Deus é Amor don a celestial blue or off-white nurse's uniform. As spiritual nurses, the obreiras perform triage on the patients in the pews. An obreira attends to the mildly afflicted with a vise-grip maneuver in which her hands, positioned at the front and back of the patient's head, force out the demon(s). Those tormented by stronger demons are sent, sometimes dragged, to the altar where the spiritual medic, the pastor, operates. Dramatizing his role as healer, the head pastor at the mother church of God is Love in Belém often led the service dressed in a bleached doctor's smock. The crude wooden canes and crutches adorning the back wall of the small foyer add to the medical imagery. Finally, the bare white walls and the harsh electric light recall the aseptic corridors of a hospital. Visitor and believer alike have entered a spiritual emergency ward.

Though they frequently employ human agents in the business of healing, Jesus and the Holy Ghost need no mediators to operate on the sick, as the following testimony graphically illustrates:

> For four years I was suffering from a disease of the liver and was getting sicker each day despite the treatment and medication. Then I made a vow to serve Jesus for the rest of my life if He would extend his healing hand over me. One night a few days later I received a visit.

Two young men dressed in white spoke to me, saying, "Your illness is serious, but don't worry. The Lord said He will heal you." The following night, in bed, I felt the Lord touch me and remove my liver. I saw that it was swollen, and then He burned it with a white flame which made a loud noise, and all of a sudden it was restored to its normal and perfect state. (Anonymous, *Estandarte* 8/92)

The supernatural surgery on the patient's diseased organ was not performed without a price. In exchange for a restored liver, the long-suffering individual first vowed to dedicate his life to Jesus, in other words to become a crente of the Assembléia de Deus. The English term "faith healing," better than the Portuguese and Spanish *cura divina*, captures the dialectic between the two components: the ailing supplicant first must have faith, must believe, that Jesus indeed possesses the power to heal the mind, body, and soul.[5] No matter how fervently the petitioner petitions, only genuine faith will stir the Supreme Physician to action.

The most efficacious manner of expressing one's faith, in accord with the mechanics of Brazilian popular religiosity, is through a vow, or, in Catholic parlance, a promessa. The type of vow made by the aforementioned liver patient recurs with such frequency on the pages dedicated to *testemunhos* in the *Estandarte Evangélico* that I have denominated it "the standard vow." Failed by traditional and modern medicine and perhaps the deities of Umbanda and Catholicism, the afflicted promises "to accept Jesus," to become a Pentecostal, in exchange for the cure of her own malady or a family member's.

The act of divine healing, in turn, inspires faith. The desperate individual seeks a supernatural cure not only because all other resources have been exhausted, but also because she has either personally witnessed an act of faith healing or heard about it through Pentecostal preaching or her network of social relationships. Moreover, the healing rituals of Catholicism and Umbanda are part of her religious formation. That the Pentecostal Jesus cures believers of their earthly and spiritual afflictions is nothing new. The novelty, rather, consists in the price and potency of the remedy. Whereas the Virgin of Nazaré and her fellow saints demand an act of ritual sacrifice for the granting of a miracle, and the Cabocla Mariana requests that her medium, the *mãe* or *pai-de-santo*, be compensated for her healing services, the Pentecostal Jesus orders the patient to convert, to be born again and become a *nova criatura* (new creature).

Since they require little of their human supplicants beyond ritualistic payment, the saints and spirits cannot provide the kind of comprehensive health coverage that the crente Jesus can. The Pentecostal convert must repent, rejecting the sinful (sick) world of "men" in favor of the righteous (healthy) world of God and his elect.[6] Adopting the ascetic moral code of classic and modern Pentecostalism, the neophyte renounces the sins of the world, manifested as the pathogens of poverty. The crente still inhabits an impoverished world but now, through an ascetic lifestyle, has the power to resist many of the contagions spawned by poverty.[7] Conversion to Pentecostalism is no panacea for the multiple viruses caused by material deprivation, but it does immunize its followers against some of poverty's more pernicious strains.

Libertação

Though not a significant factor in the conversion stories of my informants, another type of faith healing has become increasingly popular since the emergence of postmodern Pentecostalism in the early 1980s. Interviews with clergy and laity, in addition to my own observation-participation in cultos, confirm the fact that after Tuesday, the day of cultos de cura divina, IURD churches in Belém and throughout the country attract the greatest number of worshipers on Friday, when services revolve around *libertação*, or exorcism. This alternative method of faith healing has had such success in the IURD that most Brazilian Pentecostal churches have incorporated it into their liturgy. Even the AD, which has traditionally preferred to keep the demons at bay rather than conjure them up to then be exorcised, adopted the practice of Friday exorcisms in 1988.

The fundamental difference between traditional faith healing and libertação lies in folk etiology. Despite regional variations, the manner in which Amazonian caboclos classify illness captures the duality of popular etiological conceptions in Brazil. On the one hand is "normal" illness or sickness sent by God. The common cold, fever, malaria, cuts, allergies, tuberculosis, nasal congestion, among other ailments, can be treated successfully by home remedies, pharmaceuticals, and doctors. "Abnormal" illness, on the other hand, also known as *pajé* afflictions (*sofrimentos de pajé*), are maladies cultivated by evil. Only a *pajé* (Amazonian healer) can treat evil eye, *susto* (soul shock), spirit attack, *boto* (magic related to the enchanted river dolphin of Amazonian folklore), and the arrow of the beast (*flecha de bicho*) (Maues 217–218). Where traditional and modern medicine fail to cure normal illness, traditional Pentecostal faith healing can prove a potent remedy. Likewise, libertação can free those suffering from abnormal sickness caused by the evil spirits that have resisted the healing powers of the pajé, mãe-de-santo, or *curandeira* (folk healer).[8] In short, cura divina heals the pathogens of the soma, and libertação expels the demons of the psyche.

Regardless of the particular type of evil spirits that worshipers blame for their distress prior to entering the austere warehouse that serves as the mother church (*sede*) of the IURD in Belém, pastors expose the demons as the familiar exús and spirits of Umbanda. As offensive as it is to many Umbandistas, the demonization of the pantheon of African-Brazilian deities strikes a resonant chord in Brazilian popular religiosity. Who in the favelas of the urban periphery has not feared the malevolence of a *coisa feita*, a work of sorcery intended to block the path (*trancar a rua*) of a rival or enemy through sickness or injury? Through faith in both the pastor and the Holy Spirit, the possessed is liberated from the yoke of the Cabocla Mariana or Tranca Rua. But only conversion and affiliation with the IURD will bring lasting and comprehensive protection from the *espíritos malignos*. And like traditional faith healing, libertação often is the first step in the conversion process.

In early December 1993, I recorded my own observation of an exceptionally animated exorcism at an IURD Friday evening service:

> The service climaxes when the pastor instructs everyone to stand up and move to the front and lateral walls. Worshipers form a huge prayer circle occupying the whole sanctuary. People clasp each others' hands, and the pastor launches into rapid-fire tongue speaking about expelling demons. His glossolalic speech whips the congregation into a frenzy. The atmosphere is electric. Tongue speaking, wailing, moaning, and shouting raise the noise to an almost intolerable level.
>
> After about five minutes, a sudden scream pierces the cacophony. A woman is possessed, jumping up and down and screaming. An obreiro grabs her by the hair and drags her to the front, where she is set on her knees and continues to gesticulate wildly and scream for the duration of the exorcism. The scene is repeated with four other women, who are also brought to the front by obreiros. Cameras rolling [the service is being filmed], the pastor steps down from the altar and, joined by the legion of obreiros, asks the believers to help expel demons from the possessed. The first possessed woman, screaming in a chilling, diabolic voice, refuses to tell the pastor her name. A tremendous struggle ensues, in which the pastor, aided by the frenzied worshipers,

FIGURE 9. "Miracles"—Items, including a cockroach and spider, expelled from the demon-possessed during exorcisms at God Is Love.

commands the demons to exit. The demon hurls all the familiar epithets heard in the streets of the a baixadas before succumbing to the
superior divine force invoked by the pastor. The woman recovers, and
everybody applauds.

Faith Healing or Fake Healing?

Because Pentecostal healing is ascribed to God and requires faith,
many nonbelievers dismiss it as religious fakery or superstition. Pentecostal
preachers are denounced as the latest vendors of holy snake oil to the naive
masses. Indeed, certain churches in Brazil have deceived congregants
through practices related to faith healing. The IURD, in particular, has been
lambasted in the national press for marketing "holy oil," supposedly from
the Mount of Olives in Israel, and Dead Sea salt. Laboratory analysis of the
two "sacred" substances exposed the unguent as common Brazilian soybean
oil and the Dead Sea salt as the same monosodium chloride with which
Brazilians liberally season their food ("O bispo não é santo" 59). Paradoxically, such stories of fraudulent faith healing in the print and electronic
media probably do more to bolster Pentecostalism than weaken it. Those
crentes aware of denunciations in the press are likely to dismiss them as
Catholic propaganda aimed at discrediting their dynamic religion. Potential
Pentecostal converts cannot afford to buy magazines or newspapers, and even
if they have heard rumors of charlatanism in Pentecostal churches, the ur-
gency of their illness overrides any doubts.

Medical malpractice, misdiagnosis, and a general disregard for the
health of the poor, more than fraud, account for a significant amount of what
Pentecostals present as faith healing. Like Nizila da Silva, who was misdi-
agnosed with ovarian cancer and then attributed negative test results to divine intervention, many of the desenganados who have vowed to become
believers in exchange for a supernatural cure can see only the healing hand
of Jesus in the resolution of their health crisis. In the following story, Joanna
Macedo, a thirty-three-year-old manicurist and member of the IURD, saw
the awesome power of God, and not extreme medical incompetence. "The
other day in the church (IURD) I heard about a man who had died of a heart
operation, and his family called the pastor there to the wake. The pastor went
and said a prayer, and they started to shut the doors. The pastor put holy oil
on the body, and that man who was in the coffin got up, and everybody was
hugging him." Once a supplicant has enlisted divine aid through a vow, she
will invariably point to Jesus or the Holy Spirit as the source of her recov-

ery. A miraculous cure from the Holy Spirit is more comforting than the possibility of medical malpractice.

Extramural recognition of the mundane sources of many instances of Pentecostal faith healing in no way diminishes the power of the religion's most universal experience. Regardless of the opinions of skeptics and non-believers, the fact that millions of Pentecostals believe that Jesus and the Holy Spirit heal on the basis of faith alone makes cura divina a subjective reality. Like the patient whose health improves because of her faith in the curative properties of the little white capsule she takes three times a day, though it is merely a placebo, the crente creates the possibility of divine healing through belief.

Unlike the placebo patient, who has only her pills, the Pentecostal has recourse to an entire community of spiritual medics, her *irmãos na fé* (brothers and sisters in faith), ready to pray for her health. Even medical science is beginning to recognize the therapeutic value of prayer. According to recent research, ritual acts, such as prayer, might actually activate the human immune and endocrine systems. Researchers are also investigating the potential medical benefits of dissociated states of consciousness, such as crentes experience in the baptism of the Holy Spirit (Cox 109).

Sealing the Vow

Having invoked the healing power of the Doctor of Doctors for an ill family member or on her own behalf, the new convert must seal her vow by publicly declaring her commitment to serve Jesus. The pastor of a small AD congregation in the baixada bairro of Sacramenta, forty-seven-year-old José Araujo rushed to the nearest AD to publicly proclaim his devotion to Jesus after his wife's cure. His voice competing with the din of hammers and saws raising the roof of his unfinished church, José explained to me how he had become a member of the Assembly of God.

> The doors began to close; things were bad. My wife got sick and couldn't do anything at home. She suffered a lot with that swelling of her face. The swelling just got worse and worse. It was then that I had a revelation, when I was working at the hospital for minimum wage. And the Lord spoke to me saying this: "Your wife's cure depends on you." I said, "What do you mean, Lord?" It was a Sunday, the second Sunday of April, 1981. It was around six in the afternoon, there at the maternity wing. That was when He said, "Your wife's cure

depends on you." I heard the voice, and I looked outside and didn't see anybody. I said, "Is that really you, Lord, speaking to me? If it is you, and you are the master of truth, if you are the savior of the world like people say you are, and you heal, I want you to take me to the place where your truth exists, and there I will accept you as my savior." On that day, the second Sunday of April of 1981, at six in the afternoon, I saw that being dressed all in white, and he was saying, "Let's go." And He went ahead, with me following. I arrived home, and my wife was lying in the hammock. That was when I told her I was going to church to accept Jesus Christ as my savior, and she said, "I'll go with you." I said, "You're sick; you can't," and she said, "No, I'm going."

So I arrived here (in the church), and when I went in they were singing that Hymn Number 15. Then the whole congregation stood up, and I said, "I want to accept Jesus as my savior." They all knew that I was a very hardened man when it came to the gospel. I had a bad reputation. And so the whole church stood up and the pastor said, "Let us pray for this citizen who wants to accept Jesus as savior." At that moment great power filled the church, but I didn't recognize it. Today I know how to discern what it was. The whole church was taken by the power of God, and that night I devoted myself to Jesus, and my name was written in the book of heaven. A week later my wife's face had returned to normal.

Most new converts, unlike José, do not customarily march into the church and assertively declare their desire to accept Jesus. More typical is the way Hezio Nazareno, the twenty-one-year-old Quadrangular, responded to the preacher's chamada.

It was a Saturday youth service, and the church was full. I had already been participating for about three months, and that Saturday, when the pastor was preaching the message for young people, God touched me through the pastor's message. God touched me, and I got up. I got up, the pastor launched [*lançou*]) the invitation, and I stood up from the pew and went to the front; and when I got there in front, I felt something, something different. God was calling me to come to Him. I always remember that touch. God was calling me. And I accepted Jesus, and it was a very good thing, like this great happiness had taken over my heart and my life.

José and Hezio represent the great majority of converts, who voluntarily go to the altar to profess their commitment to Jesus, but a small minority are coerced to the front of the church through pressure from both family and pastor. In the small houses of prayer, many preachers will direct their conversion call at individual visitors when they see that no one is accepting their invitation to embrace Jesus. At several services I myself felt enormous pressure to respond to the call directed at "our friend from America." I was able to resist, but some worshipers, afraid of disappointing the pastor and their family, ambled to the altar, despite serious misgivings. Pressure from crente family members, friends, and pastors impelled one-fifth of my respondents to accept the pastor's invitation. Most tended to be adolescents at the time of their conversion. Despite their coerced conversion, most viewed it as an irreversible ritual, an act of God's will, if not their own. In the case of Luiza Andrade, a fifty-eight-year-old unemployed doméstica and mother of nine children, her Assembleiano brother-in-law "volunteered" her for Jesus.

> Then the pastor asked who wanted to accept Jesus, but I kept silent. I didn't say anything, and my brother-in-law said this: "Brother, my sister-in-law wants to accept Jesus." Ay, I got so angry. So as not to contradict him, I went against my will. Then he said, "Come and kneel here. We are going to pray for you," and I knelt, filled with anger, and so did my husband. We accepted Jesus, you know, and when the service was over, I asked my brother-in-law why he had called me, because I didn't want to be a crente. "Ah, but you already are one, and now you are going to stay here and live with me, because if you don't you will stray." So I stayed in his house for around a month, and my relatives explained what it means to be a crente, and I became firmer in the faith.

Washing Away Sin (Sickness)

In publicly proclaiming their devotion to Jesus, José, Hezio, and even Luiza initiated the official conversion process. After the culto, the church secretary records the neophytes' names and eventually forwards them to the Central Temple, where functionaries register the new converts' vital statistics on index cards. Converts spend the next few months in preparation for the ritual that symbolizes their official affiliation with the church: baptism.

Preparation for baptism varies greatly across denominational lines but typically involves instruction in the fundamentals of the faith via Sunday school, home visits from church workers, and regular attendance at worship services.

In the classic churches and in some modern ones, where believers are expected to separate from the world, the three or four months between the public conversion and baptism also serve as a probationary period. Home visits and instruction from established members socialize the neophyte into the doctrinal, attitudinal, and comportmental norms of the faith. Behavioral norms are of particular concern to Assembleianos and those belonging to churches where crentes must externalize their inner transformation, declaring themselves creatures of God and not the sinful world. In addition to renouncing all vices, men must replace the uniform of the torrid baixadas, a bare chest, brightly colored athletic shorts, and plastic sandals, with long pants, preferably dark-colored, and a shirt, long-sleeved for Sunday worship. Likewise, girls and young women must divest themselves of the rayon halter tops and revealing shorts and miniskirts that identify them as faveladas. In their crente uniform, composed of a dark, knee-length skirt, any modest blouse on hand, and waist-length hair, often tied up in a bun, the girls and women proclaim their allegiance to Jesus, effectively removing themselves from the sexual economy of the rua.

Having acquired the fundamentals of the faith and learned proper crente conduct during the short probationary period, the new convert is ready to become an official, card-carrying member of the church through baptism by immersion.[9] Some converts, however, preferring informal affiliation to official membership or ineligible due to their marital status, remain congregants (*congregados*) for several years or even the duration of their life as believers.[10] Congregants of the AD in Belém constitute approximately 40 percent of all those who regularly attend worship services and participate in church activities.

Maintaining that the decision to accept Jesus must, in part, be a rational one, Pentecostals reject the Catholic and mainline Protestant practice of infant baptism.[11] Instead, Pentecostal pastors usher baptismal candidates into a tank of water that in the diminutive temples of the shantytowns is not much larger than a small bathtub but in the mother churches of the metropolis, such as the Central Temple, reaches the size of a backyard swimming pool. Baptisms in the AD, due to the church's centralized bureaucracy, take place only at the Central Temple on a quarterly basis. Divided by sex into two single-file lines, between two hundred and three hundred baptismal candidates, cloaked in simple cloth robes, patiently wait their turn to descend into the cool water.

Once in the tank, candidates profess their commitment to Jesus, and then, in the name of the Father, Son, and Holy Ghost, the pastor immerses the convert in the cleansing water. The convert emerges from the water a new creature and an official member of the church, her worldly sins left to drown at the bottom of the tank. Claudia Souza, the AD member who was raped by her uncle, conveyed the purgative and transformative nature of baptism by immersion. "For me it was a great experience. You feel like you're burying all your sins, that the water is cleansing. It's like everything, all that filth, is left in the water. You become a new person, a new creature. You feel very happy."

Claudia and her coreligionists have poignantly illustrated the relationship between conversion and healing. A health crisis, typically physical illness, leads the afflicted individual to accept Jesus in exchange for a cure. Brazilian Pentecostals, of course, do not conceptualize the *voto* (vow) as an exchange, but the contractual agreement, according to the mechanics of popular religion in Brazil, is the most effective way to implore the gods for something. The Pentecostal God, however, demands a much higher price from his supplicants than a pilgrimage or some other act of ritual self-sacrifice. The Pentecostal God commands the petitioner to convert, to turn away from the old world of sin (sickness) and commence her spiritual and physical renewal. The *Deus todo poderoso* (omnipotent God) of the crentes does not transform the world but, through conversion, restores the health of his believers and inoculates them against the most common diseases of poverty.

CHAPTER 4

Health Maintenance: Spiritual Ecstasy and Mutual Aid

❧

Being Pentecostal means being a person filled with power, a different kind of person, a person who lives in communion with God. Because in order to have power, we have to live in communion with God. So a Pentecostal is a person full of power, a person of real power. When a crente really prays hard for a person possessed by demons, the demons leave right away, and when we pray for a sick person, the illness goes away.
  —Sandra Andrade, twenty-five-year-old Assembleiana
  and high school student

$\mathcal{S}$andra, speaking on what it means to be a Pentecostal, identifies the essence of her evangelical faith: power. Whether emanating from the secular or sacred, power instills in its possessors a sense of the possible. That Portuguese and Spanish, as Romance languages, employ the same word for the noun "power" (*poder*) and the verb "to be able" (*poder*) reveals much about the nature of power. To possess power is to be able to exercise some degree of control over one's environment. The greater the power, the larger the environment one is able to influence. Of course, spiritual and temporal power are not perfectly interchangeable, but as evidenced by the Pentecostals of Latin America, spiritual strength can be harnessed for secular purposes.

More specifically, it is the experience of divine power in their everyday lives that defines Latin American Pentecostals. From glossolalia to their personal relationship with Jesus, crentes live and express their faith in terms of *poder divino*. For example, baptism in the Holy Spirit, the experiential and doctrinal core of Pentecostal religion, is first and foremost an act of explosive power. If the cathartic eruption of spiritual baptism were contained within the walls of the temple, as some scholars argue, *crença* would have nothing to offer *populares* in their daily struggle to survive. But the walls separating the sanctuary from the street cannot contain the spiritual blast within. Believers carry the force of the spirit with them, out of the church and into casa and rua. There, in their everyday lives, the poor, from the baix-adas of Belém to the *ciudades perdidas* (shantytowns) of Tijuana, employ the power of the Spirit to cure the afflictions of poverty and immunize them-selves against future infection. This chapter examines how, after the initial cure through conversion, converts are able to access sacred power through both the Holy Spirit and the community of believers and exert it to repair the damage inflicted by the violence of material deprivation. Put differently, what did Sandra Andrade mean when she told me "being Pentecostal means being a person filled with power"?

Baptism in the Holy Spirit

Crentes, like Umbandistas and popular Catholics and all practitioners of popular religion in Brazil, elevate the experiential component of their faith over the doctrinal. In response to my question about illiteracy being a bar-rier to leadership positions in the AD, Neuza Sá (the widowed crente who opined that Catholic priests cannot be good counselors) stressed the domi-nance of the spirit over the letter. "If a person has faith in God, nothing is difficult. I have seen many people who don't know how to read preach re-ally well. But there are many who know how to read but can't preach, be-cause they want to preach by the letter. The true gospel is the one preached through practice and biblical stories, not by the letter."

Ecstasy is one of the principal ways in which Pentecostals receive the power of the Spirit. In contrast to cerebral historic Protestantism, which en-gages the psyche more than the soma, the Pentecostal culto aims at body and soul. The Pentecostal God is not a remote figure to be contemplated in si-lence but a dynamic force to be experienced by the entire being, both psy-che and soma. Pentecostalism provides its followers with several means of achieving spiritual rapture, but none is as potent as baptism in the Holy Spirit.

Although not as universally experienced as faith healing, baptism by the Holy Spirit is such a fundamental part of Pentecostal identity in Brazil that those who have not received it feel less than spiritually whole and often express doubts about the vitality of their faith. Pentecostal belief in baptism by the Holy Spirit derives from biblical references in the Gospels and the Acts of the Apostles. John the Baptist, baptizing believers in the river Jor-dan, preached, "I baptize you with water; but he who is mightier than I is coming, the thong of whose sandals I am not worthy to untie; he will bap-tize you with the Holy Spirit and with fire" (Luke 3.16). Indeed, Pentecostals take their name from the first instance of the spiritual baptism, when the disciples, gathered together on the feast of Pentecost (literally, "fifty days," i.e., after Passover), were possessed by the Holy Spirit. "When the day of Pentecost had come, they were all together in one place. And suddenly a sound came from heaven like the rush of a mighty wind, and it filled all the house where they were sitting. And there appeared to them tongues as of fire, distributed and resting on each one of them. And they were all filled with the Holy Spirit and began to speak in other tongues, as the Spirit gave them utterance" (Acts 2.1–4). In opposition to traditional Protestants and Catholics, who regard spiritual baptism as a significant but purely historical event, Pentecostals affirm that the same power bestowed on the disciples almost two millennia ago is available to today's believers.

Spiritual baptism, along with conversion, emerged as one of the defining moments in my informants' life histories. Some Belenense Pentecostals could not recall the number of children they had but remembered the precise moment of their *batismo no Espírito Santo* and described it with as much detail and emotion as if it had occurred just hours before our interview. Almost four-fifths (79.4 percent) of my interviewees had been baptized by the Holy Spirit, usually several months after becoming members but sometimes many years later.

Spiritual baptism provides a phenomenological bridge to the new faith for poor Brazilians familiar with spirit possession in African-Brazilian religion. Like the Umbandista "horse" or medium "ridden" by its spirit, the crente is taken by and filled with the power of the Holy Spirit. Though the term "possession" in Brazilian Pentecostal discourse denotes demonic invasion of an individual, Pentecostals receiving spiritual baptism are clearly "possessed" by the power of the Holy Spirit. In psychological terminology, the baptized lapse into a dissociated state of consciousness, marked by ecstatic utterances, clonic spasms, and explosive bodily energy. Perhaps the phrase "spiritual orgasm" best captures the climactic ecstasy of the event.

The great power that crentes experience during spiritual baptism is often expressed in language borrowed from two other sources of ecstasy and altered states of consciousness: drugs and sex. Assembly of God Evangelist Antonio Amolina related his baptism in the Holy Spirit in terms of the injections administered in ubiquitous Brazilian pharmacies for everything from the common cold to "nerves": "Look, I felt the power like a force that descends over you, like when you feel bad and someone comes and 'applies' a strong injection and then you feel energized. You want to say 'Alleluia' and 'Praise God,' shaking from His power. It is a very special force that overcomes you, a power that people say cannot be put into words. It's something that happens only once in a lifetime."

While the evangelist employed medical metaphors to convey the power he felt, Ovidio Pinheiro, the seventy-seven-year-old retired night watchman and doorman at a small AD church in the bairro of Terra Firme, described his baptism in terms of the sedating effect of alcohol, one of the most common sources of altered states of consciousness on the urban periphery. "I felt anesthetized, like when you're plastered [*porre*]. I felt so full of power when the Holy Spirit operated on me. I was in a chair when the light struck me, and I blanked out and fell to the ground. But I didn't feel anything; I felt, like, anesthetized, filled with power and speaking in tongues. Later, when it was over, we got up and ended the service. A brother said, 'Look, you're covered with blood.' And when I went back to church the next day, I was healed."

Metaphors of drug-induced ecstasy also permeate Pentecostal women's accounts of baptism, but more salient is a subtext of eroticism largely absent from male narratives. In Latin American Pentecostalism, as well as most branches of Christianity throughout the world, the Holy Spirit is a decidedly masculine being; it penetrates the believer, injecting her with seminal power. Although male sexual identity in Brazil is not as rigidly constructed as in other parts of Ibero-America, the erotic imagery expressed in female baptismal narratives would, due to the Holy Spirit's masculine identity, take on homoerotic subtones in the male narrative. The image of the Holy Spirit as a supernatural and superlative lover also complements the popular female conception of Jesus as the consummate husband, the loyal spouse who would never abandon his wife and, despite great hardship, always provides for his family. The men in Rosilea Garcia's life, particularly her alcoholic father, lacked the potency of the Holy Spirit, which baptized her during a prayer service at the IURD. "Look, I felt a very intense light, you know. I felt hands. I felt like praying but not the same way other people were, and I began to talk to God, and it seemed like I was trying to touch, to encounter, to embrace God, you know. It seemed like He wanted to speak only with me, you understand? It was like He wanted to be only with me that night. It was a very, very beautiful thing, a new experience for me. I confess to you that when I went to sleep that night, I had a beautiful dream of God."

Forty-three-year-old civil servant and Assembleiana, Julite Pantoja, wearing only a towel, received a more eruptive Holy Spirit in the intimacy of her bedroom.

I was so lost in heavenly prayer that I didn't even realize that I had finished my bath. I entered my bedroom and kneeled, wearing just a towel. But when I began to pray again, something happened: all my words came out in the tongues of angels, in foreign tongues. It was really an explosion of the Holy Spirit in my life. I couldn't control myself, and from so much tongue speaking, the sisters began to come to my room and saw that I was being baptized by the Holy Spirit. It was complete joy [*gozo*]).[1] During the rest of the day, I couldn't even look at the sky or feel my own breathing, because I felt God in everything. When I looked up at the sky, there were foreign tongues. I would look at a tree, and there were foreign tongues. I felt an intense fire inside me. It really was a marvelous day for me, an unforgettable experience. Now I no longer have any doubts about baptism by the Holy Spirit.

Thus, baptism in the Holy Spirit infuses crentes with a tremendous sense of power through *ekstasis*, or the sensation of being taken out of their normal state. The dissociated state of consciousness induced by spiritual baptism allows believers to transcend their oppressive social locus. Like the hypnotic effects of psychotropic drugs and sex, spiritual baptism suspends ordinary time and place, allowing the believer to float in an extraordinary sacred space, devoid of the demons of quotidian poverty. Analyzing possession trance, anthropologist I. M. Lewis identifies the harsh social reality that engenders the need for escape and release. "The circumstances which encourage the ecstatic response are precisely those where men feel themselves constantly threatened by exacting pressures which they do not know how to combat or control, except through those heroic flights of ecstasy by which they seek to demonstrate that they are the equals of the gods" (Henney 101). But the ecstatic power of the trance is not merely an opiate-like flight from reality. Rather, spiritual baptism also fills believers with the strength to face a harsh reality and persevere.

The power transmitted by the Holy Spirit also serves as divine protection from both natural and supernatural evil. Reflecting the clientelism that continues to characterize Brazilian social, political, and religious relationships, the Holy Spirit operates as a sort of divine patron, offering protection in exchange for service and loyalty. In addition to its role as the ideal lover and spouse, the Espírito Santo is also the perfect *patrão*, who demands unswerving fealty from his clients in return for the security of sustenance. With little defense against rising crime, unemployment, and prices, the need of poor Brazilians for supernatural protection from societal evil has increased sharply.

The testimonial pages of the *Estandarte Evangélico* record the growing demand for a supernatural protector. It is not until the early 1980s that stories of divine protection appear regularly, though still overshadowed by myriad accounts of faith healing. Much of the testimony relating to protection involves home burglary. Under the front-page caption "Thief Puts Down Stolen Object upon Seeing Bible," one Assembleiano, in particular, testified that a thief who had broken into his home exited promptly upon seeing an open Bible on the kitchen table but not before penning a note admonishing the family to keep the back door locked. A photograph of the homeowner holding his Bible accompanies the story (8–9/72).

Psalm 91 is the quintessential statement of divine protection for Brazilian Pentecostals. Obreiras at the IEQ mother church in Belém would distribute printed copies of the cherished psalm with the heading "Psalm 91 Divine Protection." Worshipers were told, "A thousand may fall at your side, ten thousand at your right hand; but it will not come near you. You will only look with your eyes and see the recompense of the wicked" (Psalm 91.7–8).

Gifts of the Spirit

Though the Pentecostal faithful experience spiritual baptism only once in a lifetime, they have continuous access to spiritual power through the gifts of the Spirit. As Bishop Macedo of the IURD writes, charismata, or the *dons do epírito* (gifts of the Spirit) are yet further proof of the power of God (Macedo 1993: 101). Prior to being possessed by the Holy Spirit, the majority of crentes adhered to the faith through the supreme gift of faith healing. Faith healing heads the category of gifts that Bishop Macedo has aptly denominated *dons de poder* (gifts of power). This category also includes the spiritual presents of miracles and faith. Due to their unspecified and rather general nature, the latter two are not as salient as others. Tongues, or glossolalia, is indubitably the apex of the second category of inspirational gifts. While Brazilian Pentecostals, especially members of the Assembly of God and God Is Love, regard the gift of prophecy with awe, a much greater proportion speak the "tongues of angels" than prophesy. Those who can simultaneously interpret the messages of tongue speakers into Portuguese possess the third type of inspirational charismata: interpretation of tongues. In contrast to the abundant gift of tongues, glossolalic interpretation is distributed sparsely. Less prominent are the three gifts of revelation: knowledge, wisdom, and the discernment of spirits. My Belenense informants tended to conflate the three under the general rubric of revelation.

Charismatic power among Brazilian Pentecostals is distributed according to the variables of sex, denomination, and ecclesiastical rank. At the time of our interviews, almost three-quarters of my interviewees claimed to be endowed with at least one spiritual gift. Glossolalia emerged as the most common gift for both sexes and all three denominations: 41.8 percent of all informants declared themselves to be active speakers of tongues. Revelation and faith healing ranked a distant second and third, distributed respectively among only 15.2 percent and 11.4 percent of all believers. The remaining gifts, with the exception of prophecy among women, were statistically insignificant.

The greatest determinant of spiritual gifts among Belenense crentes is denominational affiliation. While 83.3 percent of all Assembleianos surveyed spoke in tongues or possessed some other form of charism, only a slight majority (54.2 percent) of Quandrangulares and members of the IURD were spiritually gifted. Those endowed with gifts followed the pattern of their Assembly brethren in claiming glossolalia more than any other *don*. Likewise, revelation and faith healing ranked as the second and third most practiced gifts.

The greater distribution of charismata among Assembleianos is at first glance a bit perplexing. One would expect, according to sociological theory, the Spirit to be weakest where the institutionalization process has developed to the fullest. As one of the nation's two oldest Pentecostal denominations, the Assembly of God stands as the epitome of the Pentecostal institution, with a salaried pastorate, seminaries, and a publishing house. Moreover, many of my older Assembly informants asserted that the Spirit had been more active in the past. But it is not only institutionalization per se that dampens the Spirit. Of equal significance is the organizational model of the church. The AD's organizational design, though centralized, has left the churches of the baixadas with sufficient autonomy to maintain the priesthood of all believers. Services in the small temples can last for up to three hours, as numerous members of the congregation ascend into the pulpit to sing a hymn, read a Bible passage or the weekly calendar, and give testimony. I, myself, was a frequent participant in Assembly cultos.

The relatively democratic and participatory liturgy of AD churches in the baixadas gives way to the more autocratic and centralized practice of some modern, and many postmodern, churches. IURD liturgy, in particular, reintegrates elements of traditional Catholic hierarchy. Responding to my observation that common members never step into the pulpit to sing a hymn or deliver a biblical message, Rosilea Garcia explained: "Look, that's not done in the Universal, because the pulpit is something very sacred in the IURD. If someone who has sinned approaches the pulpit, a malign spirit can strike him down. So that's why no one goes to the pulpit to preach or pray. The only time a person can step into the pulpit is when the pastor calls him to give testimony."

Functioning as Weberian priests, albeit charismatic ones, pastors of the IURD, and the IEQ, to a lesser extent, mediate ecstatic power in a manner that is only seen in the larger churches of the AD, especially the central temples. Postmodern Pentecostals are not so much the practitioners of spiritual gifts as the beneficiaries of them. Exorcism and faith healing in the IURD are gifts possessed by pastors and practiced on ordinary believers. Most members have been healed or exorcised, but very rarely have they themselves been used by God to cure another person. Hence, the power of the "priests" accounts for much of the denominational difference in the distribution of spiritual gifts. Postmodern Pentecostal pastors have appropriated much of the power of the Spirit for themselves, leaving the laity as passive beneficiaries of the clergy's charismata.

The distribution of charismata also depends on the variable of sex. In every denomination women are more endowed with spiritual gifts than men. Of my total group of informants, 80 percent of the women were spiritually gifted, compared to 62.5 percent of the men. Factoring in denominational differences, AD women manifested charismata twice as often as men of the IURD and IEQ. My female interviewees spoke in tongues and received revelations from God and the Holy Spirit twice as often as men did. Swiss sociologist Christian Lalive D'Epinay also found Pentecostal women in Chile to be more charismatic, especially glossolalic, than their male counterparts (203).

The unequal allocation of spiritual gifts between the sexes is a function of power and culture. It is the socially weakest who, in compensation for their temporal impotence, most seek spiritual power. And in twentieth-century Brazil favelada and rural women, particularly *negras* and *mulatas*, stand the furthest from the center of power. Not only victims of classism and racism, poor Brazilian women suffer material and psychic stress owing to their subordinate position in a patriarchal society. Without husbands or boyfriends to bring home a meager paycheck, they frequently live in abject poverty. Adding to the need for spiritual release from mundane suffering is cultural conditioning which endows women with greater sensitivity to perceive and feel the

Spirit. The majority of Spiritist mediums, Umbandista parents-of-the-saints, and Catholic healers are women, since the spiritual realm in Latin America is predominantly feminine. Men may direct the ecclesia, but women have greater access to the *spiritus*.

Although faith healing is the most common spiritual gift received by Brazilian Pentecostals, glossolalia is the charism most often practiced by ordinary members. In its first form, tongue speaking serves as a seal or proof that a believer has been baptized by the Holy Spirit. If a crente does not manifest angelic utterance during or shortly after spiritual baptism, then the baptism is rejected as illegitimate and perhaps the work of lesser spirits than the Spirit itself. The second type of ecstatic speech usually erupts spontaneously during prayer.[2] A few of my informants even broke into glossolalia during our interview.

In the temples of Belém and the rest of Brazil, glossalalic speech sounds remotely similar to Hebrew. I suspect that tongue speakers unconsciously transmogrify biblical words of Hebraic and Aramaic origin into ecstatic utterance. A common speech pattern shared by most Brazilian crentes suggests that glossolalia, as researcher Marion Aubree argues, is learned behavior (1074).[3] Pentecostals, however, believe glossolalia to be a divine tool in which the Holy Spirit uses the faithful as media to broadcast its message. Lacking the gift of interpretation, most crentes must have an interpreter translate the speech into Portuguese.

That those whose social voice is muted by the *poderosos* (the powerful) should speak so loudly and fluently in the language of the Spirit is not surprising. Spiritual language allows the poor to speak like saints and not like *populares* whose Portuguese is denigrated and ridiculed by the elite guardians of culture. Glossolalia, then, is not "the language for people without language," as some have posited (D'Epinay 199). Deviating from the correct language of official society, popular Portuguese possesses a wealth of colorful idioms and slang that is no less language than the polished speech of the scholastically educated. Rather than "language for people without language," glossolalia is speech for those whose tongue is tied by official society, particularly poor women of color. When an entire congregation bursts into charismatic utterance, it is the amplified female voices that send the researcher scrambling for his ear plugs.

Besides tongues and faith healing, what Assembleianos collectively refer to as "revelation" is the only other spiritual gift of any practical significance. Prophecy, while technically an inspirational gift, tends to get lumped under the rather ambiguous rubric of revelation. An essentially female phenomenon, revelation transforms believers who are deprived of official means of communication, such as regular postal and telephone service, into divine messengers, God's spokeswomen. Dreams and visions, the materia prima of Brazilian popular religiosity, are powerful media through which God reveals himself to crente women of the baixadas.

Bishop Macedo's accurate perception of prophecy as a tool of female subversion applies equally to the dreams and visions of revelation. What is often revealed to women are the sins and transgressions of men, particularly their husbands. A vision allowed forty-two-year-old homemaker and Assembleiana Noemi Pessoa to perceive her husband's philandering:

> Before my husband took up with that woman, I had a vision of an enormous ball floating over the church. It was a day when I was praying in church, and that ball was very black and went by making a lot of noise. When I finished praying, I spoke with a sister, and she told me that I was going to pass through some type of tribulation. I prayed and prayed for the Lord to reveal the meaning of that vision to me. A lot of time passed, and my husband was already with that woman, but I still hadn't found out. It was years later that I found out about his lover, at the end of their relationship. It was better that way because my suffering was less. When they told me about his lover, it was then that I came to understand the meaning of that black ball that I saw years ago.

The dreams and visions associated with the gift of revelation grant crente woman the moral authority to challenge the sinful behavior of both Pentecostal and non-Pentecostal men. Sometimes the fear of divine retribution provoked by prophecy is enough to cause a man to desist from his errant ways. Armed with the moral authority of revelation, Pentecostal women discover a powerful new weapon for confronting a cheating husband or wayward pastor. Like his prominent colleague Bishop Macedo, Pastor-President Paulo Machado felt sufficiently threatened by uncontrolled revelation and prophecy that in a weekly administrative meeting in late 1971 he admonished members not "to frequent the homes of certain sisters and brothers with the intention of finding out the will of God about certain matters. Such behavior must be banished from the church" (Acts 1971).

Less subversive is the only other significant spiritual gift that is practiced on a regular basis. Faith healing, in addition to its central role in the conversion process, continues to be the primary kind of charism experienced by the mature believer. Although the crente has recovered much of his physical, psychological, or spiritual health through conversion, the world of material deprivation continues to spawn pathogens from which permanent access to cura divina provides considerable protection. The afflicted adherent has access to the healing hands of the pastor and the curative prayers of an entire congregation of believers.

One of the great paradoxes of Brazilian Pentecostalism's prize gift of the Spirit is that it is received much more than actively practiced. In other words, the great majority of my informants had been healed through faith, but only a small minority (11.4 percent) had been "used" by the Holy Spirit as healing agents in the cure of another person. The gift of faith healing appears to be limited to pastors and exceptionally devout believers, usually female. With the exception of Page (227), who argued that pastors monopolized all forms of charismata, no other research on Latin American Pentecostalism has addressed the question of the distribution of spiritual gifts.

Lacunae in the research notwithstanding, the institutional need to control charismatic power explains the unequal distribution of the practice of faith healing. In a religion that thrives because of faith healing, the power of the pastor depends greatly on his talent as a healer. He claims that he himself does not cure; the Holy Spirit merely uses him as a vessel. But the Pentecostal preacher known for performing powerful cures will attract standing-room-only crowds. In contrast, the preacher lacking curative charismata might find himself pastoring a reduced flock. In summary, while many experience the benefits of Pentecostalism's most valued gift, the greatest power is reserved for the privileged few who administer it.

Hymns of Healing

Although technically not a spiritual gift, Pentecostal music merits consideration as a potent source of ecstatic release, particularly for women. In my interviews, I asked my informants what things gave them the most pleasure in life. In third place, after only church and family, women most frequently cited sacred music as their greatest joy. Men also respond to the rousing hymns but generally did not attach as much significance to music. So fundamental is music to Pentecostal liturgy in Brazil that it typically composes two-thirds of the culto. Background mood music soothes the soul when worshipers are not singing such hymns as "Cristo Cura, Sim!" (Christ Heals, Indeed!) and "Jesus Me Tirou da Lama" (Jesus Pulled Me Out of the Mud).

Pentecostal churches in Brazil and throughout the world have been extraordinarily adept at incorporating local folk and popular music into the wor-

FIGURE 10. Healing rhythms.

ship service. The sensual rhythm of *carimbó* suffuses many of the hymns sung at the small AD temples in the baixadas of Belém.[1] In churches where youth groups actively participate in the music, hymns are often popular tunes from the radio and soap operas which have been set to evangelical lyrics by Protestant recording artists. No church has perfected this process to the degree that the IURD has. Sentimental songs by Leandro and Leonardo (the kings of *sertanejo* pop) and by Roberto Carlos and the lively theme from the Xuxa television show aid cristãos of the Universal Church of the Kingdom of God in achieving spiritual ecstasy. One Assembleiana, Maria Santos (forty two year old homemaker), was even cured through a hymn.

> Now, my voice isn't one of those finely tuned voices, but it's the voice that God gave me to sing with. In fact, the Lord cured me through hymns. When I lived in the interior, I was sick and depressed, with terrible headaches. One day I had a really bad headache, so I lay down and began singing a hymn, and when I was in the middle of it, I began to get happy, and the Lord began to speak to me. He said He was going to make me happy, that He was with me, that He was taking care of me, and that I should feel His presence. And then Jesus did the job right away. Jesus always works miracles with me through hymns.

The Congregation as Mutual Aid Society

If charismata and baptism in the Holy Spirit inject crentes with a spiritual force that allows them to more effectively cope with the everyday crises of poverty, then the church community functions as a mutual aid association, providing material and psychological assistance to members in need. The congregation, however, does not supplant the family as the primary network of mutual aid among poor Brazilians. Rather, the church community serves as an additional network which members can access if and when kin relationships fail. Sociologist Bryan Roberts's discovery in the late 1960s that evangelical churches were one of the few types of voluntary associations functioning on the urban periphery of Guatemala applies to the slums and shantytowns of Brazil as well (754). Left to fend for themselves by an indifferent, if not antagonistic, state, the urban poor must create their own mutual aid associations. In late twentieth-century Brazil, Pentecostalism stands out as one of the principal organizations of the poor.[5]

The Templo Central of the AD in Belém has sporadically practiced institutional charity through food drives and medical and legal clinics. Yet it is not primarily as a religious institution but as a community of believers that the church practices mutual aid. Of the 73.9 percent of my informants who had accepted some type of material aid through the church, the vast majority had received it as an offering from fellow members, rather than as a direct donation from the Central Temple. At most of the services I attended in the baixadas, the pastor would ask the congregation to make a special offering for a crente family in crisis, usually related to health or employment. Many worshipers probably knew which brother(s) or sister(s) in faith would receive the donation, but the pastor, out of respect for the family's dignity, maintained their anonymity. Maria Santos was saved from ignominious suffering by her fellow believers.

> So I had to have an operation, and two weeks later my husband fell ill with a lung problem and couldn't work. The brothers and sisters couldn't believe how skinny he got. But I believe that this was all so God could act in our lives. So at that time there was a very good-hearted pastor, and when my husband got sick, the pastor gathered the church together and told them that we needed help from the church and that they shouldn't deny us aid. And thank God; it was a blessing, wasn't it? We never lacked anything at home. God even used people who weren't crentes to help us. One sister made sure that we always had some meat at home. Her husband worked with meat, and she would bring meat home for us. Another sister would bring a liter

of milk each day. So I thank God that everything is the fulfillment of His word. After a couple weeks, he [her husband] recuperated and began to work again for Jesus, as well as for us.

Poor Pentecostals also aid each other without pastoral mediation. A liter of milk might arrive at the home of an unemployed crente before the pastor is even aware of the situation. Although Brazilian Pentecostalism does not abolish ecclesiastic hierarchy, its rejection of the Catholic *compadrio*, or godparent, relationship in favor of a community of "brothers and sisters in faith" allows the member to experience the small- and medium-size congregation as an extended family. Roseline Nascimento, a twenty-seven-year-old Assembleiana and high school student, contrasted the anonymity of her old faith with the fraternity of her new one. "It's different because in our church we are a family, everybody knows each other. Not like the Catholic church, where everybody leaves right after mass and no one knows each other."

But not all congregations are like Roseline's in the bairro of Guamá, where believers, as rural migrants from the interior of the state, share the bonds of culture and social class. Outside the relatively homogeneous AD congregations of the baixadas, the larger, more differentiated churches, such as the AD's Central Temple and the sede of the IURD (strategically located across the street from Belém's long-distance bus terminal), do not permit the same degree of mutual aid. Here the congregation as family rarely exists. Instead of congregating in small groups outside the temple to socialize after the culto had ended, worshipers at the large churches scampered to catch the bus home. At the conclusion of services at the IURD sede, people were in such a hurry to get home that I had to dart about frantically to arrange two or three interviews. In marked contrast, crentes at churches in the slums were so eager to be interviewed that I could only meet with a small fraction of all who wanted to narrate their life histories.

Another less common but notable function of the Pentecostal network of mutual aid is as a job bank. Of my interviewees, 16.3 percent, mainly men, had found work through church contacts. Several of the women worked as domestic servants for middle-class crente families, and a few of the men earned minimum wage as security guards and janitors at the Central Temple. Despite some employers who complain that Pentecostal workers have their eyes fixed on heaven instead of the task at hand, crentes seem to have earned a reputation in Brazil for honesty, sobriety, and peacefulness, traits that privileged Brazilians normally do not attribute to the *povão*, or rabble. The wife of a well- known Brazilian sociologist, overhearing my conversation with her

husband on Pentecostalism, explained that she hired only evangelical dó-
mesticas because they do not steal and drink nothing stronger than *guaraná*
(the national soft drink, flavored with and named after the caffeinated seeds
of an Amazonian shrub). Corruption scandals involving prominent Pentecostal
pastors and politicians may have tarnished the crente reputation for honesty,
but in the early 1990s pastors continue to serve as employment agents, rec-
ommending certain church members to employers.

Possibly even more consequential than the material benefits derived
from church membership is the psychological and spiritual support provided by the community of believers. Assembled by the common diseases
of poverty, believers experience healing power in the hymns and prayers of
the congregation, in the exchange of embraces, and in visits from their spiritual brothers and sisters. Even in the poorest churches, on invasion sites
where some people worship barefoot, the passionate hymns and moving testimonies exude a sense of solidarity that proclaims, "Yes, we are the down-
trodden of the earth, but with the Holy Spirit and each other, we are spiritual
victors" (author's adaptation of an IEQ pamphlet entitled "Proclamation of
Victory"). The congregation as a spiritual and psychological solidarity network is especially important to crente women. Prayer circles and women's
groups often resemble the psychological support groups for abused and battered women that have proliferated in the United States during the last
decade. Temporarily removed from the stress of their impoverished homes,
women, gathered in prayer, carve out an alternative space where they com-
fort each other and vent their frustrations. As Darcy Neves, a twenty-nine-
year-old member of the IURD and nurse's assistant, explained, much of the
discussion in women's groups centers on marital and domestic strife. Responding to my question regarding the predominance of women in her
church, Darcy said:

> Look, the majority of women who attend church have problems with
> their husbands. These are the problems that most afflict them. For ex-
> ample, sometimes the husband suddenly "arranges" another woman
> out there. So at church we have prayer groups and through prayer, God
> removes the other woman from her path.[6] Also the majority of women
> at church are young women, and most young women have emotional
> problems. A wife often has problems with her husband when he drinks
> too much, and they fight constantly. And so here at church we get to-
> gether to pray and through prayer, God blesses the couple.

Thus crentes are further able to reclaim and preserve their health
through the spiritual and ecclesiastical tools of charismata and mutual aid.

Pentecostals, in achieving spiritual ecstasy through baptism in the Holy Spirit, the gifts of the Spirit, and music, temporarily transcend their oppressive reality. Believers, imbued with spiritual force, no longer regard the demons of want as so formidable. Tranca Rua continues to block the crossroads of the baixadas, but crentes, filled with the Spirit, pass intrepidly through the numerous socioeconomic roadblocks on the back streets of the urban periphery. Pentecostalism also infuses its followers with the power to hurdle the countless obstacles of ubiquitous poverty as members of the community of believers. As active constituents of congregations in the baixadas, the faithful create mutual aid societies that complement the primary network of kin relationships. For the favelado struggling to stay afloat in the low tide of material deprivation, the church as community provides the material, spiritual, and psychological succor that can make the difference between health and illness.

CHAPTER 5

Health Maintenance through Ideology and Morality
❦

*B*razilian Pentecostalism, in addition to mutual aid and spiritual gifts, dispenses a potent ideological remedy for the recovery and maintenance of health. A dualistic theology that divides the world into good and evil provides crentes with both ideological and practical tools for preventing and combating illness. On the ideological plane, the theological dualism of Pentecostalism furnishes adherents with a powerful and comprehensive etiology of the diseases of the baixadas. A worldview organized by such polarities as world and church, carnal and spiritual, house and street, darkness and light, believer and nonbeliever, to name a few, provides a clear road map for individuals attempting to negotiate the innumerable obstacles of life in the slums.

At the level of praxis, Pentecostal Manichaeism posits an uncompromising ascetic moral code that requires converts to renounce their worldly ways. As servants of God, believers must forswear the earthly vices that circulate freely through the streets of the baixadas: alcohol, tobacco, prostitution, soccer, philandering, thievery, and carnival—one of the greatest evils of all. Since much of this "sinful" behavior pertains to conduct associated with the male prestige complex, a poor Brazilian male who converts faces a much larger rupture with secular society than does his female counterpart. In effect, by converting and abjuring vice, men relinquish a significant part of their culturally constructed masculine identity.

Pentecostal doctrine then supplies converts with the spiritual and ideological tools to construct a healthier identity, one which better equips them to battle the tenacious demons of deprivation. Though the break is less traumatic for women, since they were less worldly prior to conversion, they are direct beneficiaries of the new moral code. Crente women whose husbands or amigos have adopted the faith find their men investing more money and time in the domestic domain. Even women whose partners do not convert are sometimes able to exert newfound moral authority over the household.

FIGURE 11. A young family of the Four-Square Gospel Church.

Should her husband oppose her new religion, perhaps even leaving her because of it, she can seek solace in the theodicy of her evangelical faith.
Based on the life histories of Belenense crentes, I will demonstrate how dualist ideology and a strict moral code of conduct allow believers to recover
and maintain their health in the midst of pervasive illness.

Pouring Out the Devil's Brew

Whereas faith healing is available to afflicted supplicants, the rigid
moral code of classic, and some modern, Pentecostal churches promotes
health maintenance primarily through the reallocation of resources from the
rua to the *lar* (home). Crentes eradicate the "contagions of the street," such
as alcoholism and sexually transmitted diseases, which plague the nonbelieving poor, by removing themselves from the contaminated *passagens*
(pathways) and *travessas* (back streets) of the slums. Men, as the principal
players in the street, are the most obvious beneficiaries of the elimination of
vice, but women also profit from the reinvestment of resources in the home.
The transfer from extradomestic to domestic spending, however, does not
begin until men withdraw from the *festa mundana*.

Like many Protestants of rural Guatemala who define their faith in terms of renouncing vice (Annis 1987: 80), Belenense Pentecostal men describe their postconversion life as the absence of worldly festa. Nearly two-thirds (65 percent) of my male informants mentioned the repudiation of vice and festa as the most important change in their lives since conversion. Missing from most anthropological analyses of *carnaval*, the greatest of all Brazilian festas, is the death, violence, and *bagunça* (disorder and confusion) that often accompany the festival, particularly in the shantytowns.[1] From one minute to the next, the same group of revelers that was swinging to the rhythm of *brega* watches in horror as a jealous boyfriend, emboldened by cachaça, plunges a knife into the abdomen of his rival, real or imagined.[2] A former heavy drinker, Assembleiano Carlos Barbosa from the invasion site of Riacho Doce, contrasted the peace he had found as a crente with the "confusion" and violence of the festa.

> I am a person who goes from my home to work and from work to the Assembly and from the Assembly back home. I'm not one to hang out in the rua, going around with women in the street. Here, there is a group that always parties every Wednesday, Saturday, and Sunday. It's really disturbing when they have their festas. People return from the parties shouting in the streets and drunk. And others fight, hitting each other all over the place. Heads of family [*donos de casa*]) come home plastered and beat their families, making so much racket that no one can sleep. These are the really diabolical things that the world offers but don't please God.

Similarly, sixty-eight-year-old Assembleiano and fruit vendor Guadiono Ribeiro described how his life had changed as a member of the AD and how it contrasted with the life of his brother, who had elected to stay in the "worldly orgy."

> If I weren't a crente, I wouldn't have anything. I would have ended up in booze and parties. I have a brother and a neighbor who is just like him. He [his brother] worked hard in the *roça* (manioc field), making a lot of farina which he would sell for money. Then he would buy clothes for himself and his family to wear to a festa, and then he would go to the festa. The party would end, and so would his money. So he never had a house worth spit. During his whole life, his house never had a bedroom and was full of holes and leaks. But we, thank God, have a tranquil life and a good house. If I weren't a crente, I wouldn't have anything, nothing at all.

Most significantly, withdrawal from the profane festa results in the exorcism of one of the most devastating demons of urban poverty: distilled spirits. Once a part of the flock, neophytes quickly learn that their new faith regards beer and cane liquor as the devil's brew. Under Section P, "Carnal Pleasures," Item P1 of the God Is Love members' rulebook states Pentecostal policy on liquor: "Drinking any type or brand of alcoholic beverage, including wine and beer, is forbidden according to the following passages of the Bible. . . ." One of the cited texts is Romans 13:13, which links wine to pugnacity: "Let us conduct ourselves becomingly as in the day, not in reveling, and drunkenness, not in debauchery and licentiousness, not in quarreling and jealousy." Punishment for the first offense warrants a six-month suspension, and the second results in one year of exclusion.

Amidst the seemingly interminable flow of liquor through the baixadas, Pentecostal men find in both doctrine and its enforcers the strength to resist the current. Fear of the fires of hell serves as an effective deterrent to those who believe in the great abyss. When this world is infernal enough, why risk eternal damnation in the next? Seventy-one-year-old retired bus driver and AD member, Alcindo Fonseca, who supplemented his meager pension by selling used clothes out of his home, illustrates how real the horror of hell is for many believers: "I'm afraid of hell. It horrifies me to think of going to hell, because the Devil is an evil gentleman [*senhor*] who comes only to destroy, rob, and kill."

But as religious pragmatists, Brazilian Pentecostals are more concerned with the here and now than the afterlife. A stronger deterrent than hellfire is peer pressure. Although few men are probably ever suspended from their churches for drinking, a crente spotted at a barzinho not only disgraces himself but also brings shame upon his family in faith. Preachers at the AD frequently remind worshipers that in the world they are each soldiers in God's army and must act accordingly.

Without Pentecostalism's moral asceticism, many male believers would be unable to resist the invitations of their comrades to share a fifth of cachaça, followed perhaps by a visit to the nearest brothel. *Camaradagem* (male camaraderie in drinking and "whoring") forms such an integral part of masculine identity in the baixadas that the man who withdraws from this decidedly male type of socializing is no longer considered a *camarada* by his friends and coworkers. Crente men often must endure mockery and taunting from their former camaradas, who view them as having surrendered to their wives' authority. Even years after conversion, many Pentecostal men find the battle against festa and vice one of the most difficult aspects of keeping the faith.

My male informants indicated "temptation" as their greatest current problem, following only financial hardship. Female interviewees, on the other hand, scarcely mentioned temptation. They were more concerned with the souls of unconverted family members. One man, André Amolina, writing to the testimonial pages of the *Estandarte Evangélico*, revealed how hard it can be, even with faith, to resist the temptations of the world.

> I was unemployed for three years and passed through great tribulation with my wife and six children to support. But now, thanks to God, I have a job. I was a happy man with Jesus and a united family. Even though I wasn't legally married, there was peace at home. One day an evil spirit came to destroy my home. The spirit said, "Leave your family and build a new home." At the time, it seemed like God's voice, but it was really the voice of the Angel of Darkness. I was about to be defeated by temptation and told my faithful companion that I was leaving her to marry the other woman. But thanks to the prayers of the church, I stumbled but didn't fall. God in His infinite mercy took my hand, and I began to feel the weight of His hand on me and wanted to resist. I almost went crazy, because the voice of the Enemy was very attractive. Knowing that I was going against God's will, I married the woman whom the Devil had offered me. But nothing turned out right. It was then that my eyes were opened. I left everything behind and married my faithful companion. Today we are a happy couple. Now there is peace in our life and home, because Christ is with us. (6/86)

Discovering the Domestic

The establishment of peaceful, if not harmonious, domestic relations is one of the most significant consequences of conversion to Pentecostalism. Having withdrawn from the "mundane orgy" of the street, crente men enter the female domain of the lar. Concern for the domestic is manifest in the husband's newfound interest in childrearing and issues of family maintenance. In her assessment of evangelical Protestantism's impact on gender roles in Colombia, Elizabeth Brusco asserts that Pentecostal belief actually replaces "machismo" as the principal determinant of spousal relations (1986: 197). In Belém, Pentecostal dualism, by demonizing the world of the street, eliminates the most destructive elements of the male prestige complex but does not go so far as to supplant it, as Brusco argues. Churches that exclude women from the pastorate and governing bodies can hardly be viewed as agents of female emancipation.[3]

At the doctrinal level, Pentecostalism strongly reinforces many traditional gender roles. In sermons and church publications, men are upheld as the undisputed heads of the family. Good Christian women must obey their husbands. In the AD quarterly journal of Bible studies, the first lesson, entitled "The Family, A Divine Institution," teaches Assembleianos that wives must be "loved and understood, mainly because they constitute the fragile sex" ("Família: alicerce da sociedade" 8). Here an intriguing paradox emerges. How can a religion that doctrinally sacralizes patriarchy extirpate the most deleterious aspects of the male prestige complex?

The answer lies in Pentecostal dualism, which views the street as the Devil's playground and church and home as sacrosanct spaces. Men, of course, must traverse the streets leading to church and work, but the path should be straight and narrow, avoiding the carnal temptations of women, wine, and song. Pentecostalism is able to reorient men from the extradomestic to the domestic not by challenging patriarchy but by demonizing the rua, the locus of the "worldly orgies" associated with the male prestige complex. Crença transforms the *rei da rua* (king of the street) into a *dono de casa* (master of the household).

A subtle linguistic shift reflects the reorientation of crente men to the domestic sphere. Pentecostal men, since they have quit the street for home and church, adopt much of the feminine vocabulary of their new loci. Carlos Mara, the member of the IURD who punched his pregnant wife in the stomach, exemplifies the sort of linguistic transformation that mirrors the move from street to home. Describing how his life had changed in the Universal Church, Carlos stated, "Everything in my life changed. I stopped fighting and nothing tormented me anymore, because I had the Holy Spirit in my life. Now I feel the presence of God, I speak in tongues, I cry, and I feel affection [*carinho*] toward people."

Home Investment: Refrigerators from Jesus

Perhaps the most profound impact of the crente man's reorientation to the domestic realm is on the economic integrity of the household. Men in the church no longer spend up to one-third of household income on vices. Money that used to disappear in the street is now available for domestic investment in such essentials as food, clothing, and transportation. Mario Marinho, a formerly suicidal thirty-three year-old-bus driver, explained in our interview how as an Assembleiano he had radically reoriented his expenditures.

> My financial situation is a thousand percent better, because before, when I wasn't a crente, you know, I spent most of my money on entertainment. I never thought about owning my own home. Festa, entertainment, the beach, movies are what I spent my money on. I didn't know how to manage my money because I didn't have any control, you understand? After accepting Jesus, I was earning one and a half minimum wages, and I began to buy this plot of land. I began to dress better socially, good leather shoes, nice and polished, dress shirts [*camisas sociais*]. And these are hard times for us Brazilians or us Paraenses, but we bought a refrigerator with cash, and I bought this Continental stove that nowadays is out of reach for a poor person and all this furniture too. I give glory to God for this, you see?

Other scholars have noted what sociologist Cecilia Mariz calls the "belt tightening" behavior of Latin American Pentecostals (Mariz 1994b and Brusco 1986). Mariz in particular argues that the Pentecostal household benefits not so much from increased wages as from diminished consumption of vices or "vanities" (1989: 217). I would argue, rather, that the Pentecostal household reallocates expenditures from the extradomestic to the domestic. More than tightening the belt a notch, crentes buy a new one with the money that previously was spent on beer. Brazilian Pentecostals do not so much reduce their total consumption as shift it from one sector to the other, from the "vice" and "vanity" of the rua to the virtue and modesty of the lar.

The same man who before conversion used to empty his pockets at bars now asks Jesus to multiply his cruzeiros so he can buy a refrigerator, one of the major icons of domesticity. José Castro, the Assembleiano who converted on account of his wife's illness, devoted an impressive part of his life history to explaining how Jesus had given him a *geladeira*. Note its prominence among José's prayer list of household appliances.

> For that refrigerator I made a petition to the Lord. On a piece of paper I wrote the following: "Lord, I need a gray refrigerator, a telephone, a new stove, and a brick house to live in, because every year I have to change the roof on my house. And you know that I am your servant. I want to testify that you are He who gives. You already gave me a new suit and a bicycle when I was returning from São Paulo.

You have already given me so many new things, and now I'm asking you for that refrigerator, new stove, and brick house. If you can't give me a new house, then you will give me the refrigerator, new stove, and telephone."

The Multiplication of Talents

The structure of the Brazilian economy severely restricts upward mobility. In fact, during the economic crisis of the 1980s most Brazilians who could not count themselves among the fortunate few who shipped their capital abroad to accounts in the United States and Europe were downwardly mobile. Many who had recently joined the ranks of the middle class slipped into poverty, while millions of the poor became immiserated. Although not immune from financial shocks, many crente households headed by Pentecostal men not only weathered the economic tempest but also ascended the ranks of their own class and occasionally even reached the lower stratum of the middle classes.

While the majority prospered through the reapportionment of resources, some of my informants actually augmented their household income. For example, thirty-three-year-old João Mendes, who became a Quandrangular in 1985, could not hold a steady job prior to his conversion. He would often arrive too intoxicated to work as a *pedreiro* (mason) at construction sites. On many occasions he returned home so late from drinking bouts with his camaradas that he would miss work altogether. Seven months after his conversion, having replaced alcoholic spirits with the Holy Spirit, João had found full-time work as a carpenter and at the time of our interview in November of 1993 was earning four times the minimum wage. No longer an actor in the theater of the street, João invests his weekly paycheck of approximately sixty-five dollars in family and church. "I bring my money home, take out what belongs to the Lord, who multiplies it, and I turn the rest over to my wife, who manages it, does the shopping, and feeds us, thanks be to God."

Pentecostalism's abrogation of the sin tax of alcohol, tobacco, and prostitution, among other vices, allows its adherents to make healthier investments in home and church. Yet, what about the case of João, who not only transferred his funds from one account to another, the extradomestic to the domestic, but also boosted his aggregate income? In other words, was João's increased earning power an epiphenomenon of his abstinence from alcohol, or does Latin American Pentecostalism, like its Calvinist predecessors in

Western Europe and Anglo-America, foster what Weber called the Protestant work ethic? On one side of the debate, represented by Mariz, scholars of Latin American religion aver that, because of the exploitative nature of the job market, no form of popular religion in Brazil affects the work ethic (Mariz 1989: 211). On the other side, David Martin (1990) regards Pentecostalism as the advance guard of a capitalist revolution sweeping through Latin America.

Pentecostals in Brazil are neither Weberian protocapitalists nor devoid of a religiously inspired work ethic. Though the AD during the last decade has embraced many of the ideological and liturgical innovations of its post-modern coreligionists, its traditional attitudes toward work diverge sharply from those of the IURD. My Assembleiano informants did not possess the Protestant work ethic in the sense that they regarded their labor as divinely inspired. Most stated that the Holy Spirit helped them bake cakes, wash clothes, or do whatever else they did to generate income, but they attached no religious meaning to work per se. As crentes, Assembleianos undoubtedly benefit from their reputation for honesty and sobriety. However, the case of twenty-five-year-old Ivanildo Farias illustrates how work often takes a back seat to prayer and church life. "To give you an idea, I used to always pray at work. I would seek the Lord wherever I was at the time, in the bathroom, or wherever. However, people would criticize me and make fun of me, but I didn't care. I only know that at noon and six in the afternoon, I would leave because those are important times in our Christian life. And I had a boss who was really more of a demon than a person. He was one of those Portuguese who was possessed not only by one demon but a whole legion of them. He was the one who stepped all over me and ended up throwing me out of my job. The Portuguese have more pacts with the Devil than they do with God."[4]

In a similar vein, José Vergolino, whose sister's friend had introduced him to the IEQ, sold his profitable french fry stand because the business was keeping him away from church. José explained how the demands of the microenterprise prevented him from practicing his faith: "I couldn't even read the Bible there. I had to attend to the customers, making sure they got what they ordered. That's why I left the french fry business." Even though at the time of our interview he had taken a steep pay cut as an appliance repairman, José was more at peace, because the flexibility of his new job allowed for greater participation in church and family life.

Whereas for members of the Assembly of God any amelioration in their employment status is more epiphenomenal than a direct result of a well-defined work ethic, cristãos of the Universal Church of the Kingdom of God enthusiastically espouse the virtues of self-employment. Paul

Freston has noted that popular Brazilian culture promotes the idea of "not giving your time to anyone else" (*não dar o tempo para ninguém*) (107). The way in which domestic servants in Brazil commonly refer to their work as *trabalho em casa dos outros* (work in other people's homes) expresses the resentment that many harbor about having to endure humiliating terms of employment.

Reinforcing this popular notion, the IURD devotes two full days of its weekly schedule of services to preaching the virtues of entrepreneurship. At Saturday services dedicated to the "greatness of God," pastors invite the afflicted to bring their "work material" to be blessed during the "prayer of faith." During the "prosperity campaigns" on Mondays, the extollment of independent work is more explicit. Preachers lead worshipers in prayer for "those who desire to be self-employed."

Carlos Mara typifies the brash young adherents of the IURD who see only the hand of Satan in poverty. Carlos answered emphatically when I asked him if he earned enough to make ends meet. "No way. Christians have to earn more. No, we are not content with what we have. We want to earn more. So I pray for that, to earn more so we can take care of our children better." To this end, Carlos not only prayed but also quit his minimum wage job as a deliveryman and, along with a brother in faith, started his own business of manufacturing the wrought-iron window coverings that protect Brazilian businesses and the homes of the privileged from the hungry masses. Adding the approximately sixty-five dollars that his wife netted as a self-employed, door-to-door apparel vendor, Carlos's household income totaled about three times the minimum wage, which represents substantial improvement, yet not enough for this ambitious young *cristão*.

Whether through the reallocation of resources or a combination of reallocation and augmentation, increased financial and emotional investment in the household dramatically improves its members' physical health. The money saved on vice is now available to buy *açaí* (fruit of the cabbage-palm), manioc meal, bread, and Amazonian fruits, the staples of the Paraense diet. The nutritional content of their diet may still be deficient, but members of male-headed *crente* households in the baixadas of Belém increase their caloric intake over preconversion levels.[5] This, of course, means a reduction in the maladies caused by malnutrition.

Ten Percent for Jesus

Believers of all denominations, in accord with biblical injunction, are required to tithe, donating at least 10 percent of their income to the church.

On account of the real abuses associated with the *dízimo*, particularly in the postmodern churches, I somewhat reluctantly include it in this section on economic health. During the numerous services I attended at the IURD and DEA in Belém pastors placed such great emphasis on the blessings of tithing that I occasionally wondered if I was at a church or a corporate fund-raising event. Lest the worshiper forget to deposit her faded and torn cruzeiro notes in the slickly produced "tithe envelope," a large red banner on the wall behind the altar, the focal point of the austere sanctuary, served as a constant reminder: "Trazerei todos os dízimos à casa do tesouro" (Bring the full tithes into the storehouse [Malachi 3:10]).

On Mondays and Saturdays at the IURD sede, pastors would spend more than half of the two and one-half hour cultos preaching, soliciting, and collecting the tithe. Across town at the mother church of Deus é Amor, on one Friday in late February 1994 three different preachers on six separate occasions asked congregants to give whatever amount of cash they could. In the rich tradition of Pentecostal histrionics, the more flamboyant of the three religious specialists held up a crisp new five thousand–cruzeiro bill and invited the faithful to give up this sum for Jesus. Cognizant of the material deprivation suffered by his flock, the crente fundraiser quickly returned the big bill to his pocket and methodically worked his way down the myriad denominations of the then battered but now extinct cruzeiro. Although she had been the treasurer of her former IEQ church, it was not until she became a member of the IURD that Rosilea Rivera discovered the profound significance of the tithe, in addition to the sacredness of the pulpit. "In the Universal the pastor said to me, 'Look, did you know that you are dealing with the lifeblood of the church? Because the offering is the sacrifice, the blood and sweat that drips from each of your faces."

The abuses notwithstanding, to see only financial exploitation in the dízimo is to lose sight of the mechanics of popular religiosity in Brazil. As Mariz points out, material investment in the sacred, whether in Umbanda, Catholicism, or *pajelança* (Amazonian shamanism), is a routine part of the religion of the poor (Mariz 1994a: 14). The same principle of exchange manifest in the vow applies to the tithe. Despite the great hardship implicit in parting with 10 percent of an already meager income, believers conceive it as a sound investment in their church and themselves. Those who are loyal *dizimistas* can expect a healthy return on their tithe in the form of spiritual and even financial dividends. Conversely, supplicants who fail to turn over their 10 percent "rob from the house of God" and can expect divine retribution. The test that Sandra Andrade applied to her dízimo reveals the principle of *troca* (exchange) that governs expenditure on the sacred. "In the first place, I tithe because I see that my salary really produces. To give you an idea, I did a test one day for Jesus. I stopped tithing for a whole month and during that month I never even saw my money, you know. It vanished! I thought, Wow, Jesus really is really making me pay. So when I give my tithe, the money produces, but when I don't give, it disappears."

Sandra's experiment also dramatizes one of the major benefits of tithing. As with the phenomenon of faith healing, whether or not the dízimista actually reaps financial gain is immaterial. What matters is her perception that she does. Consequently, she will tend to ascribe any material or spiritual gain to her fidelity with the tithe. Given that she probably has watched her money multiply through the restructuring of her life since adhering to charismatic Protestantism, it follows that she would regard her loyalty to the church, symbolized by the tithe, as the source of her economic progress. Contrariwise, failure to turn over part of her income to the church that restored her health signifies a serious breach in the contractual agreement which can result in spiritual and material degradation.

An additional advantage of tithing relates to the constant theme of power. To be poor is to be on the receiving end in the calculus of class relations. In the baixadas of Belém residents accept hammocks and tee shirts from politicians soliciting their votes and occasionally donations of food and clothes from religious or charitable organizations. Their status as receivers, objects of charity, contributes to their feeling of powerlessness. In contrast, the act of giving often implies the power of becoming a creditor (Oro in Mariz 1994a: 14). In the United States, while many members of the middle class donate their blood at blood drives organized by the Red Cross, some of the urban underclass are driven by poverty to sell their plasma for twenty to thirty dollars a pint. In marked contrast to North American "lumpen," Brazilian Pentecostals in the act of tithing experience the power of being donors, of fortifying the "lifeblood" of their church. Thus, despite the abuses and manipulation of the tithe in some churches, its positive impact on the health of Pentecostal households is undeniable.

Jesus as Husband and Father

Heretofore, much of the analysis of the positive impact of moral asceticism and ideological dualism has focused on crente households, families in which both spouses or amigos belong to the church. In Belém, this type of household predominates among married believers. Pentecostal women whose husbands or amigos share their faith represent the majority of married or amigada female believers. Of my married female informants 62.5 percent had crente husbands, most of whom (60 percent) had converted after marriage. United with their spouses by a common religion, these women experience the twin benefits of their own conversion and their partner's. However, the majority of Pentecostal women are either single or married to *incrédulos* (unbelievers) who in the best of scenarios respect the new order in the household imposed by their crente wife and in the worst violently oppose "their woman's" demanding faith.[6] How do these women whose spouses have not become believers or who have no stable relationship with a man recover and maintain domestic health through Pentecostal dualism and moral asceticism?

Besides the various church organizations that serve as women's support groups, female adherents draw on the ideological power of their faith to manage domestic discord. Pentecostalism's view of the patriarchal nuclear family as a divine institution reinforces and sacralizes traditional Brazilian sex roles. As the primary nurturer and caregiver, the crente wife and/or mother is not merely performing her culturally prescribed function; she is doing God's work. Antithetically, her husband or amigo who squanders the family income on vice serves the Enemy. AD Bible lessons on the Christian family single out marital infidelity as particularly diabolical. "Above all, conjugal fidelity is a divine and unconditional demand" ("Familia: Alicerce da sociedade" 46). Therefore her pietistic religion grants her the moral authority to challenge her husband's devilish conduct. If he reforms his behavior as a result of the conviction of her faith, she has won a major victory in the struggle for domestic health. But if her mate continues his sinful ways or even turns against her on account of her new faith, the crente woman possesses two ideological tools that enable her to cope with domestic strife.

Those crente women who are unable to domesticate their husbands are likely to divest from their conjugal relations to invest in their relationship with Jesus. Early in my research, it became evident that many women stuck in dysfunctional relationships looked to Jesus for the succor and support that their mates were incapable of providing. Having been abandoned by her husband over thirty years ago and left with four young children to raise on her own, Enedina Pires, a sixty-six-year-old Assembleiana from the bairro of Condor, stated that she wanted nothing more to do with men. "I am Jesus' bride." Jesus also became the father of her children. "All my suffering, the tears that I shed because of him [her ex-husband], I turned over to Jesus. Jesus was the one who raised my children with me. He was always with me, help-

FIGURE 12. A single mother of the IURD and her children.

ing me and supporting me." Several other women declared that they would
not trade Jesus for anything, including their husbands.

Paradoxically, Pentecostalism in Brazil, while bolstering the patriarchal model of family, concurrently provides a legitimate refuge from the dysfunctional household unit. Elizabeth Brusco, one of the first scholars to
examine the impact of Latin American evangelicalism on the household and
gender roles, posits that charismatic Protestantism appeals to Colombian
women because it "places the private realm of home and family at the center of both women's and men's lives" (1993: 149). This is a perceptive observation of the transformation that occurs in a crente household, but the large
minority of Pentecostal women in Belém and throughout Latin America
who are married or amigada to nonbelievers with no interest in creating a
lar evangélico actually give primacy of place not to the domestic but to the
extradomestic, yet feminine, realm of church and spiritual family.

Through praying, proselytizing, and singing, afflicted wives escape
from their indifferent or abusive husbands and are free to develop their relationship with the real object of their desire, Jesus. For instance, Luiza Andrade, whose brother-in-law "volunteered" her for Jesus, sought refuge from
her alcoholic and womanizing husband in her AD church on the invasion site

called Riacho Doce. "At church I forget about the problems at home: my husband, children, drunks, sickness, and neediness. It's a different environment. I feel good there, and it gives me the strength to go back home and deal with problems."

Rather than healing domestic conflict, the practice of her faith can actually exacerbate the strife between a Pentecostal woman and her incrédulo husband. He may resent her for spending considerable time away from home and accuse her of neglecting her domestic duties. Even more seriously, omnipresent *ciúmes* (jealousy) may lead a non-Pentecostal husband to suspect his wife of flirting or infidelity with a pastor or male church member. Given the widespread press coverage of the sexual escapades of televangelists Jimmy Swaggart and Jim Bakker, coupled with the popular association of both the Catholic and Umbanda priesthood with homosexuality, the Pentecostal pastor is often perceived as a sexual threat by nonbelieving men. In extreme cases, such as that of Silvia Santos (whose spouse torched her Bible and favorite blouse), the husband's opposition can turn violent and ultimately lead to separation or divorce. As traumatic as the dissolution of a marriage or long-term relationship can be, most of the divorced, separated, or abandoned crente women I interviewed believed that they had made the right decision in choosing Jesus over their spouses. The declaration "Eu não troco o meu Jesus por nada" (I wouldn't trade my Jesus for anything) punctuates the life histories of many of my female informants.

The Colorblind Spirit

Since the Black population of Belém is small compared to that of the Northeast and Southeast, the question of Pentecostalism's particular attractiveness to African Brazilians is not as relevant in the Amazon basin. According to 1980 census figures, merely 3.2 percent of Belém's population is Black (*preta*) (IBGE 1980a: 46–47). In comparison, national figures put Brazil's Black population at 4.9 percent (IBGE 1992: 261).[7]

Nonetheless, I did make a concerted effort to interview several Black Pentecostals whom I met at various churches in the shantytowns. As elsewhere in Brazil, people of predominantly African phenotypes tend to rank among the poorest of the poor in Belém, occupying the most marginal lands, earning the lowest salaries, and having the fewest years of schooling. In the words of Enedina Pires, the African-Brazilian Assembleiana who declared herself the bride of Jesus, "We *morenos* [Blacks, in this context] always get the worst of everything. It's always that way." Unlike their caboclo neighbors in the baixadas who hail predominantly from the interior of Pará, the great majority of African Brazilians whose acquaintance I made at scores of churches were recent migrants or first-generation Paraenses who had come originally from Maranhão and Amapá. Owing to both racism and the fluidity of racial categories in Brazil (especially compared to the United States), only one of my informants identified himself as *preto* (Black).[8] The most commonly used term was *moreno* (brown or Black, depending on the context); the next most common was *pardo* (brown).

Although church walls are not thick enough to totally prevent the racism of the world from entering the sanctuary, they are sufficiently sturdy to insulate African Brazilians from the most insidious manifestations of racial discrimination. Dualist Pentecostal ideology, which rebukes the world as the Devil's lair and upholds the church as the house and family of God, provides sufficient rupture with secular norms for Black Brazilians to feel more accepted there than in most other sectors of society, whether sacred or secular. This, however does not imply that the *espíritos malignos* of racism have been completely expelled from the houses of prayer.

An incident involving one of my key contacts in the AD and a personal friend, Evangelist Antonio Amolina, illustrates how not all crentes check their racist baggage at the temple doors. In late May of 1994 the staff of SETAD, the AD seminary in Belém where Evangelist Antonio taught Old Testament, organized a farewell party for a colleague who was returning to his native state of Piauí to head a Pentecostal theological institute in the state capital, Teresina. During the gift-giving ceremony several of his brothers and sisters in faith remarked that despite his *cara feia* (ugly face), brother Antonio was a wonderful person and devout crente. Though no Adonis, Evangelist Antonio is a handsome man who, standing six feet tall towered over his caboclo coreligionists. The articulate young evangelist's "ugly face" was owing not to any physical deformity but to its blackness. In a country where blue-eyed, blond Xuxa is the paragon of physical beauty, African Brazilians are often considered homely.

Despite such incidents of racism in the church, the fact that Evangelist Antonio had rapidly ascended the clerical ladder of the AD to become the director of a seminary at the young age of thirty-three reveals the extent to which Pentecostalism has diverged from societal norms. In civil society, it would have been extremely difficult for Antonio as a preto to achieve the kind of professional success he has had in the church. As the former pastor-president of the AD in Recife was Black, Antonio can realistically aspire to the same position in Piauí. In contrast, how many African-

FIGURE 13. An African-Brazilian Assembleiana with her grandchildren.

Brazilian governors or archbishops has the Northeast or the rest of Brazil ever had? As of November 1993, the state legislature of Bahia, where 80 percent of the population is Black or mulatto, seats not a single African-Brazilian lawmaker, and only eleven hold office in the 503-member Chamber of Deputies (Masland 31).

Evangelist Antonio was able to rapidly rise through the ranks of the Assembly because dualist Pentecostalism, in opposition to secular society, values the quality of the spirit over the color of the flesh. Church status, while still related to race, depends less on skin color than on charisma. African Brazilians are often thought of as spiritually gifted. However, my informants, unlike those of anthropologist John Burdick, did not regard their African-Brazilian brethren as more spiritually potent (1990: 479).

Crença may not cure the scourge of racism, but it provides a space and community where African Brazilians are immune from its most malignant forms. Many Black believers regard Pentecostalism as a haven from the racism they experienced in the Catholic church. One incident in particular caused Assembleiano Alcindo Fonseca to abandon the religion of his childhood. "My father had put me in the parochial school, and I was the best student in my class. And, you know, the best student had to study to become a priest. So I studied as hard as I could, and when it came time to choose, the bishop came and picked another student who was dumber than me, but he was White and I was Black. "

I then asked Alcindo what his skin color had to do with not being selected for sacerdotal training, and he replied, "I was Black, so I wasn't suitable [*não servia*]." Similarly, seventy-one-year-old Assembleiana Alayde de Jesus's godmother dissuaded her from studying to be a religious. "When I was a kid I wanted to be a nun. I said I was going to be a nun when I was only nine. But I still remember to this day: my godmother said I couldn't be a nun, because they, the Vatican, wherever that is, don't accept people of color [*gente de cor*] to be nuns, not at all. That hurt me. Since then, you know, I got an inferiority complex and sometimes I still have it."

The ideological transformation of one of my pardo or caboclo informants illustrates the reason that another one of my African-Brazilian interviewees feels so "at home" in her AD congregation. Fidelis da Silva, a twenty-nine-year-old AD member and self-employed appliance repairman, told me that he was "prejudiced against Blacks before accepting Jesus." He went on to say that in the AD racism does not exist, because "the Lord does not discriminate against people." Conversion to Pentecostalism does not imply the extirpation of the individual roots of racism, but it does uphold the ideal that a sincere follower of Christ cannot judge others on the basis of skin color. Sufficient numbers of non–African-Brazilian crentes have joined Fidelis in reforming their racist attitudes and behavior that Sandra Andrade, the young Black Maranhense who experimented with her tithe, declared the following: "Let's say it [racism] doesn't completely disappear, but it's one of the main things that led me to accept Jesus and feel as good there as if it were my own home. Everybody there treats me so well, not like out there in the world."

Sandra's dichotomy between church and home on the one hand and the world on the other captures the essence of Pentecostal health maintenance. On the ideological plane, dualist theology constructs the stark polarities of church/home versus world/street. The latter is the Devil's lair, where the Enemy and his minions offer nothing but disease, destruction, and death. In glaring contrast, the former is the province of God, where the Doctor of Doctors heals the wounds of the world. To put his faith into practice, the crente must leave the orgia mundana for the festa of the Spirit. In removing himself from the street, the believer reduces his exposure to its contagions, thereby maintaining his health.

PART III

The Church as Institution

CHAPTER 6

Authoritarian Assembly: Church Organization

❦

 T hus far I have focused on the microlevel of the individual believer, but to remain only at the individual and personal level would be to myopically lose sight of the larger picture of the extraordinary appeal of Pentecostalism among the poor of Brazil. At the macrolevel, Pentecostal churches are more differentiated than the close-knit congregations of the baixadas. The larger denominations, in particular, have developed into established religious institutions, with sizeable bureaucracies, professional staff, and seminaries.

Employing Latin America's largest Pentecostal denomination as a case study, the next two chapters will examine the AD in Belém as a religious but rational organization seeking to further institutional interests both internally and externally. Chapter 7, which concerns political relations with the state, will consider the exercise of power beyond the gates of the Templo Central, while the present one investigates the internal organizational structure of crente churches. Specifically, I seek to explain how an ostensibly authoritarian and centralized organization allows ordinary members to participate in church life to such a high degree.

Though the AD conducted worship services in Belém for over half a century, it was not until the late 1960s, with the ascent of Paulo Machado to the pastor-presidency, that the church began the profound institutionalization process that continued apace in the early 1990s. Prior to Pastor Paulo's tenure, the AD already claimed more members than any other Protestant denomination in Belém, but it lacked the type of organizational features characteristic of the mainline churches. During his twenty-five years at the helm of the oldest, and one of the largest, Assembly of God ministries in Brazil, Pastor Paulo has transformed a once loosely organized charismatic church into a bureaucratic religious institution. In its theological and musical training programs, bureaucratic division of labor, and profound concern for civil status the AD now resembles its mainline brethren more than it does the independent Pentecostal denominations of the slums.

The paradoxical term "participatory authoritarianism" best describes the organizational model of the AD in Belém. At the apex of the administrative pyramid, decision-making power is concentrated in the hands of the pastor-president. At the ample base, common members involve themselves in the daily activities of the church through a wide range of low-level offices and positions. Though excluded from participation in the decision-making process and the exercise of ecclesiastical power, a critical mass of members feel as though they are an integral part of the church through active engagement in the plethora of church activities and organizations. An inspection of the top of the pyramid will illuminate the often obscured exercise and distribution of church power.

The Ministerio

The internal organization of the *ministerio*, the top administrative organ of the AD in Belém, dissimulates the concentration of power in the office of pastor-president. On paper it appears that the eighteen pastors, sixteen evangelists, twenty-four presbyters, seven deacons and 150 *dirigentes* (pastors of local congregations) who compose the ministerio actively collaborate with the *pastor-presidente* in the decision-making process. In reality, the head of the church decides on important matters behind closed doors with a cabal of pastors. The pastor-president and/or his representatives then present the ministerio with resolutions for pro-forma discussion and rubber-stamp approval. Since upward mobility in the AD depends heavily on the good graces of the "Pentecostal Pope," church officers, while they may question the form and style of a resolution, are usually careful not to challenge its content.[1] The exclusion of the great majority of church officers from the formulation of ecclesiastical policy does not mean that they derive no prestige or power from the exercise of their office. Most of these men, who hold no civil office, earn status and dignity through the titles of *diácono* and *dirigente*, among others.

The Pentecostal Pontiff

Hoffnagel's analogy of the pastor-president of the AD in Recife with the patrão of secular society also applies to the church's chief officer in Belém (78). Normally chosen by his outgoing predecessor and then "elected" unanimously by the ministerio, the pastor-president governs the church au-

tocratically. He rewards those whom he perceives as loyal clients with ministerial appointments, making them the *capatazes* (foremen or overseers) of
the crente flock. Those branded as disloyal or potential subversives are
pushed to the institutional margins, either through exile (assignment in the
interior of the state) or restriction to an office at the congregational level.

Among ordinary members, Pastor Paulo elicits a mixture of reverence
and resentment. Assembleianos who had received the pastor in their homes
or had merely exchanged a few words with him found a way to insert it in
their life histories, even when I did not inquire about him. However, I observed little of the quasi-devoted behavior described by Hoffnagel in Recife.
Not once did I see a portrait of the supreme believer in an informant's home.
Yet his daughter, State Deputy Claudia Machado, graced the walls of several crente homes in the form of a calendar that her campaign workers had
distributed as political propaganda.[2] A number of my informants, in fact, expressed outright hostility toward their spiritual patron, most commonly for
what they interpreted as a breach of the patron-client relationship. Doralisy
Coelho, a twenty-one-year-old single mother and one of the poorest Pentecostals I interviewed, did not mince words when I asked her if she had ever
received material aid from the church.

> Only a bottle of cooking gas. In my congregation people are poor, like
> me. They have little to give. But in the Templo Central, they say, the
> pastor is rich there—isn't he? I don't know what to tell you. . . . He
> has a car, he has everything. He isn't needy. When I went there to ask
> for help renting a room, they didn't respond. I spoke with Pastor
> Paulo's wife. I spoke with her, and she told me she would talk to her
> husband, but she kept me waiting and waiting. They never contacted
> me or called me. So I said, Damn her [*maldita*]! They could fall at
> any moment and end up in the same situation that I'm in. At that point
> I saw that I would have to struggle alone and not be humbling myself
> before others. I humble myself only before God.

While most of the fold do not harbor such intense resentment as Doralisy,
the image of an obedient flock blindly following their pastor does not con-
form to reality.

Ministerial Rank

Ministerial rank in the AD depends on proximity to the center of
power, the Templo Central. Pastors and evangelists based at the Central

Temple and its appendage, SETAD, constitute the pastoral elite. As salaried clerics, pastors and evangelists manage the affairs of the mother church, such as directing administrative departments, teaching at the seminary, visiting congregations in the interior of the state, and performing the ecclesiastical rites of communion, marriage, baptism, and burials. Since the requirement a decade ago that all members of the ministerio earn a three-year seminary degree, the large majority of pastors and evangelists are graduates from SETAD or a similar theological institute. While holders of both offices perform essentially the same functions, pastors earn slightly more money and enjoy slightly higher prestige than evangelists.

The middle tier of the church governing body includes deacons and presbyters who, as unsalaried officers, operate closer to the satellites than to the mother ship. The presbyter's main responsibility is to serve as a liaison between the Central Temple and the houses of prayer. In the early 1990s, two presbyters were assigned to each of the ten congregational areas in Belém. Ranking below presbyters, deacons circulate among a small number of congregations, collecting financial offerings for delivery to the Central Temple, distributing communion, and ensuring the maintenance of the physical plant. Deacons also serve as liaisons but on a lower level. Though unsalaried, men in these positions are usually compensated for their considerable travel expenses.

At the bottom rung of the ministerial hierarchy, dirigentes pastor the 165 AD houses of prayer in Belém. Under the supervision of deacons and presbyters, these local congregational leaders are pastors in all but name. They conduct weekly worship services, counsel congregants, and direct lay officers—in addition to holding day jobs, since they too are compensated only for transportation costs. Until 1974, the ministerio placed no limits on the duration of a dirigente's tenure. Pastoring the same congregation for several years, he had ample time to develop close ties with his flock. However, the politically astute pastor-president perceived the dirigentes as potential threats to his authority and decided to separate them from their power base, the local congregation. Emulating the organizational model of the AD in Recife, Pastor Paulo instituted the *rodizio*, in which dirigentes rotate from one church to the next every six months (Assembléia de Deus em Belém 1986: 50).

The Centralization of Ecclesiastical Power

The rodizio formed part of the pastor-president's overarching strategy to centralize and concentrate power in his office without alienating the laity.

In a move that revealed great political and organizational savvy, Pastor Paulo implemented the rotation of dirigentes while simultaneously decentralizing the Sunday evening service. From the church's inception, the most important culto of the week had always been held only at the mother church. Members throughout the city would walk great distances or pay relatively high bus fare to hear their charismatic head pastor preach the word of God. However, Pastor Paulo, conscious of the demographics of church growth and the financial hardship exacted by transportation costs to the Central Temple, permitted the thirty-two congregations to hold their own Sunday evening services (Assembléia de Deus em Belém 1986: 50). Thus, Belém's most influential Pentecostal was able to increase his control over the dirigentes and facilitate church growth in the baixadas where the great mass of Assembleianos lived.

The expansion of the Sunday culto to the local congregations, however, would prove to be the sole exception to the policy of centralization. Through a series of reforms enacted in the church bylaws (Estatutos da Igreja), the pastor-president further restricted the autonomy of the local congregations. To accomplish his authoritarian project, Pastor Paulo recruited an Assembleiano well versed in the abrogation of individual and collective rights, a major general in the Brazilian army (Gomes, personal interview). The first amendments to the bylaws in November of 1977 were specifically intended to thwart schismatic movements, a common occurrence in Pentecostal churches. Article 22, one of the first amendments adopted, prohibits the congregations of Belém from "organizing themselves autonomously, respecting the centralization of the Church." The ambiguity of the language leaves the door wide open for ministerial intervention in the affairs of the local congregations.

Concurrently, Article 23 sought to preclude dirigentes from developing power bases beyond city limits: "Congregations will not make or receive visits from outside the city or state without previous authorization from the ministerio." Of even greater significance, Article 24 called for the ministerio to draft a set of congregational regulations and submit them to "the church" for approval.[3] In Orwellian fashion, the only amendment of 1977 mentioned in the church's own history is offered as evidence of the "decentralization of power" that Pastor Paulo has purportedly led. After citing the bylaw article authorizing the creation of five new administrative departments, the church historians wrote: "With this decentralization, the pastor-president is better able to supervise work and devote himself more freely to the spiritual dimension of the church" (Assembléia de Deus em Belém 1986:

48–49). Further legislation in 1989 accelerated the pace and scope of the centralization process. Completing the neutralization of the dirigentes, Article 27 excluded both deacons and dirigentes from ministerial meetings dealing with "delicate matters." Of course, Pastor Paulo would be the one to determine what constituted a sensitive subject, and in 1989, when the pastor was more deeply involved in state politics than ever, "delicate matters" abounded.

Bureaucratization

The bylaw reforms of 1977 and 1989 also reflect the bureaucratization of the Belenense AD. A 1977 amendment organized the church into five administrative departments (*secretarias*). Then, after more than a decade of vertiginous growth, the original five departments were reorganized and expanded to eleven: Administration, Evangelization, Finance, Pastoral Counseling, Spiritual Counseling in Hospitals, Works, Social Assistance, Media and Culture, Planning and Technical Support, and Music. While pastors and evangelists coordinate the day-to-day operations of each sector, major decisions are taken only after consultation with the chief pastor. For example, the presbyter who maintained membership records at the Central Temple had to obtain permission each time I wanted to examine a new document.

Of the eleven departments, the first three, Administration, Evangelization, and Finance, stand out as the most indispensable in the management of ecclesiastical affairs. The pastor-president appoints his most trusted pastors to direct these three sectors and involves himself in details of their daily business to a greater extent than in other departments. The Administration department, like its secular counterparts, is charged with the coordination of personnel. In addition to staffing the office of the head pastor, it coordinates the contracting, discipline, and dismissal of church employees. Prior to the legislative reforms of 1989, Finance and Administration were consolidated in a single department. However, a rapidly expanding financial base required a cadre of accountants and secretaries to control and monitor the cash flow.

Another impetus behind the creation of the Finance department was the amendment to the bylaws mandating the remittance of offerings collected in the satellite congregations to the Templo Central. This measure eliminated the modicum of financial independence that local congregations had once enjoyed. Finance also controls the purse strings of the Evangelization department, which, in turn, contributes to church coffers. This sector's former name, Missions, more accurately conveys its charge of missionizing at the national and international level. Few Brazilian churches rival the missionary zeal of the AD in Belém. Before the church had even proselytized the Paraense capital, one of its members in 1914 had returned to Portugal, his native land, to convert his Catholic compatriots (Assembléia de Deus em Belém 1991: 4).

Eager to boost the church's local and national prestige and coffers, Pastor Paulo greatly intensified missionary activity. From 1968, when his tenure began, to 1991, a total of ninety-seven married missionary couples had spread the Pentecostal gospel of health in Brazil and abroad. The majority of the forty-four couples sent abroad received assignments in the Andean countries (predominantly in Ecuador), but two, in a historical role reversal, journeyed to the United States to proselytize Portuguese and Brazilian residents. Most of the fifty-three couples granted national assignments carried out their mission work in the neighboring state of Piauí, but three journeyed to the Amazonian interior to recruit Indians to their salvation army (Assembléia de Deus em Belém 1991: 9–10).

Congregational-Level Positions

The increasingly authoritarian and bureaucratic model of organization has not critically affected growth, since there are myriad opportunities for the ordinary member to participate in church life. Statistics on my survey population reveal an impressively high level of engagement in church organizations. Almost four-fifths (79.5 percent) of my informants had held a church position at some time since converting, predominantly in their local congregations. Slightly less, 72.7 percent, exercised a *cargo* (office) at the time of our interview. Both institutional sexism, which excludes women from ministerial office, and the gender gap resulted in a higher ratio of male officeholders: 88.5 percent of crente men had served the church at least once in an official capacity, while 75.8 percent of women had.

The abundance of organizations at the congregational and intercongregational level provides seemingly limitless opportunities for active engagement in church life. Besides performing a ministerial function or working on a volunteer basis in one of the eleven administrative departments, members can serve in the following organizations: Adult Choir, Youth Choir, Young Adult Choir, Sunday School (and its multiple departments organized by age group), Band, Visitors, Youth Groups, and Prayer Circle. Common members, with very few exceptions, first hold office at the congregational level and then, if inspired and deemed worthy by their organizational superiors, gradually ascend the ranks of the ecclesiastical hierarchy. Since church doctrine bars them from ministerial service, women have a much shorter ladder to climb.

The lowest positions occupied by men in the AD serve as apprentice-ships for the ambitious and charismatic and, for the majority who never be-come ministerial officers, as a meaningful way to serve their church. Shortly after joining the church, men deemed responsible and serious members are often offered the job of *porteiro* (doorman or usher). Since the position re-quires no reading, any man can perform its simple tasks. Like his heavenly counterpart Saint Peter, the porteiro guards the gate separating the assem-bly of saints from the *gente do mundo* (people of the world). During the short period of prayer that precedes regular cultos, he ensures that only members and *congregados* enter the house of prayer. Those of my contacts who ac-companied me to services in the baixadas always made a point of introduc-ing me to the doorman before entering the sanctuary.

In the past, when Catholic mobs frequently disrupted services, the porteiro also acted as a security guard. Now, the persecution having ended, the main intruders are boisterous drunks wandering in off the street. Gaudi-ano Vieira explained to me that his job is most demanding during carnaval, when the number of intoxicated revelers multiplies. Like *seu* (a colloquial form of *senhor*) Gaudiano, many of the doormen at the temples I visited were sexagenarians and septuagenarians whose illiteracy precluded them from promotion to *auxiliar* (congregational assistant) or dirigente. Nevertheless, the porteiros I interviewed took great pride in their positions and were held in esteem by their congregations.

After proving himself worthy to his ecclesiastical superiors, a literate porteiro is invited to assume the highest congregational office of auxiliar. Rather than performing a specific function like the doorman, the auxiliar does what his title implies: assisting in whatever capacity his local congregation requires. Many serve as youth leaders, directing the youth group or teach-ing Sunday school. They also usher worshipers to the pews and collect their tithes and offerings. The auxiliar who favorably impresses the ministerio has a good chance of becoming one of its members by advancing to the position of dirigente. In 1986, six hundred auxiliares attended the 109 temples of the AD in Belém (Assembléia de Deus em Belém 1986: 62). By 1993 there were approximately eight hundred for the city's 165 *casas de oração* (Paulo Machado, written interview).

Women's Organizations and Participation in Church Life

Though excluded from the centralized decision-making apparatus of their church, women empower themselves through participation in a set of

FIGURE 14. A visitadora of the Assembly of God.

organizations more focused on proselytory and spiritual work than administrative affairs. This sexual division of labor undoubtedly reinforces the
stereotyped gender roles of Brazilian secular society. Nevertheless, for many
women, the church provides them with their first opportunity to engage in
extradomestic activity independent of their husbands or amigos. In Buenos
Aires, researcher Monica Tarducci discovered that church work allowed
many Pentecostal women to venture out of the home alone for the first time
since being married (77). Belenense crente women, though not as cloistered

as Tarducci's Argentine informants, were likewise able to expand their social horizon as *servas de Deus*.

The great majority of my female informants had held office in at least one of the following four groups: prayer circles, visitadoras, choir, and Sunday school. The predominantly female choirs allow women to express themselves musically, while the other three organizations, in varying degrees, promote leadership and communication skills in settings practically devoid of men. Founded in 1931, the Visitors are the church's front line troops in the battle to win the world for Jesus. In pairs, women with a Bible in hand traipse through the alternately sun-baked or flooded shantytowns, visiting the homes of recent converts (*novos convertidos*) and sick church members and congregants. They also proselytize door to door but far less often than they minister to the converted. In 1990 the church's 1,340 visitors made 92,190 house calls in Belém, almost quadruple the number in 1972 (Relatório Anual).

In attending to ailing Assembleiano brothers and sisters, visitadoras realize their church's mission of health through faith while sharpening their skills as healing agents. Adelaide Correia Lima, one of the first visitadoras, who joined the AD in 1926, described how she and her team of spiritual nurses would keep an infirm sister's household intact while she convalesced. "When we got to a sister's home and found her sick, without any food, with crying children et cetera . . . , we would get to work, cleaning the house, washing clothes, making *caribé* [manioc pap], and bathing the children. If the sister had nothing to eat and no money for medicine, we would provide her with the money the missionaries had given to us for that purpose. Only later would we open the Bible and read the word of God, followed by a prayer. Normally, the Lord would operate, curing the sick and resolving problems" (Assembléia de Deus em Belém 1986: 130). Admittedly, sister Adelaide's work as a visitor reinforced her gender role as caregiver and nurturer, but the fact that she was performing it beyond the walls of her own home in an era when such extradomestic activity was rare for married women attests to the liberating element of Brazilian Pentecostalism.

When they are not working as health agents, visitadoras hone their communication skills monitoring recent converts. Figures from the annual reports show that only a fraction of the number of people who accept Jesus in the AD ever become members. From 1969 to 1992 only one new member joined the church in Belém for every twelve that proclaimed Jesus as their Lord and savior. In 1992, for instance, of the 17,634 who responded to the preachers' chamada, only 1,674 became members (Relatórios Anuais 1969–1992). Factoring in congregados, the ratio of "decisions for Christ" to new members drops to about seven to one. A small percentage of those who choose not to affiliate with the AD seek out other denominations, but the majority never follow through on their public acceptance of Jesus.

Many go to the front of the church not to become Assembleianos but to receive miraculous cures. Pentecostal preachers, particularly in the AD, exert tremendous pressure on those who go forward to accept Jesus as well. Thus, thousands of supplicants insincerely profess their commitment to the Supreme Physician in order to receive his healing power. Others, like some of my informants, are compelled by zealous family members or friends to take the trip to the altar. Lucila de Silva, a seventy-two-year-old AD member from the bairro of Guamá, confirmed the statistical story told by the annual reports. In her three decades as a visitadora she has been unable to locate hundreds of "new converts." Avoiding censure and direct confrontation, many who "make the decision" but have no intention of becoming crentes give a bogus address and sometimes a bogus name to church officers.[4]

The purpose of visiting recent converts and new members is to put the former on the path to membership and ensure that the latter are complying with the norms of their new faith. Both tasks require considerable power of persuasion on the part of the visitor. In the case of a novo convertido, the visitadora must remind her of the public commitment she made to serve Jesus. Alluding to the terrible tribulations that others who have broken their vows have suffered, the visitor plays on the reluctant convert's fear of divine retribution. Visitadoras also call on new members, especially when their conduct is the subject of church *fofoca* (gossip). If the visit produces no positive results, then the visitors report the case to their dirigentes or deacons for further consideration.

More than the visitadoras, the prayer circles (*círculos de oração*) are the main venue through which Assembleianas participate in the life of the church beyond regular worship services. Though not officially a women's organization, the prayer circles are de facto feminine groups. Only one of my male informants had ever belonged to a circle, and the few times I went in the company of a female contact, I felt out of place as the only man present. Each congregation has a prayer circle that meets at least one day a week, often at noon. Groups from five to thirty women, depending on the size of the church, gather to pray and read the Bible. Without the presence of men, the prayer meetings often take on the tenor of support groups, similar to those for afflicted women in the United States.

The sisters facilitate an extraordinary amount of faith healing in the intimacy of the prayer circles. Benedita Barreto Bitencourt, for example, brought her seven-month-old son to a meeting, where the sisters' prayers cured him of his chronic fainting spells (*Estandarte* 11/73). Members of the circles also have the opportunity to develop their leadership and communication skills. Like all other AD organizations, no matter how small or informal, the circulos are run by a governing body of appointed officials. Hence, a woman whose ambitions exceed common membership can aspire to the positions of president, vice president, et cetera. Even those who never become officers improve their public speaking skills by leading prayers and reading biblical passages.

Another position which is not exclusively female but attracts a disproportionate number of women is that of Sunday school teacher. With an estimated enrollment of fifteen thousand students, both young and adult, the AD *escola dominical* faces a continuous demand for instructors at all levels (Relatório Anual 1992). Since the ministerio organizes classes according to sex and age groups, Assembly women teach only their peers and young children. After dirigentes, Sunday school teachers are the principal disseminators of church doctrine and behavioral norms. Students learn the fundamentals of the faith and proper Christian conduct for both within and beyond temple walls (Guimarães 242). In continuity with secular society, where women constitute the overwhelming majority of primary school instructors and bear the main responsibility for childrearing, many of my female informants had taught children from the ages of five to fourteen in the Departamento Infantil. To an even greater extent than the two aforementioned groups, Sunday school provides a space, again segregated from men, where women can develop their pedagogical, oratorical, and leadership skills.

Recovering Dignity

Perhaps one of the premier benefits of holding ecclesiastical office for both sexes is the sense of dignity derived from it. As residents of the urban periphery, my informants are excluded from positions of authority in secular organizations. Outside the baixadas, in the city center and the media, they appear as nameless populares at best, as *marginais* if accused of criminal activity. I recall how heads turned when Eliel, my main contact in the AD and friend, entered the chic Italian restaurant where I had invited him to dine. It was not Eliel's attire that caused the "gente fina" to stare but the dark complexion of his skin and his Indian phenotype. Normally, those in Belém of Eliel's physical appearance are the waiters and busboys, not the diners, in such exclusive establishments. Unfazed, Eliel proceeded to my table, where he tried lasagna for the first time. In stark contrast to his cold reception at the restaurant, in the congregations of the baixadas Eliel, as a deacon, commands respect and is warmly received. There he is not only a brother in faith but an articulate young leader who will probably rise through the ranks of the ministerio.

The majority of crentes, who hold no position in the church, also find dignity and meaning attending worship services and engaging in ecclesiastical activities. In harmony with the cultural predilection for festa, in any given week some AD organization commemorates the anniversary of its founding or celebrates a graduation. From late 1993 to early 1994, the AD in Belém was in almost a constant state of festa, celebrating Pastor-President Paulo Machado's quarter-century at the helm of the denomination's oldest church in Brazil. Thanks to a Quandrangular businessman who owned most of the billboards throughout the city, hundreds of larger-than-life portraits of Pastor Paulo announced his anniversary to Belenenses.

Whether honoring their spiritual leader or observing the anniversary of the local choir, active members invest a significant amount of time in church activities. Including attendance at cultos, my interviewees of all three denominations participated in church events and meetings an average of 4.7 times a week. Levels of participation were the same for both sexes. The few scholars who have collected data on levels of engagement in Latin American Pentecostal churches tend to confirm my findings. British historian and Pentecostal Joanne Pepper determined that Assembly women in Recife participate in church meetings on average three times a week, with one-third of the surveyed population going every day of the week (225). Measuring only attendance at worship services, Edwin Aguilar and his colleagues found Salvadoran Protestants taking part in cultos 2.4 times a week, twice the rate of their practicing Catholic compatriots (127–128). Similarly, 84 percent of Protestants in Rio de Janeiro said they attended church on a weekly basis (Fernandes 1992: 14). Such high levels of participation reflect, among other things, the respect and solidarity that crentes experience in their churches. Faceless masses in secular society, they are embraced as brothers and sisters in the church.

Templo Central or Banco Central?: Institutionalization

Although the spiritual festa continues, many older believers see cracks in the wall separating the house of the Spirit from the orgy of the street. The world and its vanities, such as music and fashion, are invading the temple and putting a damper on the Spirit. Young girls in short skirts, teenage boys blasting *música carnal* during the culto, and dirigentes who preach theology instead of the Word are some of the more obvious signs of the growing "disobedience" in the church. Neuza Sá, who became an Assembleiana in 1954, lamented the adulteration of the "pure gospel" in which she had been raised. Replying to my question about whether she had noticed any changes in the AD, she said: "Yes, the gospel has become adulterated [*misturado*]. I was raised in the pure gospel. Today, no, you enter the church and see short skirts, styled hair, makeup, and painted nails. When I was growing up, you never saw this in the church. I was raised with my long skirt and long hair. Today even the pastor's wife has her hair cut, and her daughters wear makeup. When I was young, crentes were crentes. Today you can't tell who's a crente and who's not, who's a crente and who's Catholic. These days those who say they are crentes even wear shorts at home!"

In a similar vein, Alcindo Fonseca criticized the negative impact of seminary training on charisma.

> These days the culto is more sophisticated. There are a lot of preachers who instead of preaching the gospel, preach theology. Twenty years ago there was no theological seminary here. Now there is. Since the opening of the theological seminary, there's many people who follow theology instead of the Bible. So the preaching has become monotonous and cold, but the preachers want people to shout "Glory be to God," when we don't feel like it. You only praise God and say "Alleluia" and speak in tongues when inspired by the Holy Spirit. But when there's nothing but talk about theology, sex, and money, the church is finished. Unfortunately that's what has been happening lately.

Part of Neuza and Alcindo's dissatisfaction with changes in the AD stems from their romanticization of the church of their youth. Neuza's statement "When I was young, crentes were crentes," echos the sentiments of many of her Assembleiano contemporaries, who, in typically dualist terms, contrast the purity of yesteryear's church with the contamination of today's. A scholar conducting research on Pentecostalism thirty years ago probably would have heard very similar complaints about the intrusion of the world into the church and about the corrupt younger generation. Yet Alcindo and Neuza were not merely waxing nostalgic for a mythical past. Rather, their perceptions of ecclesiastical change also reflect the reality of the institutionalization process, which shifted into high gear during Paulo Machado's pastor-presidency.

The current chief Assembleiano has over the past two and a half decades transformed the AD in Belém from a large church into a sprawling religious institution. In addition to the founding of the seminary alluded to by Alcindo and discussed in chapter 3, the Central Temple stands as a monumental symbol of the church as institution. According to Pastor Paulo, the plan to build a new mother church was conceived in a revelation he received from God on a Sunday in 1979 (*Estandarte* 4/88). In actuality, the idea originated in the 1950s with the first Brazilian pastor-presidente Francisco Pereira do Nascimento (Assembléia de Deus em Belém 1991: 11), but it took a man of Paulo Machado's vision and administrative acumen to convert the revelation into reality.

Construction of Amazonia's largest Protestant temple began in 1979, only a few months after the historic revelation, and nine years later, in April of 1988, Belém's chief crente invited his flock to the inauguration. "Come to the inaugural banquet, because your day has finally arrived," proclaimed the pastor-president on the front page of the *Estandarte* (4/88). Eager to see the fruit of their multimillion-cruzado contributions, thousands of Assembleianos, joined by Protestant brethren and curious onlookers, marched through the city streets in a commemorative parade.[5] The AD journal of record announced the event in which "Belém stopped to see the people of God pass by, three kilometers of Pentecostals invading the streets" (*Estandarte* 5/88). What Belenenses saw was a four-story monolith that replicated the modernistic austerity of Oscar Niemeyer's Brasilia. The imposing concrete and glass structure occupies seventy-two hundred square feet and seats five thousand worshipers (*Estandarte* 4/88).

The "Cathedral of Faith," as it is often referred to in church publications, announces to both crentes and incrédulos alike that the Assembly's "day has arrived." Located in the heart of Nazaré, one of the city's most exclusive districts, the Central Temple is the embodiment of the institutional church. Only the arched windows on the upper level save the church from being mistaken for the corporate headquarters of a private firm. Indeed, when the guard policing the black wrought-iron gates surrounding the temple required me to hand over my *cédula* (identity card) to gain entry, I felt as if I were registering to visit IBM or some other multinational corporation.[6]

Even more perplexing for the first-time visitor is the presence of moneylenders on church grounds. Since 1990 a local branch of the Bamerindus bank has been operating on church property a mere ten yards from the temple. For obvious reasons, church officials were less than candid about the financial arrangement that allowed one of the chief representatives of the material world to conduct its business on hallowed ground. Nevertheless, church records reveal that the bank, in exchange for the right to lend money in a strategic location, agreed to defray half of the publishing costs of an unspecified "informational bulletin" (Acts 1990).[7]

Given the dualistic nature of Pentecostal ideology, one would reason that this glaring symbol of institutionalization, the presence of moneylenders on church grounds, would alienate many members. However, organizational dualism mitigates the effects of ideological dualism. A mirror image of dualistic Brazilian society, the Templo Central is the hegemonic metropolis that embodies the spiritual and material aspirations of the Assembly elite. With considerable investments in the material world, middle-class worshipers at the mother church feel more comfortable with a reduced level of tension between the sacred and the profane.

A world apart, in the satellite congregations of the baixadas, those who have known only sickness and deprivation in the *mundo* seek to raise the barriers between church and street.[8] The majority of my informants had visited the Central Temple at least once, but transportation costs and the rarefied atmosphere there keep ordinary members within the orbit of their local houses of worship. Thus, the physical and social distance between the metropolitan temple and its congregational hinterland allows the latter to escape the brunt of the institutionalization process. While the wall separating the shantytown churches from the world has begun to crack, the one surrounding the mother church disintegrates rapidly. If the history of Protestantism in Europe and the United States provides any clues, the fractured congregational wall will also eventually crumble.

Employing the AD in Belém as a case study, I have demonstrated how the organizational model that I have denominated "participatory authoritarianism" has facilitated astronomical church growth. As the ideal patrão, the pastor-president counterbalances the autocratic exercise of power with rewards to his loyal clients in the form of ministerial office. Men who possess some measure of charisma and who exhibit fidelity to their head pastor can gradually ascend the ranks of the ministerio. At the base level, myriad opportunities to participate in church life, either as a congregational officer or ordinary member, allow believers to recover their dignity without feeling the full impact of the monopolization and centralization of administrative power. But the same institutionalization process that has brought the moneychangers into the Central Temple has also, albeit at a much slower pace, dampened the Spirit in the satellite congregations of the baixadas.

CHAPTER 7

CHAPTER 7

From the Assembly of Saints to the Legislative Assembly: Pentecostal Politics in Pará

❦

*A*fter decades as mere spectators and bit players in the political arena, Latin American Pentecostals unexpectedly burst on to center stage with the military coup d'état in Guatemala that brought General Efrain Rios Montt to power in March of 1982. Immediately upon assuming office, the former Sunday school teacher at the Pentecostal-affiliated Word Church declared he had been anointed by God to pacify Guatemala (Pixley 9). In Sunday telecasts, the dictator-cum-televangelist justified his escalation of the ethnocidal war against the guerilla insurgency (Stoll 1990: 203). Rios Montt recast the battle against leftist rebels as a holy war pitting his Christian soldiers against the atheistic forces of evil. Guatemalan Pentecostals and fundamentalist evangelicals enthusiastically enlisted in Rios Montt's Plan Victoria '82 which rounded up hundreds of thousands of highland Indians and forced them to relocate from their ancestral villages to concentration camps modeled on the strategic hamlets that the United States had utilized in its war in Vietnam. Protestant individuals and organizations, such as the Summer Institute of Linguistics, collaborated in the general's extermination campaign, serving as strategic liaisons between the army and civilians in the "model villages." Ministers from the Prince of Peace Church and the Full Gospel Church of God even served as mayors and military commissioners in the three municipalities of the embattled Ixil Triangle in Quiché (Pixley 9). In short, the first Pentecostal head of state in Latin America, supported by the majority of the Protestants in the country, sent thousands of Guatemalan civilians to their graves in the name of God.

Three years after Rios Montt's ouster, the emergence of a charismatic young congresswoman in Brazil proved that not all Pentecostal politicians were ethnocidal neofascists. Elected in 1986, Carioca Benedita da Silva made history in becoming both the first African-Brazilian woman, and the sole female among thirty evangelicals, to be elected to the Brazilian Congress. Da Silva, like millions of her compatriots, had converted to Pentecostalism through an experience of divine healing. She says that after two unsuccessful operations, the Holy Spirit cured her of breast cancer during a Sunday service at the AD twenty-six years ago (personal interview). As both congresswoman and senator from the Workers' Party (PT), da Silva has championed the cause of dispossessed African Brazilians, workers, women, and favelados. Many of her evangelical colleagues in Congress have criticized her for showing greater loyalty to the PT than to her church, but Senator da Silva remains the most prominent example of the possibility of Pentecostal engagement in leftist politics.

That two practitioners of the same faith can fall at opposite ends of the political spectrum belies the idea of uniform Pentecostal political action in Latin America. Pentecostalism has grown to the point where it includes both fascists and socialists among its ranks. However, these two high-profile Pentecostal political actors represent the ideological extremes of a continuum on which the great majority of Pentecostal political action falls somewhere in the middle. In contrast to much recent scholarship, which in the politics of Benedita da Silva and her *petista* (member of the Workers' Party) coreligionists sees the "revolutionary" and "subversive" potential of Latin American Pentecostalism (Garrard-Burnett and Stoll, Burdick, and Mariz), this chapter posits that Pentecostal political action in Brazil and most of Latin America tends to avoid the two extremes but is closer to the right of center than to the left. Employing the AD in Belém as a case study, I will argue that Brazilian Pentecostalism reinforces the political status quo by engaging in the clientelistic politics that predominate in the republic. Although religious and political ideology plays a role, personal and institutional interests form the core of Pentecostal politics.

Pará's First Pentecostal Congressman

For fifty years the AD in Belém remained on the sidelines of state and municipal politics. Governors and congressmen in search of votes would visit the Templo Central on special occasions, but the church had no elected representative to advance its interests. Furthermore, Pentecostal doctrine at the time rejected politics as a *coisa do mundo* (worldly thing) that could contaminate its practitioners. Political events of 1962, however, reveal that inexperience and a lack of mobilization, much more than doctrine, kept the AD out of the business of governing for half a century. Antonio Teixeira, a prosperous Portuguese immigrant who had joined the AD in 1947, became the first Pentecostal state deputy to serve in the Legislative Assembly of Pará. Backed by the influential Paraense senator Catete Pinheiro, Teixeira was elected as a member of the centrist PTN (National Labor Party) and switched to ARENA (the National Renovating Alliance) after the military coup in 1964 (Teixeira, personal interview).

Just months after Teixeira's election, the AD in Belém received its first government funds. Paraense federal deputy Gabriel Filho delivered US$600,000 in cruzeiros to Pastor-President José Pinto for an unspecified purpose (Acts 1962). A year and a half later, Teixeira's alliance with his political mentor paid off. Senator Pinheiro, in a telegram to the head pastor, shared the news that he had placed US$500,000 in the federal budget of 1964 for construction of an AD high school, the Colegio Evangélico Samuel Nystrom (Acts 1964).

Deputy Filho and Senator Pinheiro's "donations" initiated a three-decade period of intermittent government funding at the federal, state, and municipal level. These two disbursements to the AD prior to the military takeover in 1964 were made according to the logic of clientelistic politics. In exchange for federal monies, the two political patrons, Pinheiro and Filho, hoped that the pastor-presidente and Teixeira would serve as electoral brokers, delivering the votes of the approximately ten thousand Assembleiano members and congregados. In Belém's religious arena, only the Catholic church could potentially marshal a larger electorate than the Assembly of God.

Teixeira, wearing both a Pentecostal and a political hat, benefited doubly as the principal liaison between church and state. From his political mentors he received financial and organizational support for his own political campaign as well as funding for his church. His church, in the person of the head pastor, reciprocated with a guaranteed electoral base. Finally, the chief crente not only received financial aid for his church but suddenly found himself playing the role of one of the city's key political brokers.

An Alliance of One: Military Indifference in the Early Years

Just as suddenly as it had offered its financial teat to the church in Belém, the authoritarian state temporarily withdrew it. From late 1963 to 1968 the AD in Belém received no funding at any level of government (Acts 1963–1968). The five-year hiatus did not arise from any anti-military rhetoric or action on the part of the AD. On the contrary, the Assembly, along with the great majority of its Pentecostal brethren, celebrated the army's triumph over godless communism in newspaper editorials and communiqués to Brasilia. Due to its North American origins and genuine fear of losing the right to worship, the AD was as rabidly anticommunist as the generals. As the democratic republic felt its death pangs in late 1963, the AD warned its flock, in apocalyptic language, of the communist beast poised to enslave Brazil and abrogate the right to worship. "The communist rulers of Cuba, East Germany, China, Czechoslovakia, and other countries are impeding the preaching of the gospel. What is our attitude toward the diabolical regime, forcefully penetrating like a powerful bull furiously charging the matador? It is obvious that Brazil is the target so that all of South America will be subjugated to the Leninist regime. The communists would rob us of our right to worship" (*Estandarte* 11/63).

On the eve of the military coup in early March 1964, Assembleiano rhetoric reached fever pitch, perceiving an impending communist takeover through the lens of dispensationalism.[1] "We can compare it [communism] to a horrible monster that crushes 900 million people in its iron grip. All of this is the fulfilling of Scripture. The end time has arrived" (*Estandarte* 3–4/64). Not the least bit disappointed by the postponement of the apocalypse, Pastor-President Alcebiades Vasconcelos in late April wired a congratulatory message to the military junta in Brasilia. General Castelo Branco, the first in a succession of military rulers, expressed his gratitude for the Pentecostal leader's support in a telegram received at the Templo Central in mid-May (Acts 1964). Joining the Belenense AD, the mouthpiece of the national church headquartered in Rio de Janeiro threw its ideological weight behind the dictatorship. An editorial entitled "Christians and False Ideologies" called for the extirpation of "satanic Marxism" from national institutions (*Mensageiro da Paz* 9/15/64). Thus, it was not due to a lack of support for their authoritarian project that the military regime suspended financial aid to the AD in Belém. Rather, the generals at this point saw no need to fund an organization that had exhibited unswerving loyalty to their cause. More significantly, during the first years of its two-decade rule, the regime could still count on the support of the nation's largest and most influential religious institution, the Catholic church.

In Search of a New Religious Client in Amazonia

The resumption of government aid to the Belenense AD in the final months of 1968 was inextricably related to the growing animus between the military regime and the Catholic church in Amazonia. Mirroring the triumph of the forces of reaction in the body politic, a conservative bloc of bishops assumed leadership of the CNBB (National Council of Brazilian Bishops), the highest authority of the church in Brazil, in October of 1964, putting an end to the control by progressives that had prevailed since its founding in 1952 by Dom Helder Camara. In contrast to its precoup advocacy of social reform, the CNBB focused more on ecclesiastical matters during the first four years of military rule (Mainwaring 48 and 83).

The retreat from social and political activism, however, came to an abrupt end in 1968, when thirty-six priests from the Regional North 1 of the CNBB (one of two Amazonian regional divisions among the thirteen established by the CNBB in 1962) demanded that their church more vigorously aid poor Amazonians displaced and disenfranchised by the dictatorship's aggressive "development" of the region (Mainwaring 84). The bishops of both Regions 1 and 2 responded to their subordinates' call for action by drafting some of the most radical episcopal statements in the history of the Brazilian church. In 1970 Dom Estevão Cardoso, along with three priests, issued a denunciation of state and private violence against peasant landholders in the strife-ridden region of southern Pará. Less than a month later, bishops of the Regional North 2, headquartered in Belém, released a statement calling for agrarian reform. By 1971 Amazonian bishops spoke in unison against military development policy and large investors (Mainwaring 87). The regime responded to church opposition with violence. Police beat, tortured, and imprisoned priests and church activists working with the poor in the Araguaia area of southern Pará (Mainwaring 89). In championing the cause of agrarian reform and socialism, the CNBB Regional North 1 and 2 had turned the formerly marginal Amazon into the focal point of church-state conflict (Mainwaring 93).

To the state, the ideological and political transformation of the Amazonian Catholic church from an integral part of the social and political status quo to an organization calling for the destruction of authoritarian capitalism meant the loss of its primary religious client. Who would bless the inauguration of government projects and confer religious legitimation on official ceremonies if the bishops and priests were now enemies of the state? Both the military governor of Pará at the time, Alacid Nunes (1966–1971), and his *padrinho* (godfather), Jarbas Passarinho, the Paraense minister of education in Brasilia, wasted no time in replacing their former religious client with one that shared their weltanschauung and, in the words of Jader Gomes, "spoke the same language" (personal interview).

Of the two military leaders, Passarinho was the principal architect of the scheme to recruit the AD in Belém to replace its archrival as the regime's main religious client in Pará and all of Amazonia. As head of the Military Command of Amazonia in Belém, Lieutenant-Colonel Passarinho had played a leading role in the coup. His reward from Castelo Branco was the governorship of Pará, an office he held between 1964 and 1966 and bequeathed to his padrinho. He had already been appointed minister of education at the acme of church-state conflict in the region but kept abreast of the situation via his political successor in Belém (Fundação Getulio Vargas 2615).

In Belém, Governor Nunes turned to the pioneering Pentecostal politician Antonio Teixeira, now a state deputy affiliated with ARENA, the official government party, to reinitiate the patron-client relationship developed six years earlier. The AD treasurer recorded the latter's willingness to reassume his old role of liaison between church and state in the form of a receipt for an "offering" made by the governor and delivered to the church by Teixeira (Acts 1968). From this first instance of military largess until the return of civilian rule in 1985, the church in Belém received substantial financial aid, political favors and the social prestige of serving as the regime's primary religious client. In exchange, the AD, headed by Paulo Machado, the most politically savvy of all pastor-presidents, delivered votes, ideological support, and divine legitimation of the authoritarian project.

"Social Subsidy" of the New Religious Client

To cement the relationship with its new client, the authoritarian regime represented by Minister Passarinho began to disburse funds on a regular basis to the Belenense church. Taking advantage of his appointed office, Passarinho normally funneled the monies from the Ministry of Education and Culture (MEC) to the AD in the form of a *subvenção social* (social subsidy) for construction of the seminary, which at the time was referred to as the Seminario Samuel Nystrom. The AD received US$36,600 for its theological institute during Passarinho's tenure at MEC. Passarinho's contributions through MEC from 1970 to 1974 amounted to US$28,035, more than three-quarters of the total amount. Both federal and state politicians accounted for the balance of the monies (Acts 1970–1974). In specifically designating funds for construction of the seminary, the regime, although accountable to only itself, could justify the subvention of its charismatic client as educational support. However, not all funds were earmarked for the biblical institute. Shortly after Deputy Teixeira's appointment as majority leader of the state legislative assembly, Federal Deputy Filho arranged to have the pastoral manse declared a "nontaxable entity of public utility" (Acts 1974).

The Central Temple, led by Pastor Paulo, provided its patron with a healthy return on its investments. While the Catholic church in Pará and throughout the Amazon basin developed into the regime's most active opponent, the AD in Belém became one of its principal supporters. During this era of severe military repression, the city's leading crente assumed the unofficial role of religious apologist and propagandist for the regime. In July of 1970, a few weeks after the church had received its first check for the seminary from Paraense Federal Deputy Gabriel Filho (ARENA), Pastor Paulo preached that crentes must respect government authorities and then proposed a day of fasting and prayer for the national and local leaders (Acts). Likewise in September, he followed his announcement of Jarbas Passarinho's US$2,128 contribution to the church with instructions for members "to pray constantly for the authorities in order that they govern in peace" (Acts 1970). Seeking to continue the clientelistic relationship at the state level, the pastor-presidente sent the following telegram to the new military governor, Fernando Guilhar, in March, 1971: "On the occasion of your ascension to the leadership of our state, we offer our sincere greetings. We pray that God bless and illuminate your government, cordially offering Psalm 20 for your meditation" (Acts).[2] Beyond prayers and praise for the military authorities, the head Assembleiano pastor also used his pulpit in the mother church to assist the regime in recruiting young Pentecostal men into the armed forces. In March of 1972 he reminded male AD youth of their "patriotic duty" to perform military service (Acts).

As the key liaison between his church and the state legislature, Deputy Teixeira doubled as both a recipient and source of ecclesiastical support of the regime. He frequently joined his fellow Portuguese immigrant Pastor Paulo in propagandizing for the dictatorial regime. For example, in commemoration of Soldiers' Week in late August 1973, the ARENA deputy rendered homage to the Brazilian armed forces. Citing 1 Peter 2:11–17, he lauded "those who deserve our recognition for the great service they have lent to our beloved Brazil."[3] He also spoke of the freedom that the AD enjoyed at the time and closed with a special prayer for the *patria* (Acts 1973). On the receiving end, Teixeira profited immensely from the head pastor's political mobilization on his behalf. Pastor Paulo regularly led prayers for "our evangelical representative." During elections, he played on members' strong sense of denominational solidarity to win votes for his influential coreligionist.

Despite the profound politicization of the AD in Belém, articles in the *Estandarte Evangélico* ironically decried the unholy mix of religion and politics. At the same time that the leader of the church was offering benediction to the regime, the church journal editorialized against pastors engaging in politics. "No one can serve two masters. If a pastor can hardly attend to church work, how can he find time for politics?" Citing Scripture, James 4:4, the anonymous author continued: "Whoever wants to be friend to the world becomes the enemy of God" (*Estandarte* 2/70).

During the second decade of the dictatorship the AD continued to enthusiastically perform its role as the regime's primary religious client. In fact, Amazonia's leading evangelical church became so closely identified with military rule that in November of 1982 the Sociedade Bíblica do Brasil (Brazilian Biblical Society) received an anonymous phone call accusing Pastor Paulo of accepting US$33,333 from the PDS (Social Democratic Party) in exchange for crente votes in the first direct elections since the military coup.[4] No evidence was ever presented substantiating the allegation, and under pressure from the pastor-president, Cremilda Teixeira, the wife of Deputy Antonio Teixeira, who had first reported the accusation of political bribery, recanted her story (Acts 1982 and Teixeira, personal interview).

Still an ardent supporter of the PDS, despite the fact that the newly elected governor of Pará, Jader Barbalho, belonged to the PMDB, Pastor Paulo continued to propagandize on behalf of the regime. The political *distensão* (liberalization) initiated in the mid-1970s had resulted in an increasing number of labor strikes and popular protests. As an unofficial evangelical spokesman for the regime, Pastor Paulo in late June of 1980 admonished his flock not to participate in "ideological articulations" or popular protests (Acts). In a telegram to both President Figueiredo and Governor Barbalho, the text of which was published in the *Estandarte Evangélico*, the region's chief crente justified bitter medicine to alleviate the critical state of the economy. "In this moment in which the global crisis strikes the Brazilian nation and requires of your Excellency measures that aren't always pleasant but are capable of promoting socioeconomic development of the country in the direction of full democracy, in my name and on behalf of the members of the Assembly of God of Belém, accept our support and admiration for the patriotic manner in which you have led this great country" (5–6/83).

Even as martial rule came to an end in early 1985, the leader of the AD in Belém participated in a four-month course at the Escola Superior de Guerra (Superior War College) in Rio de Janeiro. Like his prominent colleagues Nilson Fanini and Presbyterian pastor Guilhermino Cunha, who had attended year-long classes in the late 1970s (Freston 158), Pastor Paulo was "brought up to date on various aspects of present-day Brazil; much of which will be useful in the work of God" (Acts 1985).

As conflict between the Catholic church and the military regime subsided during the second half of the 1970s, government funding of the AD diminished but did not end. Between 1975 and 1979, the only significant amount was US$2,375 from MEC for a primary school administered by the church in the bairro of Sacramenta. Although the flow of cruzeiros to the Central Temple had been reduced to a trickle, Governor Alacid Nunes, honoring the church on the occasion of its sixty-eighth anniversary, reminded Assembleianos of the significance of their support. "I could not miss this event where I know that prayers will be offered to heaven in constant supplication for the state and its leaders" (Acts 1979).

Renewed Church-State Conflict, Renewed Funding

A new period of conflict between church and state ended the five-year drought in government subsidies for the AD in Belém. Once again Jarbas Passarinho, who was now the senate majority leader (PDS) and one of the progressive church's most vehement and visible opponents, was at the center of the fray. Because the church had continued to involve itself in the land conflicts of the Tocantins-Araguaia region and had sided with the urban squatters in Belém in their clash with the state in August 1981, Senator Passarinho singled out the progressive church as the PDS's greatest problem, denouncing it as having declared war against capitalism and opted for socialism (Fundação Getúlio Vargas 2615–2616).

Even before the powerful senator had lambasted the progressive church in September, the pastor-president of the AD had in August already received US$824 from MEC via Senator Filho and a phone call from an unnamed federal deputy requesting church documents for the "future liberation of funds" (Acts 1981). Less than a year later, Senator Passarinho siphoned US$2,913 from SUDAM (Superintendency of the Development of the Amazon) to Etelvina Bloise, the church's shelter for elderly indigents (Acts 1982). Though the monies from SUDAM diverged from the agency's stated goal of developing the region through tax incentives to corporate firms, who in the regime would deny the strategic importance of funding a faithful religious client?

In addition to monies from SUDAM, Governor Nunes loosened state purse strings, contributing US$1,666 to construction of the Templo Central from 1980 to 1982 (Acts). The governor's "offering" of US$938 to partially underwrite the cost of electrical installations in the new temple marked the end of an era for the AD in Belém (Acts 1982). In retaliation for Pastor Paulo's support of the PDS in gubernatorial elections, the new governor, Jader Barbalho of the PMDB, cut off the financial pipeline to the AD. No more state money would flow into the Central Temple until two years after the return of formal democracy in Brazil.

Continuing Clientelism under Civilian Rule

Although the return to civilian rule eliminated the AD's military patron, clientelistic relations with the state would continue, albeit in a different form. Under the dictatorship the church had profited immensely from electing one of its own members, Antonio Teixeira, to the state legislative assembly. If the pastor-president could mobilize his flock to send a few more Assembleiano deputies to the Paraense legislature or even to Brasilia, the church would increase its bargaining power with the state. To this end, the presidents of the AD state conventions meeting in Brasilia in April of 1985 decided to back official church candidates in the congressional elections of 1986. The same church that had condemned the political arena as the Devil's playground until the late 1970s was now calling on its adherents to claim their piece of the political pie before the "Catholic-Spiritists" devoured it all, depriving evangelicals of their hard-earned religious freedom (*Mensageiro da Paz* 5/82).

In Belém, the AD shed all pretense of political disengagement and launched an aggressive campaign to elect its own representatives at the federal, state, and municipal levels. Writing four months before the 1986 elections, Assembleiano Joanyr de Oliveira instructed his brothers and sisters in faith to vote for evangelical representatives (*Estandarte* 7/86). Two months later, under the slogan "Evangélico Vota em Evangélico," the AD mouthpiece urged members to vote for their crente brothers rather than "worldly, spiritist, homosexual, Catholic, and communist candidates" (*Estandarte* 9/86).

In the same month Pastor Paulo introduced AD candidates for federal and state deputy Eliel Rodrigues and Mario Freitas to worshipers at the Central Temple and stressed the importance of voting for "domésticos da fé" (sons of the faith). Brazil, he preached, would become "self-sufficient" with men of such strong spiritual values in power (Acts 1986). The flock responded to their pastor's call, sending Eliel Rodrigues to Brasilia as the state's first Protestant federal deputy. Mario Freitas lost to an incrédulo, but AD member Raimundo Santos (PFL) from Paragominas and Quandrangular Guaracy Silveira (PFL) from the Paraense capital replaced the ailing Antonio Teixeira in the state legislature.

The Bancada Evangélica

Pentecostal political strategy had proven extremely successful not only in Pará but throughout the nation. An entire bloc of evangelical politicians known as the *bancada evangélica* was elected to the legislature. In the 1987–1991 legislature, Protestant federal deputies doubled their numbers over the previous one. Most significantly, Pentecostals increased their ranks by a factor of ten, claiming twenty of the thirty-four seats occupied by Protestant deputies. With thirteen legislators, the AD comprised 38 percent of the bancada evangélica and 65 percent of all Pentecostal representatives. Baptists followed a distant second, with seven federal deputies, and the Four-Square Gospel Church, with two, was the only other Pentecostal denomination sending more than one representative to Brasilia (Freston 192–193).

In Brasilia, Deputy Rodrigues, like most of his Protestant cohorts, put forth a conservative political agenda. A firm supporter of the Brazilian military, Deputy Rodrigues in his two terms (1987–1994) championed the same causes as the Christian right in the United States. What he condemned as problems that he linked to sin, such as AIDS ("God's punishment for unnatural sex"), pornography, and tobacco received the bulk of his legislative attention. Indians, whom he labeled the nation's largest *latifundistas* (owners of landed estates), and environmentalists also ranked high on the deputy's hit list for their alleged usurpation of national sovereignty in the Amazon basin. During our four-hour interview, Rodrigues launched into a tirade against Federal Deputy Benedita da Silva when I solicited his opinion of his petista sister in faith. He considered her more of a communist than a crente for refusing to sign his proposal condemning the persecution of Christians in the Soviet bloc and for her defense of homosexual rights.

Tension between Politician and Preacher

Animosity between Pastor Paulo and Deputy Rodrigues meant that the head of the church in Belém had to look to state and municipal government for financial assistance. According to Rodrigues, friction between the two started in 1981 when he presented his proposal of running for federal deputy on the PMDB ticket to the pastor-presidente. The latter vehemently opposed the idea on the grounds that Rodrigues's affiliation with the opposition party would upset relations with PDS stalwart and congressional majority leader Jarbas Passarinho. The chief crente had been lobbying the Paraense senator for authorization to purchase a radio station and believed Rodrigues's candidacy would drive Passarinho from the bargaining table (E. Rodrigues, personal interview).

Ignoring his pastor's advice, Rodrigues ran as a candidate of the PMDB, not for ideological reasons but to avoid competition with two other evangelicals affiliated with the PDS. Without the backing of the Pentecostal power broker, Rodrigues lost the election. Tension persisted when the retired Air Force engineer ran again in 1986. In the name of church unity, Pastor Paulo publicly backed Rodrigues, but relations between the two further deteriorated when the federal deputy's son-in-law, a charismatic young pastor and seminary professor in the Belenense AD, provoked a minor schism by leaving the church in 1989 to found his own Pentecostal community. Hundreds of discontented middle-class Assembleianos from the Templo Central followed Pastor Gedilson into his Comunidad Evangélica Integrada da Amazonia (Amazonian Integrated Evangelical Community) founded in 1990 (Negreiros and G. Rodrigues, personal interviews).

In an ironic turn of events, Deputy Rodrigues's only major material contribution to the church was the radio station that Pastor Paulo was attempting to procure through Jarbas Passarinho. After years of little progress in the matter, it became clear to Deputy Rodrigues that the radio station was not a high priority for Senator Passarinho. Despite his resentment of the senior pastor of the AD, Rodrigues obtained authorization from the Ministry of Communication for the church in Belém to run its own radio station (E. Rodrigues and Gomes, personal interviews). Pastor Paulo signed the contract and made a one hundred thousand–dollar down payment toward the purchase of Radio Guajará in September 1993 (Acts). The station had already begun broadcasting by the time of my arrival in Belém in mid-September.

Friction with Deputy Rodrigues forced the pastor-president to look to city hall and the state legislature for the church's share of government largess. The AD reclaimed a portion of the pork barrel in 1987, but civilian government proved to be less generous than the generals. Since the conflict between the state and the Catholic church had ceased with the return of formal democracy, the AD in Belém was no longer needed as a strategic religious client. However, the size of the electoral base represented by the church (approximately sixty thousand members and congregants in 1987) meant that state and municipal elected officials risked their political future in ignoring the interests of the AD. Moreover, elections in 1982 had apparently shown that Assembleianos tended to toe the political line of their pastor-presidente. Eighty-five percent of the AD members in Belém polled by researcher Richard Pace voted for ARENA. Many considered the PMDB communist and thus diabolical (40).

Protestant Governor, Pentecostal Pork

The five-year hiatus in government largess ended with the ascendancy of a crente to the governorship of Pará. The state's first Protestant governor, Helio Gueiros, was the son of pioneering Presbyterian minister Antonio Teixeira Gueiros, who, as a friend of Paulo Machado and contemporary of Nels Nelson, had pastored the only church of his denomination in the state capital. Although not a regular practitioner of his faith, Governor Gueiros played on evangelical solidarity and engaged in patronage politics to ensure the church's support. Some of the governor's more salient contributions were five tons of food for lunch at the church's vacation Bible school, a new piano and organ, and the use of a Ford Belarme from SUDAM (Acts 1987–1989). To disguise these illegal donations, church accountants practiced statistical sleight of hand. The government money received for purchase of the musical instruments appeared in church ledgers as a contribution toward the procurement of food (Gomes, personal interview). Similar accounting legerdemain concealed the arrangement with SUDAM (Acts 1988).

Evangelical ties with the new governor notwithstanding, the church's principal source of government funding in the late 1980s was not the state of Pará. Rather, the *prefeitura* (prefecture), headed by Spiritist mayor Coutinho Jorge, invested heavily in the Templo Central. Thanks to the political acumen of church member Sebastião Bronze, who served as a *vereador* (councilman) in the city council, the AD succeeded in securing public funds for construction of the Central Temple. In July of 1987 the mayor agreed to foot the US$84,746 bill for the laying of the sidewalk around the mother church. As a measure of gratitude, the church awarded plaques to both the mayor and the municipal secretary of works (Acts 1987).

The resumption of government subsidies in 1987 led Pastor Paulo to readopt his former role of one of the main religious apologists and propagandists for the political and economic status quo. In April of 1988, one month after Governor Gueiros had "donated" the piano and organ, the head pastor organized a *culto de ação de graças* (service of thanksgiving) on behalf of the

Paraense head of state. In addition, at the inauguration of the new temple in the same month, the pastor-president praised the governor for being the best the state had ever had (Acts 1988).

Chosen by God: The AD and the Presidential Election of 1989

As Pastor Paulo delivered paeans to elected officials from the pulpit, the church was about to enter a new, more profound phase of politicization with the presidential elections of 1989. From the dais of the mother church and the pages of the *Estandarte Evangélico*, the pastor and his trusted representatives attempted to mobilize the AD community in support of presidential candidate Fernando Collor de Melo and the pastor's own daughter Claudia Machado, who was running for state deputy. The pastor's decision to throw his institutional weight behind the campaign of the Alagoense karate champion formed part of a national Pentecostal strategy to elect Collor.

PT candidate Luis Inacio da Silva (Lula), as a socialist and friend of the progressive Catholic church, had to be defeated at any cost. Rumors of the dire consequences of a victory for Lula spread like wildfire through the crente communities of Belém and the rest of the nation. Many of my informants told me that as president, Lula would have converted evangelical churches into schools and sent believers to concentration camps. Young Doralisy Coelho had even heard that the Paulista petista planned to exterminate African Brazilians.

Fearing not ethnocide but a sinister Catholic-communist alliance, national leaders of the largest Pentecostal denominations marshaled their spiritual and material resources on Collor's behalf. Church officials formed the Movimento Evangélico Pro-Collor headed by Assembleiano federal deputy Salatiel Carvalho (PRN) and pastor Jeziel Gusmão. The duo coordinated the Collor campaign among evangelicals (Mariano and Pierucci 100). While the evangelical movement stumped for Collor, individual denominations launched an aggressive campaign to demonize Lula. Quadrangular pastor and State Deputy Daniel Marins (PTB) circulated two thousand copies of an open letter to evangelicals listing ten reasons not to cast ballots for Lula. Marins warned his coreligionists that a Lula victory could mean armed struggle (Mariano and Pierucci 100).

Reflecting on his own role in politicking for Collor, José Wellington, president of the General Convention of the Assemblies of God in Brazil, stated the following in a 1992 interview with Mariano and Pierucci: "We can't deny that it was the evangelicals who elected Collor. His victory came from the AD, whether he recognizes it or not. I never said this to him, and I will never hold it against him, because I did it out of my own free and spontaneous will. When we saw Lula was going to win, and he really was going to, the AD mobilized throughout Brazil. Where I couldn't go personally, I called. I called all over Brazil, saying the situation is such and such" (101). According to Pastor Caio Fabio, president of the Associação Evangélica do Brasil, the AD incurred significant expense not only making telephone calls in support of Collor but also promoting rallies on his behalf (Fabio, personal interview).

Back in Belém, the chief crente commander organized the local AD campaign for Collor. Preaching in the Templo Central, he led prayers for candidate Collor. And on the eve of elections in mid-November 1989, the head pastor, reading from the pulpit, defined communism in such terms that no believer would exit the sanctuary without having associated Lula with the atheistic doctrine (Acts 1989). Dirigentes of the congregations in the baixadas, taking their cue from Pastor Paulo, also instructed believers how to vote. Dirigente José Araujo, whose wife's cure led him to convert, explained how he advised his congregation to vote according to evangelical principles. Responding to my inquiry regarding whether he had told believers how to vote, he said:

> No, I asked them to do the following: I said, "Well, as leaders of the Pentecostal movement and church leaders, we have to counsel those who listen to us. We have a responsibility to teach the word of God. We have the right to know what is good for us. First, pray, opening your Bible. Pray for Jesus to illuminate whom you should vote for and what you should do to avoid negative consequences. Listen up, look what you're doing. We are members of a church. Are you going to vote for people who aren't friends of the church? You already saw their declaration on TV. You know who the enemies of the church are, don't you? So we aren't going to contribute to the downfall of our own church. So what are crentes, who have the Spirit of God in their lives, going to do? Pray to the Lord for illumination, for advice on whom to vote for. Don't let yourselves vote for the man who later will come to shut the doors on the gospel."

I then asked if the "man" to whom he was referring was Lula, and he continued: "Yes, Lula, because I told them that the man from the PT is the pits [*da fossa*]. They don't like crentes. So we oriented them on the eve of the election. We oriented all the people whom we teach the word of God to. I'm certain that no one voted for Lula."

Throughout the nation, believers heeded their pastors' advice and made a crucial contribution to Collor's electoral victory. An overwhelming 70 percent of the evangelical voting population in Brazil cast their ballot for the dashing young "friend of the gospel" (Fabio and da Silva, personal interviews, and "Disputa pelos evangélicos"). Support for Collor among Pentecostals in Belém was even stronger. Eighty-three percent of my informants voted for the telegenic candidate, while a mere 4 percent surreptitiously marked an *X* next to the name of the "enemy of the gospel," Lula. The remaining 13 percent either abstained (11 percent) or left their ballot blank (2 percent). Claudia Souza, the Assembleiana who earlier described her baptism by immersion, revealed why she and many of her Pentecostal brethren preferred Collor. "Many people both in the church and outside say Lula is a communist. The pastor advised us to vote for Collor because of that communist stuff. At election time the dirigente always says in church that we have to vote for the right person. To tell the truth, I don't know what communism is. I know that he always spoke about communism, that we had to be careful. I don't know what communism is, but I voted for Collor."

All in the Family

Even more than he had for Collor, the pastor-president in Belém attempted to mobilize the church in support of his own daughter's campaign for state deputy. As scholar Paul Freston indicates, it is common practice for AD pastor-presidents in Brazil to encourage their progeny to seek elected office as a means of increasing their own political capital and social prestige. Two of the twenty-seven post-1987 evangelical federal deputies were the sons-in-law of pastor-presidents, and a third was the son of a head pastor (Freston 200). The retirement of AD political pioneer Antonio Teixeira in 1986 due to illness and the conflict-ridden relationship with Eliel Rodrigues sent Pastor Paulo scrambling to fill the void in political representation in the late 1980s. As the seasoned patrão of the AD, whom could Pastor Paulo trust more than his own kin to represent his interests in the state legislature?

The story of Claudia Machado's political ascent not only synthesizes the classic elements of clientelism and nepotism but also reads like a melodramatic Brazilian *novela* (soap opera). Sent to seminary in São Paulo by her father, Claudia met a young man and conceived a child out of wedlock. Seminary authorities discovered her sin and promptly expelled her (Negreiros and Gomes, personal interviews). She then returned to Belém, where her status as a single mother must have provoked a minor scandal, though, predictably, there is no written record of it. Eager to end her ignominious situation, Claudia quickly married Nilson Gomes, a recent convert who had ruined his modeling career through drug addiction. Shortly after their marriage, his father-in-law put Gomes in charge of the *Estandarte Evangélico*; Desafio Jovem, the church's drug rehabilitation center; *Boas Novas no Lar* (Good News at Home), a half-hour evangelical program on TV Guajará; and the regional office of the revitalized Brazilian Evangelical Confederation (Confederação Evangélica do Brasil)(*Estandarte* 12/87–1/88).

Meanwhile her father had named Claudia his personal secretary at the Central Temple and director of both the Department of Education and the Department of Culture and Social Assistance. In April 1988 she started her own column in the church journal managed by her husband. Common members were unaware that the heavy political content of Claudia's articles presaged the imminent launching of her first campaign for elected office. Five months after the creation of her column, the *Estandarte Evangélico* announced: "In Belém an Evangelical Woman Runs for Deputy Mayor." A photograph of the beaming candidate standing next to her running mate for mayor, IEQ pastor and state deputy Guaracy Silveira (PDC), accompanies the text (*Estandarte* 9–10/88). Despite Claudia and Silveira's disappointing fifth-place finish, the pastor's daughter had increased her name recognition both within and outside the evangelical camp (C. Machado, personal interview).

Undaunted by the failed mayoral bid, the Machado-Machado-Gomes trio drew heavily on the financial and material resources of the church to support Claudia's campaign for state deputy. The pastor-presidente began to lay the institutional groundwork for his daughter's candidacy in 1989 with an historic modification of church bylaws. To legalize ecclesiastical support for Claudia's campaign, the head pastor eliminated from the church statutes the following sections of Article 9, adopted in 1977: "The church will not tolerate any political activity, nor will it allow its members to use the denomination to be elected to any political office. Church members who hold or aspire to hold public elected office cannot be elected to any administrative position in the church." The revised version of Article 9 prohibits only the use of church property for political campaigns, a regulation which Pastor Paulo flagrantly violated in backing Claudia's run for office.

The chief crente's strategy for electing his daughter to the state assembly was not limited to legal machinations. He also sought a financial-political benefactor to partially underwrite Claudia's campaign, given that AD pockets were not deep enough to finance the kind of media blitz that a successful campaign required (Negreiros and Gomes, personal interviews). Had his personal fortune been greater and his relationship with the head Assembleiano less contentious, Deputy Rodrigues would have been the natural choice for the role as Claudia's patron. Instead, Pastor Paulo turned to wealthy Belenense businessman and nonbeliever Wagner Spindola to take Claudia under his financial and political wing. In return, the pastor guaranteed Spindola the church's ample electoral base (Acts 1989, Negreiros and Gomes, personal interviews).

While her father cemented political alliances and modified church by-laws, Claudia unofficially launched her campaign with the founding of an AD organization denominated "Belém Urgente." Belém Urgente's stated purpose was to aid the needy of the church through the collection and distribution of foodstuffs, clothing, and medicine. In reality the "philanthropic organization" was created as the principal campaign vehicle to drive Claudia to the portals of the state assembly. Well versed in the mechanics of clientelistic politics, impoverished Assembleianos understood that the "donations" they received from "Professor Claudia" were not without a price. In exchange for a kilo of beans or pair of shoes, they were committing themselves to vote for "a name of faith and work" (Negreiros and Gomes, personal interviews, and *Estandarte* 1990).

Throughout the election year of 1990, the PRN candidate used her column in the church paper to urge participation in her campaign vehicle. A few months after her election at the end of year, Belém Urgente ceased operations. When I queried her regarding the nature of the organization, Deputy Machado categorically denied that it had ever been anything more than a philanthropic church agency. Moreover she ironically lamented the fact that "unfortunately in the state of Pará politics are still very clientelistic" (C. Machado, personal interview).

In addition to the candidate's self-promotion, her husband and father turned church media and the ministerio into axles of the campaign vehicle. Nilson Gomes, as director of the *Estandarte*, editorialized on behalf of his wife's candidacy. In the same issue that announced official AD support for the crente candidate and her nonevangelical running mate, Wagner Spindola, Gomes answered the title question, "Why Should You Choose Evangelical Candidates?"

> How can we disobey the wise counsel of God, electing a stranger to
> lead us when we can choose our brothers and sisters, who think like

us, who pray like us, who serve the same God, and sit with us in the same pews where we worship? Only the influence of the Devil makes the crente prefer to defeat his brother in faith and elect a stranger when both are vying for the same position. How could it be possible that a crente would prefer to vote for a stranger? Only out of envy, jealousy, or lack of love, because he sold or rented his conscience for future favors and crumbs given out by corrupt politicians [*politiqueiros*] on the eve of elections. Vote right. Vote according to the pastor's advice. (*Estandarte* 8–9/90)

Gomes somehow failed to perceive any "diabolical influence" in his own backing of the incrédulo Spindola over AD member Eliel Rodrigues for federal deputy. Moreover, his own wife was distributing political "crumbs and favors" in the baixadas while Gomes denounced such behavior as *politicagem* (corrupt politics).

Leaving his son-of-law in charge of coordinating printed political propaganda, the senior pastor of the AD ordered his subordinates at the radio station leased by the church to fill the airwaves with news about candidate Machado. Stoves, refrigerators, and other household appliances were awarded over the air to callers who could correctly answer questions about Claudia (Negreiros and Gomes, personal interviews). Deputy Rodrigues later complained bitterly about being denied access to AD radio for his own campaign (personal interview).

All other efforts to elect his prodigal daughter to public office pale in comparison to the pastor-president's edict in a ministerial meeting in early 1990. Risking clerical mutiny, the AD leader presented Claudia as the official church candidate and ordered those who refused to support her campaign to resign from the ministerio (Rodrigues, Negreiros, and Gomes, personal interviews). According to dirigente José Castro, who attended the meeting, a young dirigente stood up and said to Pastor Paulo: "Pastor, then I must turn my congregation over to you, because I have a prior commitment with Jonas [a rival candidate] for whom I have worked for a long time. I could never betray my friend. The pastor might not be aware, but I have a contract with him. But I will instruct my family to vote for Claudia, even though I can't." Castro explained that after the meeting had adjourned, Pastor Paulo approached the audacious dirigente and told him that he appreciated his sincerity and that he therefore could remain a member of the ministerio. It appears that while the great majority verbally agreed to comply, most AD officers did not carry out their pastor's orders.

Despite her access to the considerable resources of her church and a well-financed campaign, Claudia Machado won office with the support of only 10 percent of Belém's evangelical electorate (C. Machado, personal interview). Moreover, with a total of approximately five thousand votes throughout the state, she was one of the least popular of the victorious candidates. In contrast, AD state deputy Raimundo Santos won office with twelve thousand votes (Santos, personal interview). The deputy attributed her relatively low vote count to a lack of support from the State Convention (Convenção Estadual) of the AD. In an interview published in the *Estandarte Evangélico* she complained that fellow Assembleiano Deputy Raimundo Santos had secured the official support of the State Convention, whereas she only had the backing of the ministerio in Belém (3–4/91).

More to the point is the question of why Deputy Machado won such a small percentage of the evangelical electorate, particularly in her own denomination? The answer, I believe, lies in the resentment that her campaign engendered among the AD masses. It is one thing to recommend an apparently God-fearing presidential candidate over a socialist nonbeliever, but another to press church resources and organizations into service on behalf of a candidate for political office when the politician is a relative of the pastor-president and has a checkered past. Fifty-eight-year-old AD member Dolcelina Passos, like many of her brothers and sisters in faith, said she did not vote for Claudia because she perceived no difference between the crente candidate's political conduct and that of nonevangelicals. "Claudia Machado came at election time looking for votes in the prayer circle, but she never returned after the election. You know how politicians are. They only show up at election time. Besides, the dirigentes thought this was very wrong." In addition, the majority of ordinary Pentecostals in Belém oppose their churches' involvement in politics. Sixty percent of all my informants said that crentes should not run for elected office, most arguing that the polluted world of politics contaminates even those who are firm in the faith. On the other hand, the majority of the 30 percent (10 percent were undecided) who approved of an evangelical presence in the political arena stated that the defense of church interests required Pentecostal representatives in federal, state, and municipal legislative bodies.

Pork and Vice: Deputy Claudia

As the first evangelical woman elected to the state legislature, Deputy Machado practiced the same type of pork barrel politics that she denounced in our interview, while pursuing a legislative agenda akin to that of Eliel Rodrigues, which identified personal sin as the root of the nation's political, economic, and social morass. Allied with Governor Jader Barbalho, the deputy worked hard to maintain her political constituency in the baixadas of Belém through such infrastructural improvements as electricity, public phones, and street lamps. Riacho Doce, an invasion site on property owned by the Federal University of Pará, was home to many Assembleianos, and it was one of the prime beneficiaries of Deputy Machado's political pork. In an undated newsletter to residents (most likely written in 1993), she wrote: "My dear friends of Riacho Doce, the installation of public lighting in your area adds to the benefits that I have obtained, together with the governor, for the Riacho Doce area."

Curiously, the Administrative Acts between 1991 and 1993 do not record any state subsidies or political favors on the AD's behalf. I suspect that the blank record does not mean that Deputy Machado was unable to obtain government largess for the church. Rather, the highly visible relationship between the deputy and her father led the AD in Belém to simply cease recording political payments and engage in further accounting legerdemain (Gomes, personal interview).

In accord with her belief that "man's spiritual condition has a much greater influence than his socioeconomic condition," Machado devoted the remainder of her legislative agenda to combating drugs, liquor, tobacco, and pornography (*Estandarte* 3/4–91). An unsuccessful proposal called for pornographic magazines to be sold in brown wrappers and only to those over the age of eighteen. Another called upon restaurateurs in the state to create nonsmoking sections (C. Machado, personal interview). A self-described political centrist—"because Christians should avoid extremes"—she migrated from the discredited PRN to the PPR (Renovated Progressive Party) in mid-1993 (C. Machado, personal interview). At the time of our interview in March of 1994, Claudia Machado was planning to run for a second term, once again in the name of "faith and work."

Thus, in 1962 the AD in Belém abandoned its seat in the bleachers to eventually become a major player in the political arena. Half a century as mere spectators at the political contest ended in the early 1960s, not because the ideology of the church had changed but because its opportunities had. Certain elected officials, particularly Senator Catete Pinheiro, began to take notice of the church's potentially broad electoral base and encouraged AD member and prominent businessman Antonio Teixeira to run for state deputy. Perceiving a golden opportunity to increase the church's power and influence, the pastor-president gave his blessing to Teixeira's candidacy.

As both Assembleiano and member of the legislative assembly, Teixeira played the pioneering role of liaison between the client church and patron state. The state, in exchange for political support and religious legitimation, rewarded its faithful client with generous subsidies. The government, however, did not maintain a continuous flow of cruzeiros to the AD. Rather, funds ebbed and flowed according to the dynamics of church-state relations. Financial aid peaked between the late 1960s and mid-1970s when the military regime, due to conflict with the Catholic church, made the AD in Belém its primary religious client. The church experienced a funding drought in the early and mid-1980s because head pastor Paulo Machado had backed the PDS gubernatorial candidate over the victorious Jader Barbalho of the PMDB.

Although church records do not document it, the AD reached its political apogee in 1990 with the election of Pastor Paulo's daughter, Claudia Machado, as state deputy. Deputy Machado, like most of her evangelical cohorts, has neither fought for a progressive new social order like Benedita da Silva nor advocated the type of fascist and homicidal regime that her coreligionist Efrain Rios Montt unleashed on Guatemala. Instead, she has bolstered the social, economic, and political status quo by engaging in the type of clientelistic relationships that largely define politics in Brazil. Although he evinced a clear ideological affinity with the military dictatorship, the pastor-president's opportunistic politics allowed him both to make the transition to civilian rule and to become a political patron in his own right. In conclusion, Pentecostal politics in Pará, as in the rest of Brazil and much of Latin America, are not about working for either a progressive or repressive new political order but about staking a larger claim in the existing system.

Conclusion

❧

$\mathcal{P}$rior to commencing my ethno-graphic interviews, I regarded Brazilian Pentecostalism as the latest mani-festation of millenarianism in a country with a rich history of apocalyptic and messianic movements. Were not the dreams of Canudos and Contestado, of a glorious new order based on divine law, reappearing in the sanctuaries of charismatic Protestantism? The possibility of such historical continuity intrigued me. Historians, I thought, had been premature in writing the obit-uary for millenarian movements in Brazil. Like the dispossessed sertanejos who followed Counselor Antonio into the backlands of Bahia almost a cen-tury ago, millions of disenfranchised Brazilians were, it seemed, flocking to Pentecostal houses of worship on the urban periphery to await the rapture of the imminent Second Coming. Moreover, I presumed that the rapidly ap-proaching millennium (the year 2000) further contributed to the dispensa-tionalist theology that seemed to be fueling the Pentecostal boom.

My ethnography of believers in Belém, supplemented by archival re-search, quickly refuted the original theory. Narrating their life histories, my informants rarely spoke of the parousia and evinced little concern with life in the hereafter. Of course, apocalyptic discourse suffused Pentecostal preaching, but in the narratives of individual crentes, the Second Coming re-ceived scant attention compared to the trials and tribulations of their every-day lives. More than the promise of having their name written in the book of life, my informants adhered to the faith out of a desperate search for an immediate solution to the health crises of poverty. Throughout the book, therefore, I have contended that Pentecostalism thrives among the poor of Brazil and much of Latin America because it offers healing to those suffer ing from the illnesses of poverty. In contrast to previous research on the pro-liferation of Pentecostalism in Latin America, I have posited that while poverty is generally a necessary condition for conversion to take place, it is not a sufficient one.

The Boom in Retrospect

That the dialectic between faith healing and the pathogens of poverty has stoked the Pentecostal boom is borne out by the history of charismatic Protestantism in Brazil. Functioning as the Hegelian thesis, a distorted model of economic development has prevented the majority of the population from meeting their basic human needs, especially health. Physical and psychosocial illness resulting from malnourishment, insalubrious living conditions, and severely restricted access to health care is one of the most common manifestations of poverty. Thus health, or freedom from disease, serves as the antithesis of distorted development. Those on the urban and rural margins, such as Angelino laundresses and Belenense domestics, who have been debilitated by poverty-related illness seek to restore their vitality through the most immediate and accessible remedies. The treatment most readily available to the poor, however, is often not the most efficacious, such as the "miraculous" root that failed to cure Amazonian lepers. It is precisely at this juncture in the quest for a cure, the failure of either a secular or supernatural health provider, that Pentecostal faith healing completes the dialectic as the synthesis of poverty-induced illness and health. Of course the Pentecostal faith as a systematic set of beliefs and practices involves more than a belief in divine healing. Nevertheless, Brazilian Pentecostal history and the life histories of my interviewees cannot be understood without comprehending the centrality of faith healing.

From its beginnings in 1910 and 1911, with the arrival of the Christian Congregation in São Paulo and the Assembly of God in Belém, Pentecostalism has effectively appealed to those whom the modernization process has pushed to the edges of society. In Belém some of the first converts to the AD were lepers, unrivaled social pariahs. The history of Pentecostalism in Brazil shows a religion whose evangelistic media became progressively more sophisticated through three stages of development. Evolving from the CC's proscription of electronic media to the IURD's acquisition of Rede Record, postmodern Pentecostalism has left its religious rivals dozing in the pews while it broadcasts its message on the small screen to millions of viewers. What surprises the observer, however, is not the rapid development of Pentecostal media but the relative constancy of the message across time and denomination. Whether in the AD, IEQ, or IURD, the fundamental crente leitmotif continues to be, "Accept Jesus as your Lord and savior in our church, and you will be healed."

Only through the life histories of my Pentecostal informants in Belém was I able to flesh out the mechanics of the dialectic that propels the Pentecostal boom. Belenense crentes, in narrating their own biographies, provided an organizational logic for interpreting the conversion process. As evangelical Christians, Pentecostals invariably order their life histories around the epic moment of conversion. Much as the Christian world has based its calendar on the birth of Christ, Brazilian believers divide their biographical narratives on the point of accepting Jesus. The two distinct periods in crente life histories, preconversion and postconversion, are separated by the relatively brief but monumental moment of conversion.

The preconversion world of my informants was a place contaminated by poverty-related illness. Expanding the concept of illness beyond its physical borders, I have identified the principal pathogens that impel people to convert as somatic maladies, alcoholism, and domestic strife. The conversion process normally commences when an illness reaches the critical stage. Typically the infirm has unsuccessfully attempted to resolve her health crisis through both secular and sacred means. Many of my informants were desenganados, that is, told by physicians that their conditions were incurable.

It is commonly at this critical stage of illness that the afflicted first hears the Pentecostal message of faith healing. A crente family member or friend offers the possibility of a divine cure to the desperate patient. But the remedy is not dispensed without a price. In accord with the mechanics of Brazilian popular religion, the supplicant must enter into a contractual agreement with the deity whom she is petitioning. Pentecostalism requires the petitioner to accept Jesus in exchange for the restoration of her health.

Accepting Jesus in practical terms means to become a Pentecostal believer and affiliate with the church that facilitated the cure. After a probationary period of between three and six months in which the convert is instructed in the fundamentals of the faith and learns the crente codes of conduct, the neophyte is ready to seal her promise to serve Jesus through the rite of baptism by immersion. Though not as charged with meaning as baptism in the Holy Spirit, converts feel reborn in the healing waters. Emerging after momentary immersion, the baptized leave their sin and sickness submerged at the bottom of the baptismal tank.

Once official members of the crente fold, believers are able to further recover and maintain their health through the spiritual and ideological force of their new faith. With the instruments of spiritual ecstasy, mutual aid, ideological dualism, and moral asceticism at their disposal, Pentecostals inoculate themselves against many of the diseases of poverty which claim countless lives on the urban and rural peripheries. Spiritual ecstasy, experienced through the gifts of the Spirit, baptism in the Holy Spirit, and music, allows believers to transcend the material deprivation of their everyday lives. Filled with the power of the Spirit, believers exorcise the demons of poverty. While ecstatic worship imbues the faithful with spiritual power, the mutual aid societies formed by the community of believers sustain individuals in moments of crisis. Since Pentecostal churches provide only minimal institutional aid to needy members, individual practitioners form networks of mutual support to help each other weather the tempests of poverty. Although the network of kin relationships remains the primary source of succor for Pentecostals, the material, spiritual, and psychological support of the local congregation can mean the difference between health and illness.

In the ideological and comportmental realms, believers further restore and preserve their health through a Manichaean worldview and an ascetic moral code. The dualism of Pentecostal doctrine divides the world into stark polarities, such as house/street and carnal/spiritual. While the dichotomies of the crente weltanschauung may seem naive to the sophisticated nonbeliever, they allow the faithful to demonize many of the diseases of poverty. Put into practice, Pentecostal dualism becomes a strict moral code that requires converts to renounce their earthly vices. Men in particular must exit the carnal drama of the street and take up roles in the spiritual theaters of home and church. In abjuring vice, men abandon some of the main behavior associated with the male prestige complex.

While the healing power that individual believers experience through conversion and active participation in church life fuels the Pentecostal boom at the ground level, ecclesiastical relations of power, both intra- and extramural, drive the expansion of the Pentecostal institution. At first it was difficult to understand how an ostensibly authoritarian and centralized model of ecclesial organization could be contributing to Pentecostal growth. How could a church such as the Assembly of God in Belém, micromanaged by a seemingly omnipotent pastor-patron allow for the spiritual development and ecclesiastical advance of ordinary members?

The key to solving the enigma emerged from the same dialectic that illuminates the conversion process. More than any other element, power lies at the experiential core of Pentecostalism. The recovery and maintenance of health through conversion and the ecstasy of the baptism of the Spirit are essentially moments of supernatural power in which the temporally impotent believer transcends his earthly station buoyed by divine force. In less dramatic fashion, an organizational model which I have denominated "participatory authoritarianism," a modified form of clientelism, preserves the privileges of the pastor-patron while increasing the status of the congregant-client. Ecclesiastical power is extremely concentrated in the office of pastor-president, but literate male crentes who demonstrate loyalty and a measure of charisma can aspire to prestigious ministerial office. Women and illiterate men, though they are barred from the ministerio, regain the dignity denied them in secular society by serving as church officers and participating in myriad organizations at the level of the local congregation. But while converts recover their dignity as Sunday school teachers and doormen, older members perceive a dampening of the Spirit. The institutionalization process has weakened the temple walls, allowing the world to come crashing through in the form of moneylenders, an emphasis on theology instead of the Spirit, and "carnal" music and dress.

The exercise of ecclesiastical power in the external world has also contributed to rapid Pentecostal expansion. Departing from the considerable amount of contemporary scholarship that sees in Pentecostalism the potential for revolutionary or progressive political action, I have argued that Brazilian crentes have carved out a significant political presence by engaging in the same clientelistic practices that pervade Brazilian politics. The kind of leftist politics practiced by former Assembleiana and current petista senator Benedita da Silva diverge strikingly from the Pentecostal norm in Brazil. In fact, her marriage to a nonbeliever gave AD leaders the perfect pretext to rid themselves of a political albatross. Neither are the majority of Pentecostal politicians in Brazil fascists, like their Guatemalan coreligionist General Efrain Rios Montt.

An examination of the political relations of the Assembly of God in Belém showed how in 1962 the church abruptly abandoned its historical position on the periphery of politics to become a major player in the Amazonian political arena. Although ideological affinity linked the church to the military regime, the opportunity to advance institutional and personal interests was the compelling factor leading the AD to supplant its archrival, the Catholic church, as the state's primary religious client. In exchange for generous subsidies at all levels of government, the pastor-president served as one of the regime's principal propagandists and apologists in Amazonia. While Pentecostal politics do not empower the rank and file faithful in the same manner as conversion and active participation in church life, they have allowed the AD, IURD, and IEQ, and other churches to a lesser extent, to expand institutionally and establish themselves as major players in the Brazilian political arena.

Beyond the Boom

One of the major advantages of focusing on a single religion rather than several is organizational depth. Whereas the researcher conducting a comparative study risks fishing in large but shallow bodies of water, the scholar pursuing just one type of species can explore the murky undercurrent. Conversely, the single-religion paradigm can leave the social scientist plumbing the depths of a deep but narrow well. In an effort to broaden the focus on Pentecostalism, I have included some discussion of its chief religious competitors, Umbanda and popular Catholicism. This, then, is the place to cross the Brazilian religious arena and ask if the conclusions drawn about the proliferation of Pentecostalism are relevant to its rivals.

By most accounts Umbanda and African-Brazilian religion in general are growing, while the Catholic church, with the notable exception of the charismatic movement, is static. Assuming that this is indeed the case and that the growth of Umbanda, while impressive, has not rivaled Pentecostal figures, it remains to be seen if the same dialectic that propels Pentecostalism might help explain the relative success or failure of its rivals in appealing to the Brazilian popular classes. The only in-depth study of these three religions (Burdick 1993) attributes the popular appeal of Umbanda and Pentecostalism to their status as "cults of affliction." Contrariwise, the declining fortunes of progressive Catholicism are ascribed to its role as a "cult of continuity," which reaffirms secular identities rather than rupturing them by offering a sacred world apart.

If the fate of popular religions in Brazil and indeed throughout Latin America is predicated on their ability to cure the afflictions of individual believers, specifically the pathogens of poverty, then we should turn our attention to the healing rituals of each faith. Perhaps the relative importance and efficacy of spiritual healing in any one particular religion can tell us much about its success or failure with the popular classes. Applied to the three main popular religions in Brazil, the model seems not only to provide insight into Catholicism's slow growth (interestingly, the dynamic charismatic movement practices Pentecostal-type faith healing) but also reveals significant differences between Umbanda and Pentecostalism. Spiritual curing plays an important part in all three religious traditions, with the important exception of progressive Catholicism, but it is only in Pentecostal practice that it becomes the experiential core of the faith. Without cura divina, the Assembly of God, among others, would have won only a few more converts than the Presbyterians or Methodists. Hence, Pentecostalism might more appropriately be viewed as a cult of healing rather than affliction.

Pentecostalism's most vibrant competitor, Umbanda, also places healing rituals at the center of its practice. Like many of my informants in Belém, Brazilians typically seek out an Umbanda terreiro in an attempt to resolve a crisis, often health-related. Assuming that the same type of problems lead the afflicted to either Pentecostal temples or Umbanda terreiros, then perhaps the latter's less spectacular growth rate is related to the efficacy of its healing rituals. In its treatment of the psychosocial wounds of material deprivation, such as alcoholism, Umbanda appears to provide continuity with secular patterns more than rupture or inversion of them. Lacking a rigid code of conduct that demonizes activities and comportment associated with the male prestige complex, Umbanda cannot offer the type of comprehensive healing found in Pentecostal churches. Most illustrative of this point are the two religions' diametrically opposed views of alcohol. While the Assembly of God requires total abstinence at the risk of censure and expulsion, Umbanda frequently condones, if it does not encourage, the consumption of beer and cachaça during services. In fact hard drinking is such an integral part of the persona of some spirits such as the Cabocla Mariana, that their incorporation into an Umbandista medium without a bottle in his or her hand seems incongruous. The terreiro, serving more to reaffirm than to invert secular drinking patterns, can provide little relief to those seeking sobriety. Thus while Brazil's most popular African-Brazilian religion does indeed gather together its practitioners on the basis of affliction and give primacy of place to healing rituals, it seems less efficient than Pentecostalism at curing some of the maladies most prevalent on the metropolitan margins.

The importance and efficacy of divine healing are much harder to gauge in Brazilian Catholicism, since the church is unofficially divided into several camps. A recent comparative study in Rio de Janeiro (Machado and Mariz) reveals that members of at least one group, the charismatics, feel more affinity with Pentecostals than with their own brethren in the progressive sector. Internal divisions aside, the present status of two of the main expressions of popular Catholicism, the progressive church and the Charismatic Renewal, would appear to be related to the role of faith healing. Of all stripes of Catholicism, the progressive church, manifested in liberation theology and Christian Base Communities, faces the greatest crisis. Participation in the

CEBs is on the decline, and the Vatican has silenced and transferred prominent liberation theologians. But the Roman offensive only partially explains the declining stock of progressive Catholicism. Of greater relevancy, perhaps, is theology that on the one hand elevates the collective over the individual and on the other advocates social, economic, and political transformation over supernatural healing. A liberationist priest, skeptical of the efficacy of faith healing, would more likely urge poor Catholics to demand more health clinics in their neighborhood than invite them to the altar to be anointed with holy oil.

Holy oil and the laying on of hands form an integral part of the Roman church's most vibrant sector in Brazil, the Charismatic Renewal. Conceived at Duquesne University in the late 1960s, charismatic Catholicism as practiced in Brazil is a Catholicized version of Pentecostalism. Only allegiance to the pope and saints distinguishes adherents of the Renewal from Pentecostals. Faith healing, baptism in the Holy Spirit, and charismata constitute the experiential core of this burgeoning movement.

Therefore the same dialectic that propels the Pentecostal boom would seem to help explain the rise and fall of the principal popular religions in Brazil. In the competitive religious marketplace, the faith that offers the most effective remedy for the pathogens of poverty will win the battle for Brazilian souls such as that of seventy-year-old Assembleiana Jovenilha Castanhal. Dona Castanhal suffered much abuse at the hands of her alcoholic and philandering husband, whose drinking bouts often left the family without enough money for food. Her husband eventually left her for another woman, but in her Pentecostal faith, sister Castanhal found the strength to overcome adversity. "When I am in need, I ask for help from my God, who can do it all. My God never lets me go a day without lunch, because I kneel every day in prayer. I ask Jesus to multiply my provisions. Jesus blesses me; He blesses my salary and our food. I tell you that since I've been a crente, I've always had what I need. Thank God that I have two pairs of shoes that my children gave me. It is the Holy Spirit who operates in our lives to free us from want, thank God."

NOTES

Introduction

1. Popular religion is the set of sacred beliefs and practices of the poor *povo* (people or folk), characterized by a high level of lay participation and emphasis on the resolution of the quotidian crises of poverty.

2. Most evangelicals in Brazil use the term *crente*, "believer," as a synonym for Protestant, as do nonevangelicals. Whereas North Americans prefer the word "Protestant" to denote both Pentecostal and mainline denominations, Brazilians favor the term *evangélico* over *protestante*. In accord with Brazilian usage, I will use the terms "evangelical" and "Protestant" interchangeably.

3. In *Followers of the New Faith*, Willems posited that Protestantism thrives because it offers a comprehensive solution to the anomie of the urban migrant. Accelerated capitalist development, manifested in unbridled industrialization and urbanization, undermined the traditional "rules for living" in rural areas, provoking mass migration to the cities. In the metropolis, the disoriented migrant created a powerful new identity as a crente. Lalive D'Epinay reached similar conclusions in *Haven of the Masses*. He found that the vast majority of Pentecostal converts in Chile were unemployed recent migrants from the countryside. Pentecostalism, he argued, recreated the familiar patriarchal social structure of the hacienda, thus providing anomic migrants with a socioreligious haven from the indifference and chaos of life on the urban periphery.

4. Within weeks of my arrival it became apparent that neither the Pentecostal Holy Spirit nor the spirits of Umbanda can compete with *futebol*, the most popular of all Brazilian forms of ecstatic release.

5. Informal employment can be classified into three types. The first type is employment in the formal sector but without the work card (*carteira assinada*) that theoretically guarantees basic labor rights. *Biscate*, or day labor, the second type, tends to employ the least skilled workers, who sell their labor on a daily basis in any branch of the economy. *Biscateiros* commonly work in construction. Mechanics and street and market vendors exemplify the third type, stable self-employment. In Belém the largest part of the work force fluctuates between formal but unstable work and biscate (Mitschein 47 and 127).

6. The Gini coefficient measures the equality of income distribution on a scale where 0 is perfect equality and 1 is perfect inequality.

7. In 1993 the minimum wage fluctuated between US$60 and US$65.

8. Invasion sites are illegal settlements formed by groups of squatters who "invade" vacant lands with the intention of establishing permanent and legal residence.

9. The male prestige complex is a pattern of conduct characterized by aggression and intransigence in interpersonal relationships (Brusco 1986: 137). Bars, brothels, and soccer stadiums provide social space where men can collectively reaffirm their masculine persona through drinking, sex, and sports.

10. Women of the IEQ were much more likely to sell cosmetics than their AD sisters, who reject makeup as a sinful vaidade (vanity). However, many middle-class Assembleianas, especially at the Central Temple, wear lipstick, base, and small earrings.

11. Richard Pace, in his research on religion and poverty in Belém, obtained similar results from his survey of Belenense Assembleianos a decade ago. Seventy percent of those surveyed hailed from the interior (44).

12. Paul Freston's assertion that 73 percent of Brazilian Protestants are urban dwellers, as compared to 67 percent of the population at large, hardly qualifies Pentecostalism as an urban phenomenon (31).

13. To preserve the original spirit of the language, interview transcripts were edited only minimally. All translations are my own.

CHAPTER 1   *A Prophetic History*

1. Pentecostalism emerged from the Holiness movement of the nineteenth century. Literal interpretation of the Bible, ecstatic worship, and asceticism characterized the believers (Anderson 28). Baptism in the Spirit is the central tenet and experience of Pentecostal religion. It is based on an event in the book of Acts in which the Holy Spirit descended on the apostles in tongues of fire, causing them to preach in languages previously unknown to them. Pentecostals claim that the Holy Spirit possesses them similarly during the spiritual baptism. A dissociated state of consciousness marked by glossolalic behavior and intense corporal gesticulations typify the experience.

2. Once a warehouse district at the edge of downtown Los Angeles, Azusa Street is presently part of the Little Tokyo quarter.

3. Anglo-Brazilian sociologist Paul Freston has located the probable origin of the Pará prophecy. Although the state of Pará was known for the Amazonian rubber boom of the late nineteenth century and early twentieth, Swedish immigrant evangelicals had another source of knowledge about the region. At the time of the prophecy, the pastor of the Baptist church in Belém was a Swedish immigrant who had come to Amazonia in 1897 from the United States. News of his mission work in Pará probably traveled to the United States in the form of reports to the Swedish Baptist community in Chicago (Freston 70).

4. The centrality of health and healing is revealed in the second article of the premier edition of the Assembly of God's first journal, the *Boa Semente* (Good Seed). Writing in 1919, Berg entitled his first article "The Lord Is Our Doctor." "I can testify that in my trips to the islands of Lower Amazonia I have seen multitudes of believers cured merely by the efficacy of prayer" (*Boa Semente* 1/18/19).

5. The free circulation of the Bible was a novelty in Catholic Brazil. The Church hierarchy, until the sweeping reforms of the Second Vatican Council in the early

1960s, denied the laity access to Scripture. Church fathers feared the consequences of unmediated lay interpretation. Many of my older Pentecostal interviewees had never seen a Bible until joining the Assembly of God.

6. These administrative records, dating from 1930 to the present, are my primary source of historical information on the AD in Belém.

7. Troelstch developed the church/sect typology in his classic work. Of some relevance to this study, the theory posits that all Christian organizations can be placed on a continuum with church and sect at opposite ends. The relationship with secular society is key in determining where a particular group falls on the spectrum. At the church end, a highly institutionalized organization provides continuity with society at large, often legitimizing secular values. In the North American context the Presbyterian and Episcopalian denominations are examples of churches. A group such as the Branch Davidians, characterized by extreme tension with the world and charismatic leadership in the Weberian sense, occupies the opposite end of the continuum. The church/sect gradient fails with such groups as the AD, which simultaneously display both church and sect traits.

8. "But if a woman has long hair, it is her glory. For her hair is given to her for a covering."

9. The IEQ's name represents the four pillars of the church's doctrinal edifice: Jesus saves, heals, sanctifies and is returning soon.

10. Tranca Rua is the most popular *exú*, or trickster spirit, in Amazonian Umbanda. Practitioners enlist the exu's aid in blocking a rival's path (*trancar a rua*) to success in business and love. Negotiating the flooded roads of Belém's slums, I encountered more than a few black candles and half-eaten plates of food, the work of Tranca Rua, left at strategic crossroads. While some Umbandistas assert that exús can also perform good works, Pentecostals regard all spirits of Umbanda and Candomblé as evil (Leacock 153).

11. Although the Brazilian masses exercised more political influence than ever during the period from 1945 to 1964, they continued to watch from the grandstand as the elite decision makers played and arbitrated the political game. In exchange for their vote, the disenfranchised electorate might be rewarded by precinct captains with a bottle of cachaça or a hammock.

12. Expanding circulation from one thousand copies at the end of 1963 to ten thousand in the late 1980s, the journal evolved from the "paper of AD youth" to "our paper" in the 1970s and most of the 1980s. The present moniker, "Belém's paper," reflects the church's social and political aspirations.

13. Institutionalization will be more fully examined in chapter 6.

14. The Weberian prophet bases his claim to authority on personal revelation and charisma, while the priest derives legitimacy from training in the sacred tradition (Weber 46).

15. "The letter kills the Spirit" is an oft quoted phrase in churches of the shantytowns.

16. ASSEHNPLELP is the local chapter of ADHONEP, a nondenominational paraecclesiastical organization affiliated with the Full Gospel Businessmen's Fellowship International, founded in 1951 by a member of the Assembly of God in the United States who was concerned that prosperous professionals were leaving the church. ADHONEP was launched in Brazil in 1975 (Freston 119).

17. *Populares* is the term employed by the Brazilian mass media and the middle and upper classes to denote the "faceless masses." Populares perceived as dangerous or threatening are labeled *marginais*.
18. In order to receive a specific blessing, such as employment or a cure, crentes must attend worship service on the same day of the week for a certain number of weeks, usually between five and seven. In late 1993 worshipers at a small IEQ congregation in the bairro of Guamá sought spiritual and material grace through the campaign of the "five keys to prosperity" conducted on five successive Sundays.
19. Rare among Pentecostal churches, the IURD follows an episcopal model of church government: bishops are the highest ranking leaders.
20. With her Barbie doll looks, Xuxa is one of Brazil's most popular television personalities. Her Disneyesque children's variety show is broadcast throughout the hemisphere in Portuguese and Spanish.

CHAPTER 2   *The Preconversion World of Illness*

1. The World Health Organization recommends a hospital bed ratio of at least 3/1000 ("Crise na saúde é ligada à economia").
2. The circulation of poor children in Brazil is well documented (see Scheper-Hughes, Leacock, and Wagley). In the shantytowns of Belém many adoptive children were sent by relatives or compadres in the interior. The composition of many poor households is in a constant state of flux. Many of the household heads among my informants, both men and women, were uncertain as to the number of people living in the house.
3. See Da Matta (1985) on the dichotomy between house and street in Brazil.
4. Over a million faithful and onlookers attended the Cirio of 1993. Estimates for the bicentennial Cirio of 1992 put the crowd at two million (*Revista do Cirio* 5).
5. According to the 1993 edition of the journal of the Cirio, one of the largest processions took place in 1855, when pilgrims filled the streets to ask the saint for protection from the cholera epidemic that had infected approximately one-third of the city's residents (*Revista do Cirio* 6).
6. To differentiate themselves from other Pentecostals and connote the universality of their "universal" church, members of the IURD eschew the term *crente* in favor of the word *cristão*, or Christian. Moreover, members of the IURD do not greet each other with the customary salutation of the AD, IEQ, and other churches: *paz do Senhor* (peace of the Lord).
7. Macumba is the more common term for Umbanda among the popular classes. Depending how it is used, it can have a pejorative connotation. My Pentecostal informants almost always spoke of Macumba and not Umbanda.

CHAPTER 3   *Conversion: Crisis, Cure, and Affiliation*

1. Before a Maranhense *mãe-de-santo* brought Batuque to Belém, Amazonian Pajelança, based on Tupi shamanism, provided an alternative source of healing for the city's residents (Leacock and Leacock 43). Many of my Pentecostal informants had consulted with *pajé* healers in their communities of the interior. Syncretic Umbanda

has integrated Pajelança healing rituals into its own ceremonies to the point that the pajé is no longer relevant in urban Amazonia.

2. Favelado men's proclivity to gravitate toward the street was particularly striking during the matches of the World Cup soccer tournament, which Brazil dramatically won. Minutes before half-time had even started, the men at the non-crente homes, where I was invited to root for Brazil, had already rushed into the street. A few would remain there, watching the game through the window.

3. The surname da Silva is so common among the Brazilian poor that I had to order my informants' life histories by their middle names.

4. I never observed spiritual conductors, such as photographs of the infirm, at any AD service. Reacting to the rich visual imagery of Brazilian Catholicism, the AD banished what it saw as "idols" from the sanctuary. The result are temples devoid of almost any visual symbols, including the cross.

5. In the common scenario in which the supplicant requests a cure for someone else, such as a sick child, the divine remedy depends on the faith of the supplicant and not on that of the child. Thus, a nonbeliever can be cured through the faith of a believer.

6. For Pentecostals the word "saint" denotes not self-sacrificial virgins or pious Good Samaritans but the common believer.

7. I hypothesize that the relaxed moral code of postmodern Pentecostalism, represented by the IURD, attenuates the churches' healing power.

8. The experience of urban poverty has changed the nature of spiritual malaise. Residents of the baixadas no longer fear the spell of the boto but are attacked by what Bishop Macedo of the IURD calls "unclean spirits" (*espíritos imundos*). Such spirits, according to the bishop, cause constant headaches, fainting spells, suicidal feelings, nervousness, undefined illness, fear, loneliness, insecurity, vice, failure, visions, and voices (Macedo 1993: 27).

9. The *cartão de membresía*, complete with black and white photo, identifies the bearer as an AD member in good standing. It serves as a domestic passport for Assembleianos visiting churches in other regions, as well as proof of membership for bureaucratic purposes.

10. Their status as *amigos* disqualifies many believers from church membership. Only when they legalize their union through marriage are the partners eligible for membership.

11. To facilitate the conversion process for Catholics and console the parents of infants who succumb to illness before their first birthday, the AD "dedicates" babies to Jesus. The brief ritual resembles a Catholic or Presbyterian christening but without the sprinkling of holy water on the newborn's head.

CHAPTER 4   *Health Maintenance*

1. *Gozo* in Portuguese and Spanish can also connote sexual pleasure.

2. Pentecostals assert that glossolalia only occurs spontaneously, but it soon became evident to me that while ecstatic utterance, particularly the kind manifested during preaching, is not rehearsed, it is often quite formulaic.

3. Aubree, examining trance behavior in Xangô and Pentecostalism, also discovered in Recife that glossolalia only occurs in groups. In Belém, however, I documented

the rare occurrence of solitary ecstatic speech, though it is hard to imagine poor urban Brazilians ever finding themselves alone.

4. Carimbó is the most popular of the regional rhythms in the state of Pará. Belenenses dance to the African-influenced music in pairs, hunched over and spinning hypnotically.

5. Scholar Diana Brown asserted that in the mid-1980s, Umbanda was also developing into a mutual aid society on the urban margins (100).

6. "Removing the other woman from her path" is also one of the principal reasons that Brazilian women seek out the spirits of Umbanda. The Umbandista incense (*defumador*) called Destranca Rua unclogs the streets of romantic and other rivals.

CHAPTER 5   *Ideology and Morality*

1. Nancy Scheper-Hughes (1992) is one of the few scholars to challenge the Da Mattian interpretation of carnival as a moment of social role inversion. In her analysis of carnival in a small city of the Northeast she discovers that the pre-Lenten celebration actually reinforces the dominant relations of race, class, and sex (Scheper-Hughes 1992).

2. Brega, whose chief exponent is "O Rei," Roberto Carlos, is a type of saccharine music popular among the urban poor in Brazil. In popular usage, the middle and upper classes employ the term to denote anything that is "low class" or tacky.

3. The IEQ, founded in Los Angeles by Aimee Semper McPherson, is the only major Brazilian Pentecostal denomination that ordains women as pastors.

4. The Portuguese are the butt of countless jokes and slurs in Brazil, especially among Pentecostals, who trace their nation's economic, political, and moral woes to the misfortune of having been colonized by a "decadent Catholic empire." Even Pastor-President Paulo Machado, who emigrated from Portugal at the age of five, was not immune to anti-Portuguese sentiment.

5. Since men tend to be the primary breadwinners, a household in which only the wife is a believer generally does not experience the kind of financial gain that a male-headed household does.

6. Latin American men, irrespective of their socioeconomic status, commonly refer to their wives and amigas as "my woman" (Portuguese, *minha mulher*; Spanish, *mi mujer*). Women do not employ what would be the equivalent term, "my man."

7. Census data tends to inflate the actual number of Whites and grossly underestimate the Black population. At the national level Blacks probably constitute approximately 25 percent of the population, while my observations in Belém lead me to place the population there near 10 percent.

8. In an attempt to dissuade Brazilians from identifying themselves to census takers as lighter-skinned than they really are, the IBGE developed a publicity campaign for the 1990 demographic census based on posters that instructed citizens not to deny their race: "Não negue sua raça."

CHAPTER 6   *Authoritarian Assembly*

1. Hoffnagel alludes to non-Pentecostals in Recife calling the AD pastor-president the "Pentecostal Pope" (102). In Belém it was among Assembleianos themselves that I heard the term.

2. Like all her political propaganda, the calendar bore Deputy Machado's slogan, "Deputada Claudia Machado: Um Nome de Fé e Trabalho" (Deputy Claudia Machado: A Name of Faith and Work).

3. In theory, the General Assembly (Assembléia Geral) is the highest governing body of the church. In practice, the assembly, meeting on a weekly basis, gives rubber-stamp approval to resolutions adopted by the ministerio.

4. This also happened to me on several occasions. Finding it too embarrassing to refuse my request for an interview, a few people intentionally gave me the wrong address.

5. Common members paid the bulk of the approximately US$500,000 bill through their contributions. The rest, as will be shown in the next chapter, came from government coffers. Donations from abroad were insignificant.

6. Cédulas are national identity cards that Brazilians use much as North Americans employ driver's licenses. As a temporary resident, I had to carry a foreign identity card, complete with photograph and fingerprint.

7. Church officials refused to divulge the details of this arrangement. Only additional investigation would reveal the identity of the "bulletin," but I suspect Bamerindus financed part of the production costs of the *Breve Histórico da AD em Belém* published in 1991.

8. Stark and Bainbridge postulate that in all religious organizations the powerful will favor lower tension with secular society while the powerless prefer higher tension (143).

CHAPTER 7   *Pentecostal Politics in Pará*

1. Dispensationalism, practiced widely among Pentecostals and fundamentalist Protestants, interprets current events according to apocalyptic Scripture. War and political upheaval, especially in the Middle East, are regarded as signs of the end of world.

2. Pastor Machado would have been hard-pressed to find a more unequivocal declaration of fealty than Psalm 20. "May he grant you your heart's desire, and fulfill your plans! May we shout for joy over your victory, and in the name of our God set up the banners! May the Lord fulfill all your petitions! Now I know that the Lord will help his anointed; He will answer him from his holy heaven with mighty victories by his right hand" (20:4–6).

3. "Be subject for the Lord's sake to every human institution, whether it be to the emperor as supreme, or to governors as sent by him to punish those who do wrong and to praise those who do right" (1 Peter 2:13–14).

4. Under the *abertura* initiated by President Ernesto Geisel in 1979, ARENA transformed itself into the PDS, while the loyal opposition party, MDB, renamed itself PMDB.

REFERENCES

Primary Sources

INTERVIEWS
Bengston, Josué. 1994. Mar. 3, personal interview.
Castro, José. 1994. Jan. 23, personal interview.
da Silva, Benedita. 1994. July 30, personal interview.
Ethnographic interviews. 1993–1994.
Fabio, Caio. 1994. July 29, personal interview.
Gomes, Jader [pseudonym]. 1993–1994. personal interviews.
Machado, Claudia [pseudonym]. 1994. Mar. 18, personal interview.
Machado, Paulo [pseudonym]. 1994. Feb. 2, written interview.
Negreiros, Eliel [pseudonym]. 1993–1994. personal interviews.
Rodrigues, Eliel. 1994. Jan. 1, personal interview.
Rodrigues, Gedilson. 1994. Apr. 7, personal interview.
Teixeira, Antonio. 1994. Jan. 27, personal interview.

CHURCH ANNALS, MEMOIRS AND JOURNALS
Atas do culto administrativo da AD em Belém (Acts). 1930–1993.
Berg, Daniel. 1987. *Enviado por Deus: Memorias de Daniel Berg*. 7th ed. Rio de
    Janeiro: CPAD.
Boa Semente, Orgao da Igreja Pentecostal, Belém. 1919–1930.
Deus é Amor. 1986. *Regulamento Interno para Membros*. São Paulo.
O Estandarte Evangélico. 1962–1993.
Estatutos da AD em Belém. 1977 and 1989.
Fichario de Membros [Membership File] da AD em Belém. 1930–1994.
Igreja do Evangelho Quandrangular. 1987. *Manual do pastor*. 3d ed. São Paulo.
Macedo, Edir. 1993. *O Espírito Santo*. Rio de Janeiro: Gráfica Universal.
———. N.d. *A libertação da teologia*. 7th ed. Rio de Janeiro: Grafica Universal.
O Mensageiro da Paz. 1930–1994.
"Principios norteadores da postura da igreja enquanto corpo de Cristo e como institu-
    ição, e de seus líderes, quando em nome dela agirem ou se expressarem sobre
    eleições para qualquer nivel ou mandatos pleiteados por seus membros e congre-
    gados." 1993. Guiding principles of the AD in Belém on political activity.
Relatórios Anuais da AD em Belém. 1968–1993.
Vingren, Ivar. 1991. *O diario do pioneiro Gunnar Vingren*. 4th ed. Rio de Janeiro: CPAD.

Secondary Sources

Abelém, Aurilea Gomes. 1989. *Urbanização e remoção: porque e paraque?* Belém: Universidade Federal do Pará.

Aguilar, Edwin Eloy, Kenneth Coleman, José Sandoval, and Timothy Steigenga. 1993. "Protestantism in El Salvador." *Latin American Research Review* 28 (2): 119–140.

Almeida, Abraão. 1982. *História das Assembléias de Deus no Brasil*. Rio de Janeiro: CPAD.

Alves, Maria da Silva. 1980. *O carnaval devoto*. Petropolis: Editora Vozes.

Alves, Rubem. 1984. *O suspiro dos oprimidos*. 3d ed. São Paulo: Edições Paulinas.

———. 1979. *Protestantismo e repressão*. São Paulo: Editora Atica.

Anderson, Robert. 1979. *Vision of the Disinherited*. New York: Oxford University Press.

Annis, Sheldon. 1988. *God and Production in a Guatemalan Town*. Austin: University of Texas Press.

Assembléia de Deus em Belém. 1991. *Breve histórico da Assembléia de Deus em Belém*. Belém: Grafinorte.

———. 1986. *História da Assembléia de Deus em Belém*. Belém: Falangola Editora.

Assman, Hugo. 1987. *La Iglesia electrónica y su impacto em América Latina*. San José, Costa Rica: Editoral DEI.

Aubree, Marion. 1985. "O transe: A resposta do xangô e do pentecostalismo." *Ciencia e Cultura* 37 (July): 1070–1075.

Barroso, Carmen. 1982. *Mulher, sociedade e estado no Brasil*. São Paulo: Brasilense.

Bastian, Jean Pierre. 1993. "The Metamorphosis of Latin American Protestant Groups: a Sociohistorical Perspective." *Latin American Research Review* 28 (2): 33–61.

Bastide, Roger. 1978. *The African Religions of Brazil*. Baltimore: Johns Hopkins University Press.

Berryman, Philip. 1994. "The Coming of Age of Evangelical Protestantism." *NACLA Report on the Americas* 27 (6): 6–10.

Berger, Peter. 1985. *O dossel sagrado [The Sacred Vessel]*. São Paulo: Edições Paulina. "O bispo não é santo." 1991. *Veja* 71 (July 17): 58–60.

Brandão, Carlos. 1980. *Os deuses do povo*. São Paulo: Brasilense.

Brooke, James. 1993. "Protestants Win Catholic Converts in Brazil." *New York Times* July 3: 1.

Brown, Diana. 1986. *Umbanda: Religion and Politics in Urban Brazil*. Ann Arbor: UMI Research Press.

Bruneau, Thomas. 1982. *The Church in Brazil*. Austin: University of Texas Press.

Brusco, Elizabeth. 1993. "The Reformation of Machismo: Asceticism and Masculinity among Colombian Evangelicals." *Rethinking Protestantism in Latin America*. Ed. Virginia Garrard-Burnett and David Stoll. Philadelphia: Temple University Press.

———. 1986. "The Household Basis of Evangelical Religion and the Reformation of Machismo in Colombia." Ph.D. diss., City University of New York.

Burdick, John. 1993. *Looking for God in Brazil*. Berkeley: University of California Press.

———. 1990. "Looking for God in Brazil: The Progressive Catholic Church in Urban Brazil's Religious Arena." Ph.D. diss., City University of New York.

Burnett, Virginia Garrard. 1986. "A History of Protestantism in Guatemala." Ph.D. diss., Tulane University.

Burns, E. Bradford. 1993. *A History of Brazil*. 3d ed. New York: Columbia University Press.

Cesar, Waldo. 1992. "Sobrevivencia e transcendencia no pentecostalismo." *Religiao e Sociedade* 16 (1-2): 46–59.

Civita, Victor, ed. 1978. *Os pensadores: Durkheim*. Rio de Janeiro: Abril Cultura.

Cleary, Edward, and Hannah Stewart-Gambino, eds. 1992. *The Latin American Church in a Changing Environment*. Boulder: Lynne Rienner.

Conde, Emilio. 1960. *História das Assembléias de Deus no Brasil*. Rio de Janeiro: CPAD.

Costa, Jefferson Magno. 1986. *Eles andaram com Deus*. 3d ed. Rio de Janeiro: CPAD.

Cox, Harvey. 1995. *Fire from Heaven*. Reading, MA: Addison- Wesley.

"Crise na saúde é ligada à economia." 1993. *Liberal*, Dec. 16.

Curry, Donald. 1968. "Luisada: An Anthropological Study of the Growth of Protestantism in Brazil." Ph.D. diss., Columbia University.

Da Matta, Roberto. 1985. *A casa e a rua*. São Paulo: Brasilense.

da Silva, Manoel Pinto. 1981. "Etude de la population des baixadas de Belém en vue de sa sédentarisation dans l'espace urbain." Ph.D. diss., Université de Paris I-La Sorbonne.

de Almeida, Abraão. 1982. *História das Assembléias de Deus*. Rio de Janeiro: CPAD.

de Lima, Delcio Monteiro. 1987. *Os Demônios Descem do Norte*. Rio de Janeiro: Francisco Alves.

D'Epinay, Christian Lalive. 1969. *Haven of the Masses*. London: Lutterworth.

de Souza, Beatriz Muniz. 1973. *Catolicos, protestantes, espiritas*. Petropolis: Editora Vozes.

———. 1969. *A experiencia da salvação*. São Paulo: Duas Cidades.

"O dinheiro é um bem." 1990. *Veja* 45 (Nov. 14): 5–7.

di Paolo, Pasquale. 1988. *A mediação political em Belém do Pará*. Belém: Grafica e Editora Universitaria, UFPA.

"Disputa pelos evangélicos." 1994. *Liberal*, May 29.

Drogus, Carol Ann. 1994. "Religious Change and Women's Status in Latin America." Working Paper 205 (Mar.), Helen Kellogg Institute for International Studies, University of Notre Dame.

Endruveit, Wilson. 1975. "Pentecostalism in Brazil: A Historical and Theological Study of Its Characteristics." Ph.D. diss., Northwestern University.

"Familia: Alicerce da sociedade." 1993. *Lições Bíblicas* 36 (4).

"A fé que move multidões avança no país." 1990. *Veja* 19 (May 16): 46–52.

Fernandes, Rubem Cesar. 1992. *Censo institucional evangélico*. Rio de Janeiro: Nucleo de Pesquisa/ISER.

———. 1982. *Os cavaleiros do Bom Jesus*. Rio de Janeiro: Brasilense.

Ferraz, Silvio. 1993. "A guerra santa dos Católicos brasileiros." *Istoé* 1232 (May 12): 48–54.

Filho, José Bittencourt. 1993. "Crescimento dos evangélicos." *CEDI* 269: 54–56.

Filho, Tacito da Gama Leite. 1991. *Seitas Neopentecostais*. Vol. 3. Rio de Janeiro: Junta de Educação Religiosa e Publicações da CBB.

Flora, Cornelia Butler. 1976. *Pentecostalism in Colombia.* Cranbury, NJ: Associated University Presses.

Frase, Ronald. 1975. "A Sociological Analysis of the Development of Brazilian Protestantism." Ph.D. diss., Princeton Theological Seminary.

Freston, Paul. 1993. "Protestantes e política no Brasil: da constituinte ao impeachment." Ph.D. diss., Universidade Estadual de Campinas.

Frigerio, Alejanro, ed. 1994. *El pentecostalismo en la Argentina.* Buenos Aires: Centro Editor de America Latina.

Fundação Getulio Vargas. 1984. *Dicionário Histórico- Biográfico Brasileiro.* Vol. 3. Rio de Janeiro: Editora Forense.

Galano, Ana Maria, ed. 1980. *Manuel da Conceição: Essa terra é nossa.* Petropolis: Editora Vozes.

Galliano, Gabriel. "Milenarismo pentecostal, pobreza urbana, e interaccion social en el gran Buenos Aires." 1994. *El pentecostalismo en la Argentina.* Ed. Alejandro Frigerio. Buenos Aires: Centro Editor de America Latina.

Garrard-Burnett, Virginia, and David Stoll, eds. 1993. *Rethinking Protestantism in Latin America.* Philadelphia: Temple University Press.

Gill, Anthony. 1994. "Religious Competition and Catholic Political Strategy in Latin America, 1962–1979." Unpublished manuscript.

Glazier, Stephen, ed. 1980. *Perspectives on Pentecostalism: Case Studies from the Caribbean and Latin America.* Washington, DC: University Press of America.

Gonçalves, Ezequiel Laco. 1990. "Uma visão do pentecostalismo: A partir das Assembléias de Deus em Campinas." Master's thesis, Instituto de Ensino Superior.

Goodman, Felicitas D., Jeannette H. Henney, and Esther Pressel. 1974. *Trance, Healing, and Hallucination.* New York: John Wiley and Sons.

Guimarães, Jose Eugenio. 1993. "Razão e religião: Pentecostais, visão de mundo e conduta." Master's thesis, Universidade Federal Rural de Rio de Janeiro.

Henney, Jeannette H. 1974. "Functions of Shakerism." *Trance, Healing, and Hallucination.* Felicitas D. Goodman, Jeannette H. Henney and Esther Pressel. New York: John Wiley and Sons.

Hoffnagel, Judith. 1978. "The Believers: Pentecostalism in a Brazilian City." Ph.D. diss., Indiana University.

Hollenwager, Walter J. 1973. *The Pentecostals.* Minneapolis: Augsburg.

"A Igreja sacode a familia." 1994. *Liberal,* Mar. 6: 9.

"Infancia brasileria está no limbo." 1994. *Liberal,* Mar. 6: 9.

Instituto Brasileiro de Geografía e Estatística (IBGE). 1992. *Anuario Estatístico do Brasil.* Rio de Janeiro.

———. 1991a. *Sinopse preliminar do censo demográfico— 1991—Pará.* Rio de Janeiro.

———. 1991b. *Censo de População por bairro—Setor urbano— Belém.* Belém: Delegacía do IBGE no Pará.

———. 1980a. *Dados comparativos da população do municipio de Belém, 1950–1980.* Belém: Delegacía do IBGE no Pará.

———. 1980b. *Bairros de Belém.* Belém: Delegacía do IBGE em Pará.

———. 1963. *Estatistica do culto protestante do Brasil.* Rio de Janeiro: Imprensa Nacional.

Ireland, Rowan. 1991. *Kingdoms Come: Religion and Politics in Brazil*. Pittsburgh: University of Pittsburgh Press.

Jardilino, José Rubens. 1993. *Sindicato dos mágicos*. São Paulo: CEPE.

Lancaster, Roger. 1987. "Thanks to God and the Revolution: Popular Religion and Class Consciousness in the New Nicaragua." Ph.D. diss., University of California at Berkeley.

Landim, Leilah. 1989. *Sinais dos tempos: Igrejas e seitas no Brasil*. Rio de Janeiro: ISER.

Leacock, Seth, and Ruth Leacock. 1972. *Spirits of the Deep*. Garden City, NY: Doubleday Natural History Press.

Lopes, J. A. Dias. 1981. "O milagre da multiplicação." *Veja* 683 (Oct. 7): 56–64.

Loyola, Maria Andrea. 1984. *Médicos e curandeiros*. São Paulo: DIFEL.

Machado, Maria das Dores, and Cecilia Mariz. 1995. "Mulheres trabalhadores e pratica religiosa." Unpublished manuscript.

Mainwaring, Scott. 1986. *The Catholic Church and Politics in Brazil, 1916–1985*. Stanford, CA: Stanford University Press.

"A Maré religiosa." 1993. *Cadernos do Terceiro Mundo* 164 (Aug.): 1–15.

Mariano, Ricardo, and Antonio Flavio Pierucci. 1992. "O envolvimento dos pentecostais na eleição de Collor." *Novos Estudos CEBRAP* 34 (Nov.): 92–106.

Mariz, Cecilia. 1994a. "Sistemas de representación, símbolo y poder." Paper presented at IV Congreso Argentino de Antropologia Social, Buenos Aires, July 19–23.

———. 1994b. *Coping with Poverty in Brazil*. Philadelphia: Temple University Press.

———. 1992. "Religion and Poverty in Brazil—A Comparison of Catholic and Pentecostal Communities." *Sociological Analysis* 53 (5): S63–S70.

——— 1990. "Igrejas pentecostais e estrategias de sobrevivencia." *Coleção Cidadania*. Bahia: EGBA/UFBA.

———. 1989. "Religion and Coping with Poverty in Brazil." Ph.D. diss., Boston University.

Martin, David. 1990. *Tongues of Fire*. Oxford: Basil Blackwell.

Marty, Martin E., and Scott Appleby, eds. 1994. *Accounting for Fundamentalisms*. Vol. 4. Chicago: University of Chicago Press.

Marx, Karl. 1964 [1844]. *On Religion*. New York: Schocken Books.

Masland, Tom. 1993. "The South Africa of South America?" *Newsweek International*, Nov.15: 30–31.

Maues, Raymundo Heraldo. 1987. "Catolicismo popular e controle eclesiastico." Vol 1. Ph.D. diss., Universidade Federal do Rio de Janeiro, Museu Nacional.

Mendonça, Antonio Gouvea, and Procoro Velasques Filho. 1990. *Introdução ao Protestantismo no Brasil*. São Paulo: Loyola.

"A miseria que mata e desagrega." 1994. *Liberal*, Mar. 26.

Mistchein, Thomas A. 1989. *Urbanização selvagem proletarização passiva na Amazonia: O caso de Belém*. Belém: CEJUP-NAEA/UFPA.

"Mobilização contra a miseria." 1994. *Liberal*, Feb. 23.

The New Oxford Annotated Bible. 1973. Revised Standard Version. 1973. New York: Oxford University Press.

Niebuhr, H. Richard. 1929. *The Social Sources of Denominationalism*. New York: Henry Holt and Company.

"Nortista vive a tragedia da fome." 1993. *Liberal*, Oct. 19.

Novaes, Regina Reyes. 1985. *Os escolhidos de Deus: Pentecostais, trabalhadores y cidadania.* Rio de Janeiro: Editora Marco Zero.

"Olhando para o norte." 1993. *Seara* 326: 20–31.

Pace, Richard. 1983. "The Churches of Poverty: Religion's Role in Distributing Aid in a Shantytown of Belém." Master's thesis, University of Florida.

Page, John. 1984. "Brasil Para Cristo: The Cultural Construction of Pentecostal Networks in Brazil." Ph.D. diss., New York University.

"Pará é recordista em micoses." 1993. *Liberal*, Sept. 24: 3.

"Pará tem 217 mil crianças indigentes." 1993. *Liberal*, Nov. 30: 4.

"Pastor ve o Brasil no primeiro mundo." 1994. *Liberal*, Jan. 3: 6.

Pastore, José. 1983. *Mudança social e pobreza no Brasil.* São Paulo: FIPE, Livraria Pioneira.

Penteado, Antonio Rocha. 1968. *Belém do Pará: Estudo de geografía urbana.* Vol. 2. Belém: Universidade Federal do Pará.

"Pentecostalismo autonomo uma inversão sedutora?" 1990. *Aconteceu* 548: 1–4.

Pepper, Joanne L. 1991. "The Historical Development of Pentecostalism in Northeastern Brazil, with Specific Reference to Working Class Women in Recife." Ph.D. diss., University of Warwick, U.K.

Pixley, Jorge. 1983. "Algunas lecciones de la experiencia Rios Montt." *Cristianismo y Sociedad* 76: 7–12.

Prandi, Reginaldo. 1992. "Perto da magia, longe da política." *Novos Estudos CEBRAP* 34 (Nov.): 81–91.

"Preocupação com evangélicos." 1994. *Liberal*, June 2: 7.

"O que diz a Biblia." 1987. *Terceiro Mundo* 102: 67–68.

Read, William. 1965. *New Patterns of Church Growth in Brazil.* Grand Rapids: William B. Eerdmans.

Read, William, Victor M. Monterroso, and Harmon A. Johnson. 1969. *Latin American Church Growth.* Grand Rapids: William B. Eerdmans.

Revista do Cirio. 1993. Belém: Agencia Ver Editora.

Roberts, Bryan R. 1968. "Protestant Groups and Coping with Urban Life in Guatemala City." *American Journal of Sociology* 73: 753–767.

Rolim, Francisco Cartaxo. 1987. *O que é pentecostalismo?* São Paulo: Editora Brasilense.

———. 1985. *Pentecostais no Brasil.* Petropolis: Editora Vozes.

Rosario, José Ubiratan. 1980. *Urbe amazonica.* Belém: Mitograph.

Rostas, Susanna, and Andre Droogers, eds. 1993. *The Popular Use of Popular Religion in Latin America.* Amsterdam: CEDLA.

Rubim, Christian de Rezende. 1991. "A teologia da opressão." Master's thesis, Unicamp.

"Saude: O dia mundial de que?" 1994. *Liberal*, Apr. 7.

Scheper-Hughes, Nancy. 1992. *Death without Weeping.* Berkeley: University of California Press.

Secretaria de estado de planejamenento e coordenação geral. 1990. *Projeto: Adequação da Região Metropolitana ao Atual Contexto Constitucional.* Belém: Governo do Estado do Pará.

Souza, Denise Gentil. 1992. "Intervenção estadual nos municipios: O caso de Belém na década de '80." Master's thesis, Universidade Federal do Pará—NAEA.

Stark, Rodney, and William Bainbridge. 1987. *A Theory of Religion*. New York: Peter Lang.

Stoll, David. 1994. "Jesus Is Lord of Guatemala: Evangelical Reform in a Death Squad State." *Accounting for Fundamentalisms*. Vol. 4. Ed. Martin E. Marty and R. Scott Appleby. Chicago: University of Chicago Press.

———. 1990. *Is Latin America Turning Protestant?* Berkeley: University of California Press.

Stoll, Sandra Jacqueline. 1986. "Pulpito e palanque: Religão e política nas eleições de 1982 num municipio da grande São Paulo." Master's thesis, Unicamp.

Tarducci, Monica. 1994. "Las mujeres en el movimiento pentecostal: Sumisión o liberación?" *El pentecostalismo en la Argentina*. Ed. Alejandro Frigerio. Buenos Aires: Centro Editor de America Latina.

Tennekes, Hans. 1985. *El movimiento pentecostal en la sociedad chilena*. Iquique, Chile: Centro de Investigación de la Realidad del Norte.

Troeltsch, Ernst. 1931. *The Social Teaching of the Christian Churches*. 2 vols. London: Allen and Unwin.

Tupiassu, Amilcar. 1968. *A area metropolitana de Belém*. Belém: IDESP.

Vingren, Ivar. 1987. *Despertamento apostólico no Brasil*. Rio de Janeiro: CPAD.

Wagley, Charles. 1976. *Amazon Town*. London: Oxford University Press.

Wagner, Peter. 1987. *Porque crescem os pentecostais?* Miami: Editora Vida.

Weber, Max. 1993 [1922]. *The Sociology of Religion*. Boston: Beacon.

———. 1991 [1930]. *The Protestant Ethic and the Spirit of Capitalism*. London: Harper Collins Academic.

Westmeier, Karl-Wilhelm. 1986. *Reconciling Heaven and Earth*. Frankfurt: Peter Lang.

Willems, Emilio. 1967. *Followers of the New Faith*. Nashville: Vanderbilt University Press.

Wilson, Bryan. 1973. *Magic and the Millennium*. London: Heinemann Educational Books.

Zaluar, Alba. 1983. *Os homens de Deus*. Rio de Janeiro: Zahar Editores.

INDEX

Note: Italicized page numbers refer to figures.

ABOUT THE AUTHOR

R. Andrew Chesnut is an assistant professor of Brazilian history at the University of Houston. He is currently editing a multiauthor work on religion in Brazil.